Provincial Offences

POLICE FOUNDATIONS PROGRAM

Ugo Capy & Erin MacCarthy

D1511644

2000
EMOND MONTGOMERY PUBLICATIONS LIMITED
TORONTO, CANADA

RICARDO LEON.

Printed in Canada.

Edited, designed, and typeset by WordsWorth Communications, Toronto.
Cover design by Susan Darrach, Darrach Design.

We acknowledge the financial support of the Government of Canada through the Book Publishing Industry Development Program (BPIDP) for our publishing activities.

Canadian Cataloguing in Publication Data

Capy, Ugo, 1950-
　　Provincial offences

(Police foundations program)
ISBN 1-55239-041-1

1. Law—Ontario.　2. Police—Ontario—Handbooks, manuals, etc.　I. MacCarthy, Erin.　II. Title.　III. Series.

KEO189.P6C36　1999　　　　349.713'024'3632　　　C99-933113-2
KF390.P65C36　1999

To my grandmother, Rita Murphy,
whose great faith and wisdom continually inspire me.

Erin MacCarthy

Contents

Preface

As a police officer, you will likely deal on a regular basis with all kinds of provincial offences. Offences created by provincial statutes and municipal bylaws are common, and to a far greater degree than criminal matters, they pervade all areas of life. The majority of citizens do not become the target of criminal investigations, but most individuals at one time or another have been stopped for provincial offences such as speeding or disobeying a stop sign.

The *Highway Traffic Act* is the most commonly encountered provincial statute. In recognition of its pervasive importance, a separate course is devoted entirely to this statute and to traffic matters in general. Accordingly, we will not cover traffic offences in this book. We will, however, look at other provincial statutes that are commonly encountered or are unique in some way.

Chapter 1 presents a detailed overview of the *Provincial Offences Act* (POA). This Act is the starting point for the investigation, prosecution, and enforcement of all provincial offences. The POA sets out the procedures applicable to provincial offences in general. Chapter 1 also examines the classification of provincial offences as part I, part II, or part III offences and traces the specific procedures applicable to each stream of provincial offence. The chapter also explains the different types of provincial offences—that is, absolute liability, strict liability, and *mens rea* offences—and describes the meanings of these terms and their respective differences. In chapter 2, the POA itself is presented.

Although the POA is an essential starting point and must be consulted at all stages, the specific charging statutes are also important. As a result, reference is made throughout this book to the interplay between the POA and the specific charging legislation. Chapters 3 to 11 of this book are devoted to various charging statutes.

There are numerous provincial statutes that give police the authority to charge individuals who breach the terms of the legislation. Unfortunately, not every provincial statute can be covered in this book. The statutes that are included in this book have been chosen either because they cover situations commonly encountered by police or because of their particular significance. The statutes that are included are: the *Liquor Licence Act*, the *Tenant Protection Act*, the *Trespass to Property Act*, the *Blind Persons' Rights Act*, the *Coroners Act*, the *Family Law Act*, the *Mental Health Act*, the *Child and Family Services Act*, and the *Police Services Act*.

To assist you in reading and understanding the statutory material, chapter objectives and a brief commentary precede each Act. The objectives not only state the goals of each chapter, but also offer direction to your reading of each Act. The commentary provides a context of the legislation, and highlights important features and issues. The most relevant sections of each statute are then reproduced, followed by helpful exercises that test your understanding of the statutory material.

Because the statutes discussed in this book relate to various and unique fact situations, police officers seeking to enforce provincial legislation will need to pay close attention to the content of the individual statutes. Though statutory language may be challenging and intricate, it is important that you learn to navigate through the kind of legislation that is dealt with in this book. For that reason, both the chapter objectives and the exercises that follow the statutory material are prepared with the assumption that you have thoroughly read and understood the excerpted legislation

Chapter 12 discusses police powers in general as well as police powers in the specific areas of arrest, search and seizure, and disclosure. The chapter also examines some common defences to emphasize the importance of police officers' appropriate use of the powers vested in them.

The book concludes with an appendix that reproduces forms that are frequently used in the enforcement of provincial offences. These forms may be photocopied so that you can do chapter exercises that ask you to complete the required documentation in a hypothetical fact situation.

Because of the wide powers that the police have in enforcing provincial offences statutes, it is important for you as a police officer to use your discretion wisely and to charge individuals only in those situations where they clearly should be charged. Warnings and other methods of community problem solving are sometimes the most effective and appropriate methods of dealing with improper behaviour. Charges should be laid only in appropriate cases. Understanding the range of provincial offences and the procedures to follow in enforcing the statutes is an essential foundation of policing in Ontario.

In conclusion, the authors hope that you will enjoy learning about the investigation and prosecution of provincial offences in Ontario and that the text and exercises within this book will be of assistance to you as you embark upon your new careers in policing.

CHAPTER 1
Introduction to Provincial Offences

CHAPTER OBJECTIVES

After completing this chapter, you should be able to:

◆ Understand what the *Provincial Offences Act* is and why it was created.

◆ Explain how limitation periods for individual provincial offences are determined.

◆ Describe the difference between crimes and provincial offences.

◆ Describe the three streams of provincial offences.

◆ Be prepared to determine, in a hypothetical fact situation, which kind of provincial offence has been committed, and to identify and complete the appropriate documentation that should be used when charging the offence.

◆ Explain the differences between absolute liability offences, strict liability offences, and *mens rea* offences.

◆ Explain how to determine, by reading an offence, what level of intention (or lack of intention) must be proved to obtain a conviction.

INTRODUCTION

The *Provincial Offences Act* (POA), enacted in 1979, is an Ontario statute that sets out the procedure for the prosecution and enforcement of offences created by provincial statutes. Although charges may be laid for offences under the POA, it deals primarily with general procedures for all provincial offences.

The POA establishes standard limitation periods, standard penalties, the proper charging documents for the issuing of process, and the standard procedures for both trials and appeals of provincial offences. The POA also sets out three streams of provincial offences and sets out a different set of rules for each type of offence. The Ontario Court of Justice (formerly the Ontario Court of Justice (Provincial Division)) is the court that has jurisdiction over the prosecution of all provincial offences.

The POA consists of nine parts. The first three parts deal with the issuing of process and are reviewed in detail below. Part IV of the Act deals with trial and sentencing procedures. Part V deals with general provisions and part VI deals with young persons. Part VII deals with appeals and other forms of review. Part VIII governs arrest, bail, and search warrants. Part IX deals with matters that relate to other statutes and applications for judicial orders.

The three streams of offences created by the POA are part I, part II, and part III offences. The proper charging documents for the issuing of process, penalties, and limitation periods are different for part I, part II, and part III offences. Part I offences are minor offences and include such things as speeding. Part II offences are primarily parking offences. The most severe penalties—including imprisonment—are reserved for part III offences, which are the most serious of provincial offences.

The Prosecution of Provincial Offences

It is essential to understand that the POA provides only the *framework* for the prosecution of provincial offences. It cannot be read alone. One must always read *both* the POA and the charging legislation—for example, the *Trespass to Property Act*—to find out exactly what time limitations, penalties, and other requirements exist.

In some cases, a section of the charging legislation, such as the *Trespass to Property Act*, is inconsistent with one of the rules in the POA. If that is the case, the section in the *Trespass to Property Act*, not the section of the POA, applies. Where the charging legislation *does not* specify the limitation periods, penalties, etc., the POA applies. For example, if the *Highway Traffic Act* (HTA) has a different limitation period from the POA, the limitation period in the HTA applies. If the *Liquor Licence Act*, for example, does not specify a limitation period, the limitation period in the POA applies. This is the case because although various offences are created under such statutes as the *Trespass to Property Act*, the charge is laid and proceeds through the court system according to the provisions of the *Provincial Offences Act* and its regulations.

The POA was passed to make the process for dealing with the prosecution of provincial offences simpler and less formal than the one followed in criminal cases. Before the POA was enacted, provincial offences were prosecuted by reference to the procedures of summary criminal matters, as specified in the *Criminal Code of Canada*. The POA introduced a new, simpler, and less rigorous framework for the prosecution of provincial offences. It eliminates some technical defences and tries to speed up the process and save money in the prosecution of regulatory matters.

It is important to recognize, however, that despite their less formal nature, prosecutions of provincial statutes are subject to the traditional laws of fairness and standards of proof:

◆ There is a *presumption* that an individual charged with a provincial offence (the defendant) is innocent unless proven guilty.

◆　The *burden of proof* lies on the prosecution.

◆　The prosecutor must *prove* each charge *beyond a reasonable doubt*.

◆　The defendant has *the right to know the charge* laid against him or her, and has *the right to make full answer and defence* to the charge.

◆　The defendant has *the right to silence*, which means that the defendant is not required to give evidence at trial.

Provincial Offences Versus Crimes

The procedural guarantees discussed above are the same as those that exist in a criminal trial. However, one of the underlying principles of the *Provincial Offences Act* is that provincial offences are different from crimes.

With few exceptions, crimes are acts that are considered morally wrong. Obvious examples of crimes are theft, robbery, assault, and murder. Although it is true that some crimes—such as criminal negligence and dangerous driving—do not necessarily involve moral blameworthiness, but deal with some form of negligent behaviour, the vast majority of offences designated under the *Criminal Code* are acts that our society considers morally wrong.

In contrast, provincial statutes deal with behaviour that is either devoid of moral culpability or behaviour that is not as morally blameworthy as the behaviour that is the subject of criminal charges. Provincial offences are sometimes referred to as "quasi-criminal" offences. There is nothing immoral about going 70 km/hr in a 60 km/hr zone, but speeding is illegal. It is an offence because of concerns that have nothing to do with morality. The purpose of speeding and other provincial offences is to protect members of society from behaviour that could have harmful consequences.

The fact that provincial offences are regulatory in nature has other consequences distinct from criminal offences. Generally, there is some public condemnation of individuals found guilty of crimes, and there are serious penalties for criminal behaviour. As a result, in order for an individual to be found guilty of a crime, generally, the Crown must prove both the *actus reus* (the guilty act) and the *mens rea* (the guilty mind). However, in some provincial offences, a defendant will be found guilty if the provincial prosecutor simply proves that the act occurred, regardless of whether the defendant intended to commit the act. The best-known example is the case of speeding. Whether an individual intended to travel 70 km/hr in a 60 km/hr speed zone is irrelevant. The actual fact of speeding constitutes the offence.

Although serious penalties—the most serious of which is imprisonment—are imposed on individuals found guilty of part III provincial offences, generally, the same level of condemnation of those found guilty of criminal acts does not exist for those found guilty of minor provincial offences.

Because of this difference, some provincial offences are classified as absolute liability or strict liability offences and do not require the prosecution to prove *mens rea*. As a result, absolute liability and strict liability offences are quite easy for the prosecution to prove. The classification of and differences between absolute liability, strict liability, and *mens rea* offences are discussed in detail below.

Provincial Offences and Public Policy

Law makers have valid concerns about the possible negative consequences of a variety of forms of behaviour. For example, an individual who speeds may cause a collision that could result in injury to citizens and damage to property. The sale of liquor to a 12-year-old child who subsequently consumes the alcohol may result in serious harm to the child. Allowing commercial fishers to catch an unlimited quantity of fish would reduce the supply of fish, and thereby reduce the food supply of a large number of people.

These are just a few examples of provincial offences—there are many others. The provincial legislature has created legislation for public policy reasons in a number of areas. Tenants are protected and the rights of landlords are curtailed by the *Tenant Protection Act*. The sale of liquor is controlled by the *Liquor Licence Act*. Both drivers and pedestrians are protected by the *Compulsory Automobile Insurance Act* and the *Highway Traffic Act*.

Each of the statutes listed above is a charging statute that sets out the specific procedures and rules that apply to offences under that statute. The POA sets out the general procedure for the prosecution and enforcement of all provincial offences.

PART I, II, AND III OFFENCES

As discussed above, there are three procedural streams of provincial offences—part I, part II, and part III. This section introduces you to the three streams of offences; discusses the special treatment of young persons; and touches on rights of appeal and review.

Part I Offences

Most minor offences such as speeding and other traffic offences (with the exception of parking offences) are part I offences. The procedure used for part I offences is sometimes referred to as a "ticketing" process. The process involves two documents: the charging document, which is called the certificate of offence, and the serving document, which consists of either an offence notice or a summons.

Unlike an information under part III, a part I certificate of offence is not sworn by a provincial offences officer before a justice of the peace. Instead, the officer needs only to sign the certificate of offence, stating his or her belief that an offence has been committed. Then, the provincial offences officer serves the defendant with an offence notice and files the certificate of offence in the court office. Alternatively, the provincial offences officer may choose to serve the defendant with a summons, which requires the defendant to appear in court, rather than with an offence notice. If the suspect is a young person (age 12 to 15), the officer must always use a summons.

The maximum punishment for committing a part I offence is a fine in the amount specified by the POA and its regulations or as prescribed by the specific statute. The maximum fine for part I offences is lower than that for part III offences. Another important distinction between part I and part III offences is that an individual who commits a part I offence cannot be sent to jail, whereas jail is a possible penalty for part III offences.

The defendant must be personally served with either a summons or an offence notice within 30 days of committing an alleged part I offence. If a summons is served, the person charged must appear in court. If an offence notice is served (the most common course of events), the person charged has several options:

1. to plead guilty by filling in the notice and mailing it back (or delivering it in person), along with the full fine;

2. to plead guilty with an explanation, before a justice;

3. to plead not guilty and have a trial; or

4. in special cases, depending on where the individual charged lives, to dispute the charge in writing.

If the defendant does not respond within 15 days, he or she is deemed not to dispute the charge. If the certificate of offence is properly completed, the defendant can be convicted in court even if he or she is not present. The defendant can also be convicted if he or she fails to appear in court if the certificate of offence is complete and regular—that is, unambiguous and clear—on its face.

Because part I offences are generally intended for use in less serious circumstances, the *Provincial Offences Act* allows shorter time limits for the service and issuance of process for part I offences than those for part III offences.

In order for a police officer to properly lay a charge under part I of the POA, he or she is required to believe that an offence has been committed. This is a lower subjective requirement than that in parts II and III of the Act, which require, respectively, personal knowledge and reasonable and probable grounds.

Part II Offences

Most part II offences are parking infractions. Usually, a certificate of parking infraction (a ticket) is used to notify the defendant. These offences generally have a fixed monetary penalty according to the type of infraction and the monetary penalty tends to be much lower than the penalties for part I and part III offences.

There are special rules for serving a parking infraction notice. Usually, a police officer simply leaves the infraction notice on the windshield of the individual's vehicle. The defendant then has two options:

1. to pay the fine out of court, or

2. to deliver a notice of intention to appear for trial.

If the defendant fails to respond within 15 days, the court may send out a notice of impending conviction. If the defendant does not respond for another 15 days after that, or fails to appear for trial, the defendant may be convicted even though he or she is not present in court if the certificate of parking infraction is complete and regular on its face.

Under part II of the POA, a certificate of parking infraction can be issued only if the officer has personal knowledge of the offence.

Part III Offences

As stated earlier, part III offences are the most serious of provincial offences. In order to determine the maximum penalty available, the police officer must check both the POA and the charging Act to see what the maximum allowable penalty is. This is particularly important because the POA sets out the maximum punishment available, unless the charging statute says otherwise. Usually, a period of imprisonment is not available. However, if the charging legislation specifies that a different penalty (including a maximum fine or a jail sentence) is available, then that penalty, up to the available maximum, will apply.

Part III procedures are much more formal than part I or part II offences—reflecting the serious nature of the charges. The informant or complainant (usually, the provincial offences officer or police officer) will usually swear the truth of the allegations before a justice (either a provincial court judge or a justice of the peace) in a document called an "information." If the justice accepts that the complainant has reasonable and probable grounds for believing that the defendant committed an offence, he or she will endorse (sign) the information. The justice will then decide whether to confirm the summons already served under s. 22 or issue a summons in the prescribed form. Where the arrest is authorized by the statute in question and where the justice is satisfied on responsible and probable grounds that it is necessary in the public interest to do so, the justice will issue a warrant for the arrest of the defendant. If the defendant is properly served, he or she must appear in court.

Procedures Applicable to Young Persons

More rigid rules and lesser penalties apply to "young persons" charged with provincial offences. The term "young person" refers to anyone who, at the time of the offence, was at least 12 years of age but under the age of

16. Anyone under the age of 12 cannot be charged with a provincial offence or, for that matter, a criminal offence.

There are a number of procedural protections unique to young persons. For example, a young person's parent or guardian must be notified right away. Another important difference is that, unlike an adult, a young person cannot be convicted unless he or she is present in court. In general, a young person's identity may not be published. Moreover, except in relation to the offence of breach of probation, a young person cannot be sent to jail. If you as a police officer are required to deal with a young person, you should refer to part VI of the *Provincial Offences Act*, which deals with young persons, and comply with all of the special rules applicable.

Rights of Appeal and Review

Rights of appeal and review exist for provincial offences matters. However, as a police officer, you will not likely be directly involved in such matters and they are not dealt with in this book. To learn about applicable rules for appeal and review, you should consult part VII of the *Provincial Offences Act*, which discusses such provisions in detail. Appeals of proceedings commenced by certificate under part I or II are heard by a judge of the Ontario Court of Justice. A further appeal is allowed only with leave of a judge of the Court of Appeal. The Court of Appeal will not grant leave to appeal unless it deems an appeal essential in the public interest or for the due administration of justice.

PREPARING THE CHARGING DOCUMENTATION

This section provides some general information about the preparation of charging documents; samples of the forms themselves can be found in the appendix. Students will find it useful, with guidance from the instructor, to practise filling out the forms as completely and as clearly as possible.

Particulars of the Certificate of Offence

A certificate of offence, like an information, should contain all of the essential elements of the alleged offence. These include:

◆ date and time of the offence;

◆ name of the defendant;

◆ location of the offence; and

◆ specific offence(s) charged.

These particulars should be recorded with care in order to minimize the chance that the defendant will be able to successfully dispute "technical" aspects of the charge. Accuracy and thoroughness in preparation of the certificate of offence also ensures that it will conform to the evidence subsequently led by the prosecution. The prosecution must prove each and every element of the offence, including date, time, and location of the specific offence. Finally, where the defendant has submitted a certificate indicating a guilty plea, if the certificate is properly prepared—that is, if it is "complete and regular on its face"—the justice can simply examine it and accept the guilty plea.

Date and Time of the Offence

Where possible, the charging officer should indicate the precise time and date that the offence occurred. In some instances, where the exact date and time are not available, the charging officer should attempt instead to provide reasonable temporal parameters for the occurrence of the offence. Besides adding precision and fairness to the case against the defendant, the offence date is also important in establishing whether or not charges were laid within the appropriate limitation period.

Identity of the Defendant

The full name of the defendant should be recorded on the certificate of offence. The defendant may also need to be identified in court, by a witness under oath. In most instances involving *Highway Traffic Act*, *Liquor Licence Act*, and *Trespass to Property Act* offences, the encounter between the police officer and the defendant is very brief. It is important that the police officer record in his or her notes a reliable description of the defendant in order to be able to identify the defendant in court. Failure of the police to identify the defendant, when no other means of identification is available, will likely result in a dismissal of the charge.

Location of the Offence

The description of the location of the offence should include the civic number, street name, city or town, township or district, and province. Jurisdiction must be established to ensure that the presiding justice has the authority to hear the charge. Most justices who are sworn into office have jurisdiction to hear provincial offences matters throughout the entire province of Ontario.

Specific Offence(s) Charged

The offence committed by the defendant must be specified. The proper wording for provincial offences is found in the schedules to Ontario Regulation 950. The proper statute, section number, and wording of the charge must be included. The elements of the various offences will be examined in discussions under those statutes.

ABSOLUTE LIABILITY, STRICT LIABILITY, AND MENS REA OFFENCES

In *R v. Sault Ste. Marie*, the Supreme Court of Canada stated that all offences—both criminal and regulatory—fall into one of three categories of offences: absolute liability, strict liability, and *mens rea* offences. The categories are differentiated on the basis of the mental or intentional element (*mens rea*) of the offence. Since the classification was introduced in 1978, the *Sault Ste. Marie* case has been considered and affirmed by other courts many times.

Most provincial offences are presumed to be strict liability offences, but it is the wording of each charge and the available penalties that determine the type of offence created. The categorization is important because whether the offence is absolute liability, strict liability, or *mens rea* will affect whether an individual should be charged for a prohibited act and how the individual will be prosecuted.

The first step in determining the *mens rea* requirement of an offence is to look closely at the wording of each charge. There will be different levels of culpability for various offences within the same statute. Of the three types of offences, absolute liability offences are the easiest to prove and *mens rea* offences are the most difficult to prove.

Absolute Liability Offences

The easiest offence for the prosecution to prove is the absolute liability offence. To prove an absolute liability offence, the prosecution need prove only that the individual committed the unlawful act. A simple example will demonstrate this concept.

If you, as a police officer, observe Susan driving 20 km/hr over the posted speed limit on a city street, you have reason to believe that Susan has committed the offence of speeding. If you charge Susan with speeding and the matter subsequently goes to trial, the prosecutor need only call you to the stand, have you give evidence about your observations on the date and at the location in question, and describe the speed at which Susan was driving. You must also identify Susan as the woman you saw commit the illegal act and, of course, give evidence of the speed limit in the area and any posted signs to this effect if the speed limit is different from the norm that applies to city streets.

Proof of the act of speeding (along with the required proof of identity, jurisdiction, and time) is all that is required to prove the offence. The fact that Susan did not intend to speed, or did not realize she was speeding does not excuse her from liability. She is guilty if the prosecution can prove that the *actus reus* (the guilty act) of speeding was committed by Susan.

There are some limited technical and procedural defences available to Susan. However, assuming that she voluntarily committed the act (that is, no one forced her to speed), she will have a difficult time defending against an absolute liability offence. For this reason, absolute liability offences are the least serious of the provincial offences.

In the case of *R v. Hickey*, the Ontario Court of Appeal held that speeding was an absolute liability offence and rejected the defence offered by the appellant that the speedometer was defective at the time of speeding. It is interesting that this defence was rejected despite the fact that the arresting police officer also confirmed at the time of the incident that the speedometer was defective. This case demonstrates well the concept of absolute liability. Liability in a speeding offence or any other absolute liability offence truly is "absolute."

Nevertheless, the prosecution must still prove that the act was voluntary in an absolute liability offence. An example will illustrate. Shelley was driving a vehicle at the rate of 50 km/hr in a posted 50 km/hr zone. She was in the driver's seat and John was in the passenger seat beside her. John suddenly forced Shelley's foot down on the gas pedal, causing the car to accelerate from 50 km/hr to 80 km/hr. Shelley was the "driver" of the vehicle and she committed the offence, but is she guilty of speeding? Clearly, the act of speeding was not voluntary. In this example, Shelley did not commit the *actus reus* because the act was not a voluntary act.

The offence is one of absolute liability if the wording of the offence clearly excludes the defence of reasonable care and clearly indicates that proof of the illegal act is all that is required to prove the charge.

In the case of *Re British Columbia Motor Vehicle Act*, the Supreme Court of Canada held that offences for which there was a possibility of imprisonment could not be classified as absolute liability offences. The wisdom of this decision is clear, because, generally speaking, it seems unreasonable to send someone to jail for an offence that an individual did not intend to commit and may even have guarded against. For example, Susan could be found guilty of speeding even if she suddenly accelerated in order to avoid hitting an animal or another vehicle. Sending her to jail for an unintentional although voluntary act would be manifestly unfair.

The *Canadian Charter of Rights and Freedoms* is the supreme law of Canada. Section 7 of the Charter states: "Everyone has the right to life, liberty and security of the person and the right not to be deprived thereof except in accordance with the principles of fundamental justice."

Generally speaking, an absolute liability offence is contrary to s. 7 of the Charter if the defendant's "liberty" is at stake. Liberty is defined in various ways but does include freedom from imprisonment. Therefore, where there is a possible penalty of imprisonment for a provincial offence, the penalty is not lawful, unless the offence can be saved under s. 1 of the Charter as a "reasonable" limit "prescribed by law [that] can be demonstrably justified in a free and democratic society."

This issue was recently revisited by the Supreme Court of Canada in the case of *R v. Pontes*. The court said that an absolute liability offence created by ss. 94(1) and 92 of the BC *Motor Vehicle Act* does not contravene the Charter. The court said that, taken together, these sections indicate that no person is liable to imprisonment for an absolute liability offence, and the non-payment of a fine will not result in imprisonment. Therefore, an individual convicted under these sections faces no risk of imprisonment and there is no violation of the right to life, liberty, and security of the person under s. 7 of the Charter.

Strict Liability Offences

The second type of offence is the strict liability offence, which lies somewhere between the *mens rea* offence and the absolute liability offence in terms of level of culpability that must be proved.

The concept of strict liability was defined in the *Sault Ste. Marie* case, discussed above. In this type of offence, the prosecution must first prove beyond a reasonable doubt that the defendant committed the illegal act(s). The *defendant* must then prove, on a balance of probabilities, that he or she took reasonable care not to commit the illegal act, or that he or she made a reasonable mistake of fact which, if true, would have rendered the act lawful.

To constitute a defence, a defendant's mistake of fact must be reasonable. Usually, the defendant must establish that he or she took all reasonable steps and made all reasonable inquiries to determine the correct information. The defendant who can demonstrate that he or she exercised reasonable care will be excused from liability.

In a sense, strict liability offences appear to reduce the onus on the prosecution to prove its case beyond a reasonable doubt, at least with respect to some of the facts. The proof of these offences can thus be somewhat difficult to understand. It is important to remember, however, that it is still necessary in any provincial offences prosecution, including one for a strict liability offence, for the prosecution to prove beyond a reasonable doubt that the defendant committed the unlawful act. It is only when the prosecution meets this requirement that the onus then shifts to the defendant to prove, on a balance of probabilities, that he or she took reasonable care not to commit the illegal act, or that he or she made a reasonable mistake of fact which, if true, would have rendered the act lawful.

If the defendant can show that he or she took appropriate steps, he or she may be excused from his or her unlawful act(s). The success of a "reasonable steps" defence will also depend on whether the defendant has been convicted of similar offences in the past. The rationale for this is clear. One cannot simply rely on this defence over and over again in similar circumstances. A "reasonable steps" defence might be used once, but on subsequent use it wears thin.

There are a variety of considerations in determining whether a defendant took reasonable care. The defendant must establish that there was no reasonable alternative to committing the offence. Of course, if an activity cannot be carried on lawfully, it should not be carried on at all, so one of the possible alternatives that will be considered is that the defendant should have done nothing—that is, not engaged in that line of activity.

Consider the example of an individual who creates his own private chemical disposal plant and then breaches a provincial offences provision in the process. The defence of reasonable care has not been met if he simply says, "I didn't have the money to hire any technical staff to maintain the plant."

The failure of the reasonable care defence in these circumstances can be traced back to the whole concept of regulatory offences. As explained above, provincial offences are regulatory offences designed for the protection of society and for the promotion of valid public interests. However, some regulations provide that they can be overridden if equivalent or higher standards of behaviour—for example, safety standards—are followed.

As a general rule, the greater the potential for serious injury or serious damage, the greater the care required. There is also a certain degree of skill expected of staff, particularly where the activities they are engaged in pose a danger to the public or to the environment.

Reasonable care also requires that an appropriate level of technology be used. Regular and appropriate maintenance must be conducted, along with proper inspections and testing.

The following example of a strict liability offence should help to illustrate how this concept works. The offence of operating a vehicle with excess weight is a strict liability offence. A defence of reasonable care might arise with this offence under very rare circumstances.

A trucking company may take all reasonable precautions to ensure that its vehicles comply with legislated weight requirements. If, however, in a dry part of the country flood conditions suddenly develop and the level of precipitation far exceeds the usual level, which in turn causes a grain cargo to exceed its prescribed weight, an event has occurred that may not have been foreseeable. The company may claim that it did exercise reasonable care, particularly if the additional cost to guard against such a rare event would have been prohibitive.

The concept of strict liability was dealt with in the case of *R v. Pontes*, discussed above. The main issue in that case was whether the offence created by ss. 94(1) and 92 of the BC *Motor Vehicle Act* was one of absolute liability or strict liability. The offence in question involved a driver operating a motor vehicle while being prohibited from driving. (As an aside, the fact that the court dealt with this question at all demonstrates the complexity of the distinction between absolute and strict liability in some cases.)

In the *Pontes* case, the Supreme Court of Canada held that the offence was one of absolute liability, not strict liability. In reaching its decision, the court looked at the wording of the charge and found that the terms "automatically and without notice" were very helpful to its determination that the offence was one of absolute liability.

Mens Rea Offences

Mens rea offences are offences in which the prosecution must prove beyond a reasonable doubt that the defendant committed the illegal act and that the defendant had a particular state of mind at the time he or she committed the illegal act. The state of mind that must be proved depends on the offence and may be intent, knowledge, or recklessness.

If the words "wilfully," "knowingly," "intentionally," or "recklessly" are used in the wording of an offence, that offence is a *mens rea* offence. *Black's Law Dictionary* defines *mens rea* as "a guilty mind; a guilty or wrongful purpose; a criminal intent; guilty knowledge and wilfulness" (Black, 1979, p. 889).

To prove a *mens rea* offence, it is not enough for the prosecution to prove that the defendant committed the unlawful act. The prosecution must also prove that the defendant intended for the act to occur or was reckless as to whether the act occurred. The prosecution may prove the defendant's state of mind by admissions by the defendant as to his or her state of mind; through testimony by others as to what the defendant said; or by inferences as to the defendant's state of mind, based on the commonsense principle that people usually intend the consequences of their actions.

It is important to remember that in the case of *mens rea* offences, both the guilty act and the guilty mind must be present at the same time. The onus is on the prosecution to prove all the elements of the offence.

Not only are *mens rea* offences the most difficult to prove of the three types of provincial offences, they are also the most serious. Of the three types of provincial offences, *mens rea* provincial offences come the closest to criminal offences, because criminal offences are also *mens rea* offences. An element of moral blameworthiness attaches to *mens rea* offences, which justifies the higher penalties, including imprisonment, that are available for them.

There are a large number of *mens rea* offences. Section 30(1) of the *Liquor Licence Act* is one example. It states: "No person shall *knowingly* sell or supply liquor to a person under nineteen years of age." The key to determining that this is a *mens rea* offence is to look at the language of the charge. The word "knowingly" introduces a mental element to the offence.

EXERCISES

■ SHORT ANSWER

1. What is the *Provincial Offences Act*? Why was it created?

2. Describe the three streams of provincial offences.

   a.

   b.

   c.

3. What is the difference between crimes and provincial offences?

4. Give examples of some common provincial offences. What statute governs each of the examples you have given?

REFERENCES

Black, H.C. (1979). *Black's Law Dictionary*. St. Paul, MN: West Publishing Co.

British Columbia Motor Vehicle Act, Re, [1985] 2 SCR 486.

Hickey, R v., (1976), 30 CCC (2d) 416 (Ont. CA).

Canadian Charter of Rights and Freedoms, part I of the *Constitution Act, 1982*, RSC 1985, app. II, no. 44.

Pontes, R v., [1995] 3 SCR 44.

Sault Ste. Marie, R v., (1978), 40 CCC (2d) 353 (SCC).

CHAPTER 2
The Provincial Offences Act

CHAPTER OBJECTIVES

After completing this chapter, you should be able to:

◆ Understand key terms defined in the *Provincial Offences Act*.

◆ State the appropriate limitation period contained within the Act.

◆ State the time and penalty limitations for part I and part III provincial offence notices.

◆ State the arrest, release, and search authorities given to police officers.

◆ Describe the processes for commencement of proceedings against an individual charged with a provincial offence.

◆ Describe the processes for commencement of proceedings against a young person charged with a provincial offence.

◆ Be prepared to apply the provisions of the Act in a hypothetical fact situation, and to complete the required documentation.

INTRODUCTION

The POA provides a comprehensive framework for the prosecution of all provincial offences. The purpose of this Act is to replace the summary conviction procedure for the prosecution of provincial offences with a procedure that reflects the distinction between provincial offences and criminal offences (see s. 2 of the POA).

Part I Offences

Part I of the Act describes the process of commencing proceedings by a certificate of offence. A police officer who believes that an individual has committed an offence may issue a certificate of offence against the defendant. The officer issues the certificate by completing and signing it—that is, certifying that an offence has been committed. He or she must also fill out either:

1. an offence notice (which lists the set fine for the given offence), or

2. a summons, in the form prescribed under s. 13.

An officer must personally serve the defendant with an offence notice or summons within 30 days after the offence occurs. When the same officer who issued the certificate of offence serves the defendant with the offence notice or summons, the officer must mark on the certificate of offence the fact that he or she personally served the document and the date on which it was served. If another officer serves the document, he or she must complete an affidavit of service. The certificate of offence must then be filed in the court office as soon as possible.

Part II Offences

Part II offences are mainly parking infractions. Where an officer believes from his or her personal knowledge that an individual has committed an offence, he or she may issue:

1. a certificate of parking infraction certifying that an infraction has been committed, or

2. a parking infraction notice indicating the set fine for the infraction.

Unlike part I offences, the officer may serve the notice by leaving it on the defendant's windshield or by delivering it personally to the person operating the vehicle at the time of the offence.

The police officer starts the proceeding by filing the certificate of parking infraction in the court office, and, if the parking infraction is against the owner of a vehicle, evidence of the vehicle's ownership.

If the matter is contested, the court may not convict the defendant unless the following are eventually presented at trial:

1. evidence of ownership of the vehicle, where the infraction is against the vehicle owner;

2. a copy of the notice of trial, with the certificate of the person who issued the notice, stating that he or she gave the notice to the defendant and indicating the date it was given; and

3. the certificate of parking infraction.

Interplay Between Part I and II Offences and a Part III Information

In addition to using the procedures set out above, there is also provision under part III of the POA for laying an information for part I and part II offences. (Only one of these methods can be used—not both.) Since proceeding by way of information is more difficult and complex and defeats the purpose of the simple procedures available in the first two parts of the Act, unless serious or unusual circumstances exist, the police will normally choose to proceed by way of certificate of offence rather than by way of a part III information. One example of a case in which a Part III information might be used is where an individual is charged with a number of criminal offences in addition to a POA offence.

Part III Offences

Part III offences are the most serious of provincial offences. Under s. 22 of the POA, where a police officer believes, on reasonable and probable grounds, that an offence has been committed by a person whom the officer finds at or near the place where the offence was committed, he or she may, before an information is laid, serve the person with a summons.

Any person who, on reasonable and probable grounds, believes that an individual has committed an offence, may swear an information before a justice. The information may be laid anywhere in Ontario. A justice who receives an information shall consider the allegations of the informant and either:

1. confirm the summons served under s. 22,

2. issue a summons in the prescribed form, or

3. where the arrest is authorized by statute and where the allegations of the informant or the evidence satisfy the justice on reasonable and probable grounds that it is necessary in the public interest to do so, issue a warrant for the arrest of the defendant.

If, however, the justice is not satisfied that a case for issuing process has been made out, he or she will

1. so endorse the information, and

2. where a summons was served under s. 22, cancel it and cause the defendant to be notified of its cancellation.

PROVINCIAL OFFENCES ACT

RSO 1990, Chapter P.33

INTERPRETATION

1. (1) **Definitions.—** In this Act,

"certificate" means a certificate of offence issued under Part I or a certificate of parking infraction issued under Part II;

"court" means the Ontario Court (Provincial Division);

"judge" means a provincial judge;

"justice" means a provincial judge or a justice of the peace;

"offence" means an offence under an Act of the Legislature or under a regulation or by-law made under the authority of an Act of the Legislature;

"police officer" means a chief of police or other police officer but does not include a special constable or by-law enforcement officer; …

"prosecutor" means the Attorney General or, where the Attorney General does not intervene, means the person who issues a certificate or lays an information and includes counsel or agent acting on behalf of either of them;

"provincial offences officer" means a police officer or a person designated under subsection (3);

"set fine" means the amount of fine set by the Chief Judge of the Ontario Court (Provincial Division) for an offence for the purpose of proceedings commenced under Part I or II. …

2. (1) **Purpose of Act.—** The purpose of this Act is to replace the summary conviction procedure for the prosecution of provincial offences, including the provisions adopted by reference to the *Criminal Code* (Canada), with a procedure that reflects the distinction between provincial offences and criminal offences. …

PART I
COMMENCEMENT OF PROCEEDINGS BY CERTIFICATE OF OFFENCE

3. (1) **Certificate of offence.—** In addition to the procedure set out in Part III for commencing a proceeding by laying an information, a proceeding in respect of an offence may be commenced by filing a certificate of offence alleging the offence in the office of the court.

(2) **Issuance and service.—** A provincial offences officer who believes that one or more persons have committed an offence may issue, by completing and signing, a certificate of offence certifying that an offence has been committed and,

     (*a*) an offence notice indicating the set fine for the offence; or

     (*b*) a summons,

in the form prescribed under section 13.

(3) **Service.—** The offence notice or summons shall be served personally upon the person charged within thirty days after the alleged offence occurred.

(4) **Signature.**— Upon the service of an offence notice or summons, the person charged may be requested to sign the certificate of offence, but the failure or refusal to sign as requested does not invalidate the certificate of offence or the service of the offence notice or summons.

(5) **Certificate of service.**— Where service is made by the provincial offences officer who issued the certificate of offence, the officer shall certify on the certificate of offence that he or she personally served the offence notice or summons on the person charged and the date of service.

(6) **Affidavit of service.**— Where service is made by a person other than the provincial offences officer who issued the certificate of offence, he or she shall complete an affidavit of service in the prescribed form.

(7) **Certificate as evidence.**— A certificate of service of an offence notice or summons purporting to be signed by the provincial offences officer issuing it or an affidavit of service under subsection (6) shall be received in evidence and is proof of personal service in the absence of evidence to the contrary.

(8) **Officer not to act as agent.**— The provincial offences officer who serves an offence notice or summons under this section shall not receive payment of any money in respect of a fine, or receive the offence notice for delivery to the court.

4. Filing of certificate of offence.— A certificate of offence shall be filed in the office of the court as soon as is practicable after service of the offence notice or summons.

5. (1) **Intention to appear.**— A defendant who is served with an offence notice may give notice of intention to appear in court for the purpose of entering a plea and having a trial of the matter by so indicating on the offence notice and delivering the notice to the court office specified in it. ...

5.1 (3) **Filing.**— A defendant who is served with an offence notice may give notice of intention to appear in court for the purpose of entering a plea and having a trial of the matter by attending in person or by agent at the court office specified in the offence notice at the time or times specified in the offence notice and filing a notice of intention to appear with the clerk of the court. ...

5.2 (1) **Challenge to officer's evidence.**— A defendant who gives notice of an intention to appear in court for the purpose of entering a plea and having a trial of the matter shall indicate on the notice of intention to appear or offence notice if the defendant intends to challenge the evidence of the provincial offences officer.

(2) **Notifying officer.**— If the defendant indicates an intention to challenge the officer's evidence, the clerk of the court shall notify the officer.

6. (1) **Dispute without appearance.**— Where an offence notice is served on a defendant whose address as shown on the certificate of offence is outside the county or district in which the office of the court specified in the notice is situate, and the defendant wishes to dispute the charge but does not wish to attend or be represented at a trial, the defendant may do so by signifying that intention on the offence notice and delivering the offence notice to the office of the court specified in the notice together with a written dispute setting out with reasonable particularity the defendant's dispute and any facts upon which the defendant relies.

(2) **Disposition.**— Where an offence notice is delivered under subsection (1), a justice shall, in the absence of the defendant, consider the dispute and,

(a) where the dispute raises an issue that may constitute a defence, direct a hearing; or

(b) where the dispute does not raise an issue that may constitute a defence, convict the defendant and impose the set fine.

(3) **Hearing.**— Where the justice directs a hearing under subsection (2), the court shall hold the hearing and shall, in the absence of the defendant, consider the evidence in the light of the issues raised in the dispute, and acquit the defendant or convict the defendant and impose the set fine or such lesser fine as is permitted by law. ...

7. (1) **Plea of guilty with representations.**— Where an offence notice is served on a defendant who does not wish to dispute the charge but wishes to make submissions as to penalty, including the extension of time for payment, the defendant may attend at the time and place specified in the notice and may appear before a justice sitting in court for the purpose of pleading guilty to the offence and making submissions as to penalty, and the justice may enter a conviction and impose the set fine or such lesser fine as is permitted by law. ...

8. (1) **Payment out of court.**— Where an offence notice is served on a defendant who does not wish to dispute the charge, the defendant may sign the plea of guilty on the offence notice and deliver the offence notice and amount of the set fine to the office of the court specified in the notice.

(2) **Conviction.**— Acceptance by the court office of payment under subsection (1) constitutes a plea of guilty whether or not the plea is signed and endorsement of payment on the certificate of offence constitutes the conviction and imposition of a fine in the amount of the set fine for the offence.

9. (1) **Failure to respond to offence notice.**— Where at least fifteen days have elapsed after the defendant was served with the offence notice and the offence notice has not been delivered in accordance with section 6 or 8 and a plea of guilty has not been accepted under section 7, the defendant shall be deemed to not wish to dispute the charge and a justice shall examine the certificate of offence and,

(a) where the certificate of offence is complete and regular on its face, the justice shall enter a conviction in the defendant's absence and without a hearing and impose the set fine for the offence; or

(b) where the certificate of offence is not complete and regular on its face, the justice shall quash the proceeding.

(2) **Where conviction without proof of by-law.**— Where a defendant is deemed to not wish to dispute a charge under subsection (1) in respect of an offence under a by-law of a municipality, the justice shall enter a conviction under clause (1)(a) without proof of the by-law that creates the offence if the certificate of offence is complete and regular on its face.

9.1 (1) **Failure to appear at trial.**— If a defendant who has given notice of an intention to appear fails to appear at the time and place appointed for the hearing, the defendant shall be deemed not to dispute the charge. ...

10. Signature on notice.— A signature on an offence notice or notice of intention to appear purporting to be that of the defendant is proof, in the absence of evidence to the contrary, that it is the signature of the defendant.

11. (1) **Reopening.**— If a defendant who has been convicted without a hearing attends at the court office during regular office hours within fifteen days of becoming aware of the conviction and appears before a justice requesting that the conviction be struck out, the justice shall strike out the conviction if he or she is satisfied by affidavit of the defendant that, through no fault of the defendant, the defendant was unable to appear for a hearing or a notice or document relating to the offence was not delivered. ...

(3) **Trial.**— If a notice of trial is given, the defendant shall indicate on the notice of intention to appear or offence notice if the defendant intends to challenge the evidence of the provincial offences officer who completed the certificate of offence. ...

12. (1) **Penalty.**— Where the penalty prescribed for an offence includes a fine of more than $500 or imprisonment and a proceeding is commenced under this Part, the provision for fine or imprisonment does not apply and in lieu thereof the offence is punishable by a fine of not more than the maximum fine prescribed for the offence or $500, whichever is the lesser. ...

13. (1) **Regulations.**— The Lieutenant Governor in Council may make regulations,

(*a*) prescribing the form of certificates of offence, offence notices and summonses and such other forms as are considered necessary under this Part;

(*b*) authorizing the use in a form prescribed under clause (a) of any word or expression to designate an offence;

(*c*) respecting any matter that is considered necessary to provide for the use of the forms under this Part;

(*d*) designating areas of Ontario for purposes of section 5.1.

(2) **Sufficiency of abbreviated wording.**— The use on a form prescribed under clause (1)(a) of any word or expression authorized by the regulations to designate an offence is sufficient for all purposes to describe the offence designated by such word or expression.

(3) **Idem.**— Where the regulations do not authorize the use of a word or expression to describe an offence in a form prescribed under clause (1)(a), the offence may be described in accordance with section 25. ...

PART III
COMMENCEMENT OF PROCEEDING BY INFORMATION

21. (1) **Commencement of proceeding by information.**— In addition to the procedure set out in Parts I and II for commencing a proceeding by the filing of a certificate, a proceeding in respect of an offence may be commenced by laying an information. ...

22. Summons before information laid.— Where a provincial offences officer believes, on reasonable and probable grounds, that an offence has been committed by a person whom the officer finds at or near the place where the offence was committed, he or she may, before an information is laid, serve the person with a summons in the prescribed form.

23. (1) **Information.**— Any person who, on reasonable and probable grounds, believes that one or more persons have committed an offence, may lay an information in the prescribed form and under oath before a justice alleging the offence and the justice shall receive the information.

(2) **Idem.**— An information may be laid anywhere in Ontario.

24. (1) **Procedure on laying of information.**— A justice who receives an information laid under section 23 shall consider the information and, where he or she considers it desirable to do so, hear and consider in the absence of the defendant the allegations of the informant and the evidence of witnesses and,

    (*a*) where he or she considers that a case for so doing is made out,

        (i) confirm the summons served under section 22, if any,

        (ii) issue a summons in the prescribed form, or

        (iii) where the arrest is authorized by statute and where the allegations of the informant or the evidence satisfy the justice on reasonable and probable grounds that it is necessary in the public interest to do so, issue a warrant for the arrest of the defendant; or

    (*b*) where he or she considers that a case for issuing process is not made out,

        (i) so endorse the information, and

        (ii) where a summons was served under section 22, cancel it and cause the defendant to be so notified. ...

25. (1) **Counts.**— Each offence charged in an information shall be set out in a separate count.

(2) **Allegation of offence.**— Each count in an information shall in general apply to a single transaction and shall contain and is sufficient if it contains in substance a statement that the defendant committed an offence therein specified.

(3) **Reference to statutory provision.**— Where in a count an offence is identified but the count fails to set out one or more of the essential elements of the offence, a reference to the provision creating or defining the offence shall be deemed to incorporate all the essential elements of the offence.

(4) **Idem.**— The statement referred to in subsection (2) may be,

    (*a*) in popular language without technical averments or allegations of matters that are not essential to be proved;

    (*b*) in the words of the enactment that describes the offence; or

    (*c*) in words that are sufficient to give to the defendant notice of the offence with which the defendant is charged.

(5) **More than one count.**— Any number of counts for any number of offences may be joined in the same information.

(6) **Particulars of count.**— A count shall contain sufficient detail of the circumstances of the alleged offence to give to the defendant reasonable information with respect to the act or omission to be proved against the defendant and to identify the transaction referred to.

(7) **Sufficiency.**— No count in an information is insufficient by reason of the absence of details where, in the opinion of the court, the count otherwise fulfils the requirements of this section and, without restricting the generality of the foregoing, no count in an information is insufficient by reason only that,

    (*a*) it does not name the person affected by the offence or intended or attempted to be affected;

    (*b*) it does not name the person who owns or has a special property or interest in property mentioned in the count;

    (*c*) it charges an intent in relation to another person without naming or describing the other person;

(*d*) it does not set out any writing that is the subject of the charge;

(*e*) it does not set out the words used where words that are alleged to have been used are the subject of the charge;

(*f*) it does not specify the means by which the alleged offence was committed;

(*g*) it does not name or describe with precision any person, place or thing; or

(*h*) it does not, where the consent of a person, official or authority is required before proceedings may be instituted for an offence, state that the consent has been obtained.

(8) **Idem.**— A count is not objectionable for the reason only that,

(*a*) it charges in the alternative several different matters, acts or omissions that are stated in the alternative in an enactment that describes as an offence the matters, acts or omissions charged in the count; or

(*b*) it is double or multifarious. ...

26. (1) **Summons.**— A summons issued under section 22 or 24 shall,

(*a*) be directed to the defendant;

(*b*) set out briefly the offence in respect of which the defendant is charged; and

(*c*) require the defendant to attend court at a time and place stated therein and to attend thereafter as required by the court in order to be dealt with according to law.

(2) **Service.**— A summons shall be served by a provincial offences officer by delivering it personally to the person to whom it is directed or if that person cannot conveniently be found, by leaving it for the person at the person's last known or usual place of abode with an inmate thereof who appears to be at least sixteen years of age.

(3) **Service outside Ontario.**— Despite subsection (2), where the person to whom a summons is directed does not reside in Ontario, the summons shall be deemed to have been duly served seven days after it has been sent by registered mail to the person's last known or usual place of abode.

(4) **Service on corporation.**— Service of a summons on a corporation may be effected by delivering the summons personally,

(*a*) in the case of a municipal corporation, to the mayor, warden, reeve or other chief officer of the corporation or to the clerk of the corporation; or

(*b*) in the case of any other corporation, to the manager, secretary or other executive officer of the corporation or person apparently in charge of a branch office thereof,

or by mailing the summons by registered mail to the corporation at an address held out by the corporation to be its address, in which case the summons shall be deemed to have been duly served seven days after the day of mailing.

(5) **Substitutional service.**— A justice, upon motion and upon being satisfied that service cannot be made effectively on a corporation in accordance with subsection (4), may by order authorize another method of service that has a reasonable likelihood of coming to the attention of the corporation.

(6) **Proof of service.**— Service of a summons may be proved by statement under oath or affirmation, written or oral, of the person who made the service.

27. (1) **Contents of warrant.**— A warrant issued under section 24 shall, (*a*) name or describe the defendant;

(*b*) set out briefly the offence in respect of which the defendant is charged; and

(*c*) order that the defendant be forthwith arrested and brought before a justice to be dealt with according to law.

(2) **Idem.**— A warrant issued under section 24 remains in force until it is executed and need not be made returnable at any particular time.

PART IV
TRIAL AND SENTENCING

TRIAL

28. Application of Part.— This Part applies to a proceeding commenced under this Act.

29. (1) **Territorial jurisdiction.**— Subject to subsection (2), a proceeding in respect of an offence shall be heard and determined by the Ontario Court (Provincial Division) sitting in the county or district in which the offence occurred. ...

39. (1) **Issuance of summons.**— Where a justice is satisfied that a person is able to give material evidence in a proceeding under this Act, the justice may issue a summons requiring the person to attend to give evidence and bring with him or her any writings or things referred to in the summons.

(2) **Service.**— A summons shall be served and the service shall be proved in the same manner as a summons under section 26.

(3) **Attendance.**— A person who is served with a summons shall attend at the time and place stated in the summons to give evidence and, if required by the summons, shall bring with him or her any writing or other thing that the person has in his or her possession or under his or her control relating to the subject-matter of the proceeding.

(4) **Remaining in attendance.**— A person who is served with a summons shall remain in attendance during the hearing and the hearing as resumed after adjournment from time to time unless the person is excused from attendance by the presiding justice.

40. (1) **Arrest of witness.**— Where a judge is satisfied upon evidence under oath or affirmation, that a person is able to give material evidence that is necessary in a proceeding under this Act and,

(*a*) will not attend if a summons is served; or

(*b*) attempts to serve a summons have been made and have failed because the person is evading service,

the judge may issue a warrant in the prescribed form for the arrest of the person.

(2) **Idem.**— Where a person who has been served with a summons to attend to give evidence in a proceeding does not attend or remain in attendance, the court may, if it is established,

(*a*) that the summons has been served; and

(*b*) that the person is able to give material evidence that is necessary,

issue or cause to be issued a warrant in the prescribed form for the arrest of the person.

(3) **Bringing before justice.**— The police officer who arrests a person under a warrant issued under subsection (1) or (2) shall immediately take the person before a justice. ...

42. (1) **Penalty for failure to attend.**— Every person who, being required by law to attend or remain in attendance at a hearing, fails without lawful excuse to attend or remain in attendance accordingly is guilty of an offence and on conviction is liable to a fine of not more than $2,000, or to imprisonment for a term of not more than thirty days, or to both. ...

45. (1) **Taking of plea.**— After being informed of the substance of the information or certificate, the defendant shall be asked whether the defendant pleads guilty or not guilty of the offence charged therein.

(2) **Conviction on plea of guilty.**— Where the defendant pleads guilty, the court may accept the plea and convict the defendant.

(3) **Refusal to plead.**— Where the defendant refuses to plead or does not answer directly, the court shall enter a plea of not guilty.

(4) **Plea of guilty to another offence.**— Where the defendant pleads not guilty of the offence charged but guilty of any other offence, whether or not it is an included offence, the court may, with the consent of the prosecutor, accept such plea of guilty and accordingly amend the information or substitute the offence to which the defendant pleads guilty.

46. (1) **Trial on plea of not guilty.**— Subject to section 6, where the defendant pleads not guilty, the court shall hold the trial.

(2) **Right to defend.**— The defendant is entitled to make full answer and defence.

(3) **Right to examine witnesses.**— The prosecutor or defendant, as the case may be, may examine and cross-examine witnesses.

(4) **Agreed facts.**— The court may receive and act upon any facts agreed upon by the defendant and prosecutor without proof or evidence. ...

47. (1) **Evidence taken on another charge.**— The court may receive and consider evidence taken before the same justice on a different charge against the same defendant, with the consent of the parties.

(2) **Certificate as evidence.**— Where a certificate as to the content of an official record is, by any Act, made admissible in evidence as proof, in the absence of evidence to the contrary, the court may, for the purpose of deciding whether the defendant is the person referred to in the certificate, receive and base its decision upon information it considers credible or trustworthy in the circumstances of each case. ...

50. (1) **Appearance by defendant.**— A defendant may appear and act personally or by counsel or agent.

(2) **Appearance by corporation.**— A defendant that is a corporation shall appear and act by counsel or agent.

(3) **Exclusion of agents.**— The court may bar any person from appearing as an agent who is not a barrister and solicitor entitled to practise in Ontario if the court finds that the person is not competent properly to represent or advise the person for whom he or she appears as agent or does not understand and comply with the duties and responsibilities of an agent.

51. Compelling attendance of defendant.— Although a defendant appears by counsel or agent, the court may order the defendant to attend personally, and, where it appears to be necessary to do so, may issue a summons in the prescribed form. ...

53. (1) **Failure of prosecutor to appear.**— Where the defendant appears for a hearing and the prosecutor, having had due notice, does not appear, the court may dismiss the charge or may adjourn the hearing to another time upon such terms as it considers proper.

(2) **Idem.**— Where the prosecutor does not appear at the time and place appointed for the resumption of an adjourned hearing under subsection (1), the court may dismiss the charge.

(3) **Costs.**— Where a hearing is adjourned under subsection (1) or a charge is dismissed under subsection (2), the court may make an order under section 60 for the payment of costs. ...

55. Included offences.— Where the offence as charged includes another offence, the defendant may be convicted of an offence so included that is proved, although the whole offence charged is not proved.

SENTENCING

• • •

59. (1) **Provision for minimum penalty.**— No penalty prescribed for an offence is a minimum penalty unless it is specifically declared to be a minimum.

(2) **Relief against minimum fine.**— Although the provision that creates the penalty for an offence prescribes a minimum fine, where in the opinion of the court exceptional circumstances exist so that to impose the minimum fine would be unduly oppressive or otherwise not in the interests of justice, the court may impose a fine that is less than the minimum or suspend the sentence. ...

60. (1) **Fixed costs on conviction.**— Upon conviction, the defendant is liable to pay to the court an amount by way of costs that is fixed by the regulations.

(2) **Costs respecting witnesses.**— The court may, in its discretion, order costs towards fees and expenses reasonably incurred by or on behalf of witnesses in amounts not exceeding the maximum fixed by the regulations, to be paid,

　　(*a*) to the court or prosecutor by the defendant; or

　　(*b*) to the defendant by the person who laid the information or issued the certificate, as the case may be,

but where the proceeding is commenced by means of a certificate, the total of such costs shall not exceed $100. ...

61. General penalty.— Except where otherwise expressly provided by law, every person who is convicted of an offence is liable to a fine of not more that $5,000. ...

PART V
GENERAL PROVISIONS

76. (1) **Limitation.**— A proceeding shall not be commenced after the expiration of any limitation period prescribed by or under any Act for the offence or, where no limitation period is prescribed, after six months after the date on which the offence was, or is alleged to have been, committed. ...

77. (1) **Parties to offence.**— Every person is a party to an offence who,

　　(*a*) actually commits it,

(*b*) does or omits to do anything for the purpose of aiding any person to commit it; or

(*c*) abets any person in committing it.

(2) **Common purpose.**— Where two or more persons form an intention in common to carry out an unlawful purpose and to assist each other therein and any one of them, in carrying out the common purpose, commits an offence, each of them who knew or ought to have known that the commission of the offence would be a probable consequence of carrying out the common purpose is a party to the offence.

78. (1) **Counselling.**— Where a person counsels or procures another person to be a party to an offence and that other person is afterwards a party to the offence, the person who counselled or procured is a party to the offence, even if the offence was committed in a way different from that which was counselled or procured.

(2) **Idem.**— Every person who counsels or procures another person to be a party to an offence is a party to every offence that the other commits in consequence of the counselling or procuring that the person who counselled or procured knew or ought to have known was likely to be committed in consequence of the counselling or procuring. ...

80. Common law defences.— Every rule and principle of the common law that renders any circumstance a justification or excuse for an act or a defence to a charge continues in force and applies in respect of offences, except in so far as they are altered by or inconsistent with this or any other Act.

81. Ignorance of the law.— Ignorance of the law by a person who commits an offence is not an excuse for committing the offence.

82. Counsel or agent.— A defendant may act by counsel or agent. ...

PART VI
YOUNG PERSONS

93. Definitions.— In this Part,

"parent", when used with reference to a young person, includes an adult with whom the young person ordinarily resides;

"young person" means a person who is or, in the absence of evidence to the contrary, appears to be,

(a) twelve years of age or more, but

(b) under sixteen years of age,

and includes a person sixteen years of age or more charged with having committed an offence while he or she was twelve years of age or more but under sixteen years of age.

94. Minimum age.— No person shall be convicted of an offence committed while he or she was under twelve years of age.

95. Offence notice not to be used.— A proceeding commenced against a young person by certificate of offence shall not be initiated by an offence notice under clause 3(2)(a).

96. (1) **Notice to parent.**— Where a summons is served upon a young person or a young person is released on a recognizance under this Act, the provincial offences officer, in the case of a summons, or the officer in charge, in the case of a recognizance, shall as soon as practicable give notice to a parent of the young person by delivering a copy of the summons or recognizance to the parent.

(2) **Where no notice given.**— Where notice has not been given under subsection (1) and no person to whom notice could have been given appears with the young person, the court may,

> (*a*) adjourn the hearing to another time to permit notice to be given; or

> (*b*) dispense with notice.

(3) **Saving.**— Failure to give notice to a parent under subsection (1) does not in itself invalidate the proceeding against the young person. ...

98. (1) **Young person to be present at trial.**— Subject to subsection 52(1) and subsection (2) of this section, a young person shall be present in court during the whole of his or her trial.

(2) **Court may permit absence.**— The court may permit a young person to be absent during the whole or any part of his or her trial, on such conditions as the court considers proper. ...

(5) **Compelling young person's attendance.**— Where a young person does not attend personally in response to a summons issued under section 51 and it is proved by the prosecutor, having been given a reasonable opportunity to do so, that the summons was served, the court may adjourn the hearing and issue a further summons or issue a warrant in the prescribed form for the arrest of the young person.

99. (1) **Identity of young person not to be published.**— No person shall publish by any means a report,

> (*a*) of an offence committed or alleged to have been committed by a young person; or

> (*b*) of a hearing, adjudication, sentence or appeal concerning a young person who committed or is alleged to have committed an offence,

in which the name of or any information serving to identify the young person is disclosed.

(2) **Offence.**— Every person who contravenes subsection (1) and every director, officer or employee of a corporation who authorizes, permits or acquiesces in a contravention of subsection (1) by the corporation is guilty of an offence and is liable on conviction to a fine of not more than $10,000.

(3) **Exceptions.**— Subsection (1) does not prohibit the following:

1. The disclosure of information by the young person concerned.

2. The disclosure of information by the young person's parent or lawyer, for the purpose of protecting the young person's interests.

3. The disclosure of information by a police officer, for the purpose of investigating an offence which the young person is suspected of having committed.

4. The disclosure of information to an insurer, to enable the insurer to investigate a claim arising out of an offence committed or alleged to have been committed by the young person.

5. The disclosure of information in the course of the administration of justice, but not for the purpose of making the information known in the community.

6. The disclosure of information by a person or member of a class of persons prescribed by the regulations, for a purpose prescribed by the regulations. ...

101. (1) **Penalties limited.**— Despite the provisions of this or any other Act, no young person shall be sentenced,

(*a*) to be imprisoned, except under clause 75(d); or

(*b*) to pay a fine exceeding $1,000. ...

104. Evidence of young person's age.— In a proceeding under this Act, a parent's testimony as to a young person's age and any other evidence of a young person's age that the court considers credible or trustworthy in the circumstances are admissible. ...

106. Arrest without warrant limited.— No person shall exercise an authority under this or any other Act to arrest a young person without warrant unless the person has reasonable and probable grounds to believe that it is necessary in the public interest to do so in order to,

(*a*) establish the young person's identity; or

(*b*) prevent the continuation or repetition of an offence that constitutes a serious danger to the young person or to the person or property of another. ...

107. (2) **Release after arrest by officer.**— Where a police officer acting under a warrant or other power of arrest arrests a young person, the police officer shall, as soon as is practicable, release the young person from custody unconditionally or after serving him or her with a summons unless the officer has reasonable and probable grounds to believe that it is necessary in the public interest for the young person to be detained in order to,

(*a*) establish the young person's identity; or

(*b*) prevent the continuation or repetition of an offence that constitutes a serious danger to the young person or the person or property of another.

(3) **Release by officer in charge.**— Where a young person is not released from custody under subsection (2), the police officer shall deliver the young person to the officer in charge who shall, where in his or her opinion the conditions set out in clause (2)(a) or (b) do not or no longer exist, release the young person,

(*a*) unconditionally;

(*b*) upon serving the young person with a summons; or

(*c*) upon the young person entering into a recognizance in the prescribed form without sureties conditioned for his or her appearance in court.

(4) **Notice to parent.**— Where the officer in charge does not release the young person under subsection (3), the officer in charge shall as soon as possible notify a parent of the young person by advising the parent, orally or in writing, of the young person's arrest, the reason for the arrest and the place of detention.

(5) **ss. 150, 151 apply.**— Sections 150 and 151 apply with necessary modifications to the release of a young person from custody under this section. ...

(7) [**Place of custody**].— Wherever practicable, a young person who is detained in custody shall be detained in a place of temporary detention designated under subsection 7(1) of the *Young Offenders Act* (Canada). ...

PART VIII
ARREST, BAIL AND SEARCH WARRANTS

ARREST

143. Officer in charge.— In this Part, "officer in charge" means the police officer who is in charge of the lock-up or other place to which a person is taken after his or her arrest.

144. (1) **Execution of warrant.**— A warrant for the arrest of a person shall be executed by a police officer by arresting the person against whom the warrant is directed wherever he or she is found in Ontario.

(2) **Idem.**— A police officer may arrest without warrant a person for whose arrest he or she has reasonable and probable grounds to believe that a warrant is in force in Ontario.

145. Arrest without warrant.— Any person may arrest without warrant a person who he or she has reasonable and probable grounds to believe has committed an offence and is escaping from and freshly pursued by a police officer who has lawful authority to arrest that person, and, where the person who makes the arrest is not a police officer, shall forthwith deliver the person arrested to a police officer.

146. (1) **Use of force.**— Every police officer is, if he or she acts on reasonable and probable grounds, justified in using as much force as is necessary to do what the officer is required or authorized by law to do. ...

147. Immunity from civil liability.— Where a person is wrongfully arrested, whether with or without a warrant, no action for damages shall be brought,

    (*a*) against the police officer making the arrest if he or she believed in good faith and on reasonable and probable grounds that the person arrested was the person named in the warrant or was subject to arrest without warrant under the authority of an Act;

    (*b*) against any person called upon to assist the police officer if such person believed that the police officer had the right to effect the arrest; or

    (*c*) against any person required to detain the prisoner in custody if such person believed the arrest was lawfully made.

148. (1) **Production of process.**— It is the duty of every one who executes a process or warrant to have it with him or her, where it is feasible to do so, and to produce it when requested to do so.

(2) **Notice of reason for arrest.**— It is the duty of every one who arrests a person, whether with or without warrant, to give notice to that person, where it is feasible to do so, of the reason for the arrest.

BAIL

149. (1) **Release after arrest by officer.**— Where a police officer, acting under a warrant or other power of arrest, arrests a person, the police officer shall, as soon as is practicable, release the person from custody after serving him or her with a summons or offence notice unless the officer has reasonable and probable grounds to believe that,

> (*a*) it is necessary in the public interest for the person to be detained, having regard to all the circumstances including the need to,
>
> > (i) establish the identity of the person,
> >
> > (ii) secure or preserve evidence of or relating to the offence, or
> >
> > (iii) prevent the continuation or repetition of the offence or the commission of another offence; or
>
> (*b*) the person arrested is ordinarily resident outside Ontario and will not respond to a summons or offence notice.

(2) **Release by officer in charge.**— Where a defendant is not released from custody under subsection (1), the police officer shall deliver him or her to the officer in charge who shall, where in his or her opinion the conditions set out in clauses (1)(a) and (b) do not or no longer exist, release the defendant,

> (*a*) upon serving the defendant with a summons or offence notice;
>
> (*b*) upon the defendant entering into a recognizance in the prescribed form without sureties conditioned for his or her appearance in court. ...

150. (1) **Person in custody to be brought before justice.**— Where a defendant is not released from custody under section 149, the officer in charge shall, as soon as is practicable but in any event within twenty-four hours, bring the defendant before a justice and the justice shall, unless a plea of guilty is taken, order that the defendant be released upon giving his or her undertaking to appear unless the prosecutor having been given an opportunity to do so shows cause why the detention of the defendant is justified to ensure his or her appearance in court or why an order under subsection (2) is justified for the same purpose. ...

SEARCH WARRANTS

158. (1) **Search warrant.**— Where a justice is satisfied by information upon oath that there is reasonable ground to believe that there is in any building, receptacle or place,

> (*a*) anything upon or in respect of which an offence has been or is suspected to have been committed; or
>
> (*b*) anything that there is reasonable ground to believe will afford evidence as to the commission of an offence,

the justice may at any time issue a warrant in the prescribed form under his or her hand authorizing a police officer or person named therein to search such building, receptacle or place for any such thing, and to seize and carry it before the justice issuing the warrant or another justice to be dealt with by him or her according to law.

(2) **Expiration.**— Every search warrant shall name a date upon which it expires, which date shall be not later than fifteen days after its issue.

(3) **When to be executed.**— Every search warrant shall be executed between 6 a.m. and 9 p.m. standard time, unless the justice by the warrant otherwise authorizes.

159. (1) **Detention of thing seized.**— Where any thing is seized and brought before a justice, he or she shall by order,

(a) detain it or direct it to be detained in the care of a person named in the order; or

(b) direct it to be returned,

and the justice may in the order authorize the examination, testing, inspection or reproduction of the thing seized upon such conditions as are reasonably necessary and directed in the order, and may make any other provision as in the opinion of the justice is necessary for its preservation.

(2) **Time limit for detention.**— Nothing shall be detained under an order made under subsection (1) for a period of more than three months after the time of seizure unless, before the expiration of that period,

(a) upon motion, a justice is satisfied that having regard to the nature of the investigation, its further detention for a specified period is warranted and he or she so orders; or

(b) a proceeding is instituted in which the thing detained may be required.

EXERCISES

■ MULTIPLE CHOICE

1. A search warrant issued under the POA is:

   a. valid until it is executed

   b. valid until the expiry date

   c. valid, no later than 21 days after its issue

   d. valid, no later than 15 days after its issue

   e. b or c

2. The authority to search without a warrant for provincial offences is found:

   a. in the *Criminal Code*

   b. in each provincial statute

   c. in neither a nor b

3. The limitation period for provincial offences is _____, unless stated otherwise in the charging statute.

   a. one year

   b. six months

   c. three months

   d. until the person is charged

■ TRUE OR FALSE

T 1. A provincial offence notice, part I, must be served personally or substitutionally within 30 days of the alleged offence.

T 2. Any person may appear before a justice and issue a certificate of offence.

F 3. POA search warrants must be executed at any time between 9:00 a.m. and 6:00 p.m.

■ CASE STUDY #1

While on radar patrol in the west end of the city, you clock a vehicle at 68 km/hr in a 50 km/hr zone on Queen St. The vehicle is stopped a short distance from where you were set up. It is a 1984 Ford Ranger, Ontario plate number AB1 423. The driver identifies himself as Alfred Abel, age 28, of 192 First St. You ask him for his driver's licence, ownership, and insurance. He tells you that he forgot his documents at home. You advise him that he is being charged with speeding 65 km/hr in a 50 km/hr zone and that you will provide him with an opportunity to bring the missing documentation to the police station within 24 hours for inspection.

Complete a part I certificate of offence for the speeding infraction. Use $2.50 per kilometre over the limit to calculate the set fine.

1. What options are available to Abel with respect to this charge?

2. How much time does Abel have to make a decision about what to do about this charge?

3. If Abel decides to contest this charge, does he have to be represented by a lawyer? Explain.

4. Abel shows up the next day at the police station with the ownership for the Ford Ranger and confesses that he does not have insurance on the vehicle. Complete the proper documentation for this offence.

5. Where did you find the proper wording for:

    a. the speeding charge?

    b. the second charge?

■ CASE STUDY #2

Two days ago, your sergeant received information that Alfred Abel of 192 First St. was observed going through a red light at First St. and Second Ave. in his 1984 Ford Ranger. Today he assigns you to visit Abel at home and to charge him with the offence. Janice Gabel, age 44, of 221 Second Ave. witnessed the incident and has indicated that she will testify against Abel. You attend at Gabel's home and find out that the Ford Ranger was proceeding north on First St., that the light for northbound traffic had been red for several seconds, and that she was just starting through the intersection when the Ranger went speeding through against the red light. Abel stopped briefly, looked at her, and then left the scene. She knows Abel because he lives around the corner from her. Gabel's mother was in the car with her and can verify everything that she said.

You attend at Abel's house and he denies everything. You advise him that he will be charged with the red-light infraction. Complete the process using the proper documentation.

CHAPTER 3
The Liquor Licence Act

CHAPTER OBJECTIVES

After completing this chapter, you should be able to:

◆ Understand key terms defined in the *Liquor Licence Act*.

◆ Explain police officer arrest, search, and seizure authorities contained in the Act.

◆ Explain the process with respect to any arrest, search, or seizure of liquor under the Act.

◆ Be prepared to apply the provisions of the Act in a hypothetical fact situation, and to complete the required documentation.

INTRODUCTION

The *Liquor Licence Act* (LLA) deals with behaviour that is commonly encountered by police officers. In fact, next to *Highway Traffic Act* offences, LLA offences are probably the most common provincial offences.

The *Liquor Licence Act* governs the purchase and consumption of alcoholic beverages. It affects many individuals of varying backgrounds and ages, and applies to all kinds of settings.

Different laws exist for minors, adults, families who drink at home, and owners of licensed establishments. There are also laws governing the use of alcohol in specific settings. There is nothing wrong with enjoying a glass of wine inside the comfort of one's home. The *Liquor Licence Act*, however, makes it illegal to carry open alcohol in a car or boat.

Even with respect to minors, the rules change depending on where the alcohol is consumed. It is not illegal, for example, for a 16-year-old child to drink a glass of wine or beer at home with his parents, but once that 16-year-old goes outside onto the street (which is a "public place"), an infraction under the *Liquor Licence Act* has occurred.

The *Liquor Licence Act* also contains strict laws governing the use and sale of liquor in stores, restaurants, and bars.

As discussed earlier, provincial offences are regulatory offences, designed for the protection of individuals and society as a whole. The public policy considerations that underlie provincial offences statutes are perhaps most clear in the case of the *Liquor Licence Act*, because this Act contains laws that attempt to protect people who, in some instances, do not want to be protected. An obvious example is a person who spends all of his or her time drinking alcohol on the street and clearly wants to be left alone. The *Liquor Licence Act* prohibits drinking in a public place, regardless of the individual's wish or belief that he or she can look after himself or herself.

PROVING A LIQUOR LICENCE ACT OFFENCE

The essential elements of an LLA offence, like any other provincial offence, must be proven beyond a reasonable doubt. These elements, or facts in issue, include:

◆ date,

◆ time,

◆ location,

◆ identity of the accused, and

◆ elements of the offence.

The elements of the specific offence are contained in the charging sections of the Act. In order to gather sufficient evidence to support the charge, a police officer must first identify the offence that was committed, locate the offence in the Act, and proceed to investigate based on the elements of the offence that require proof in court.

The date and time of an offence are usually simple enough to prove. Proving location will often be straightforward as well, but not always, because the legislation creates different rules for different types of locations. For example, when an offence is committed near a location that is usually considered a private place, the police officer must take special care in describing the location in his or her notes and in the charging documents so as to avoid a challenge on this issue in court.

The identity of a person charged under the *Liquor Licence Act* can be established by the officer as witness pointing to that person in court. The officer will often be able to support the identification by testifying that he or she requested and examined the accused's identification documents.

Because many LLA charges relate to the age of the accused, special care must be taken in establishing age. If the accused refuses to produce identification or to admit that he or she was under 19 years of the age at the time of the offence, the accused's mother may be required to give testimony as to when the accused was born. Where an accused does admit his or her age at the time of charging, it is important for the police officer to note exactly how the accused identified himself or herself and gave his or her age, because this may become a point of contention in a court proceeding.

It is often necessary to establish that the accused was intoxicated at the time of the offence. The most commonly accepted evidence of intoxication is the police officer's observation of a strong smell of alcohol on the accused's breath. (It is not necessary, nor is it generally possible, to attempt to identify the specific type of alcohol detected.) This observation is often corroborated by evidence of other observed signs such as:

◆   staggering and physical clumsiness or lack of motor coordination;

◆   swollen and/or bloodshot eyes;

◆   slurred speech; and

◆   obnoxious or aggressive behaviour.

THE ROLE OF OTHER LEGISLATION

Finally, when investigating an LLA offence, police may sometimes need to take into account the application of other legislation. For example, intoxication is often a factor in crimes involving violence or disturbance of the peace, and criminal charges may need to be considered. In other cases, officers may need to rely on other provincial legislation to resolve an alcohol-related conflict. For example, where the owner of a licensed establishment has requested that an intoxicated patron leave the premises and the patron refuses to leave, police can rely, in appropriate circumstances, on their arrest authority under the *Trespass to Property Act* to remove the patron from the premises.

LIQUOR LICENCE ACT

R.S.O. 1990, Chapter L.19

1. Definitions.— In this Act,

"alcohol" means a product of fermentation or distillation of grains, fruits or other agricultural products, and includes synthetic ethyl alcohol;

"beer" means any beverage containing alcohol in excess of the prescribed amount obtained by the fermentation of an infusion or decoction of barley, malt and hops or of any similar products in drinkable water;

"Board," "member of the Board" and "employee of the Board" means the board of the Alcohol and Gaming Commission of Ontario or the Registrar of Alcohol and Gaming, as the case may be, as set out in the regulations made under the *Alcohol and Gaming Regulation and Public Protection Act, 1996*;

"government store" means a government store established under the *Liquor Control Act*;

"licence" means a licence issued under this Act;

"liquor" means spirits, wine and beer or any combination thereof and includes any alcohol in a form appropriate for human consumption as a beverage, alone or in combination with any other matter;

"manufacturer" means a person who produces liquor for sale;

"municipality" means a city, town, village or township;

"Ontario wine" means,

   (a) wine produced in Ontario from grapes, cherries, apples or other fruits grown in Ontario, the concentrated juice of those fruits or other agricultural products containing sugar or starch and includes Ontario wine to which is added herbs, water, honey, sugar or the distillate of Ontario wine or cereal grains grown in Ontario.

   (b) wine produced by the alcoholic fermentation of Ontario honey, with or without the addition of caramel, natural botanical flavours or the distillate of Ontario honey wine, or

   (c) wine produced from a combination of,

      (i) apples grown in Ontario or the concentrated juice thereof to which is added herbs, water, honey, sugar or the distillate of Ontario wine or cereal grains grown in Ontario, and

      (ii) the concentrated juice of apples grown outside of Ontario,

in such proportion as is prescribed;

> O. reg. 74/91, s. 1, part; O. reg. 163/96, s. 3
>
> "operating day" means the period during which liquor may be sold and served in accordance with subsections 25(1) and (2), beginning at 11 a.m. and ending at 2 a.m. or 3 a.m. on the following day.

"permit" means a permit issued under this Act;

"prescribed" means prescribed by the regulations;

O. reg. 547/90, s. 3

PRIVATE PLACE

3. (1) For the purposes of clauses 30(13)(a) and 31(2)(c) of the Act, "private place" means a place, vehicle or boat described in this section.

"regulations" means the regulations made under this Act;

"sell" means to supply for remuneration, directly or indirectly, in any manner by which the cost is recovered from the person supplied, alone or in combination with others, and "sale" has a corresponding meaning;

"spirits" means any beverage containing alcohol obtained by distillation;

"wine" means any beverage containing alcohol in excess of the prescribed amount obtained by the fermentation of the natural sugar contents of fruits, including grapes, apples and other agricultural products containing sugar, and including honey and milk. …

LICENCES AND PERMITS

5. (1) **Licence or permit required.**— No person shall keep for sale, offer for sale or sell liquor except under the authority of a licence or permit to sell liquor or under the authority of a manufacturer's licence.

O. reg. 546/90, s. 8(2); O. reg. 163/96, s. 1

CLASSES OF LICENCES

8. (1) The following classes of licences to sell liquor are established:

1. A liquor sales licence authorizing the sale and service of liquor for consumption on the premises to which the licence applies.

2. A mini bar licence authorizing the sale and service of liquor from a dispenser in a room rented as overnight accommodation on the premises to which the licence applies.

(2) The following endorsements to liquor sales licences are established:

1. A brew pub endorsement authorizing the sale and service, for consumption on the premises to which the licence applies, of beer manufactured by the applicant.

2. A wine pub endorsement authorizing the sale and service, for consumption on the premises to which the licence applies, of wine manufactured by the applicant.

3. A caterer's endorsement authorizing the applicant to sell and serve liquor for an event held on premises other than the premises to which the liquor sales licence applies.

4. A room service endorsement authorizing the applicant to sell and serve liquor to persons registered as guests in a facility that rents overnight accommodation adjacent to the premises to which the licence applies.

5. A mini bar endorsement authorizing the sale and service of liquor from a dispenser in a room rented as overnight accommodation in a facility adjacent to the premises to which the liquor sales licence applies.

6. A golf course endorsement authorizing the sale and service of liquor to golfers for consumption on the playing area of a golf course.

(2) **Soliciting orders.**— No person shall canvass for, receive or solicit orders for the sale of liquor unless the person is the holder of a licence or permit to sell liquor or unless the person is the holder of a licence to represent a manufacturer.

(3) **Delivery for fee.**— No person shall deliver liquor for a fee except under the authority of a licence to deliver liquor. ...

10. (1) **Licence to deliver.**— A person may apply to the Board for a licence to deliver liquor. ...

19. (1) **Special occasion permit.**— A person may apply to the Board for a permit authorizing the holder thereof to sell or serve liquor on a prescribed special occasion.

(2) **Requirements.**— An applicant for a permit for a special occasion is entitled to be issued the permit except if,

(a) the applicant would not be entitled to the issuance of a licence to sell liquor for any ground under clauses 6(2)(d) to (g) or subsection 6(4) or (4.1); or

(b) the premises for which the permit is applied are disqualified under section 20. ...

O. reg. 389/91, ss. 2 and 3

SPECIAL OCCASION PERMITS

2. The following classes of special occasion permits are established:

1. A sales permit authorizing the sale and service of liquor.

2. A no-sale permit authorizing the service of liquor without charge.

3. An auction permit authorizing the sale of liquor by way of auction.

3. For the purpose of subsection 19(1) of the Act, the following are the prescribed special occasions:

1. A reception for invited guests only that is conducted without the intention of gain or profit.

2. A fundraising event for the advancement of charitable, educational, religious or community objects conducted by,

i. a charitable organization that is registered under the Income Tax Act (Canada), or

    ii.   a non-profit association or organization for the advancement of charitable, educational, religious or community objects.

3. An event of provincial, national or international significance or an event designated by a municipal council as an event of municipal significance.

4. A trade show or consumer show at which the major themes, exhibits and demonstrations are directly related to an aspect of the hospitality industry and conducted without the intention of gain or profit and to which,

    i.   in the case of a trade show, only persons involved in the hospitality industry and their guests are permitted, and in the case of a consumer show, the general public is admitted.

5. An event at which market research on a liquor product will be carried out by or on behalf of the manufacturer of the product.

6. An event designated by the municipal council or by a delegated official of the municipality as a community festival and conducted by a charitable organization registered under the Income Tax Act (Canada) or by a non-profit association or organization for the advancement of charitable, educational, religious or community objects.

7. An auction conducted by or on behalf of,

    i.   a charitable organization that is registered under the Income Tax Act (Canada),

    ii.   an administrator or executor of an estate acting within the scope of his, her or its duties, or

    iii.   a Sheriff acting within the scope of his or her duties.

RESPONSIBLE USE

27. Unlawful purchase.— No person shall purchase liquor except from a government store or from a person authorized by licence or permit to sell liquor.

28. Unlawful gift.— No manufacturer or employee, agent or licensed representative of a manufacturer shall give any liquor to any person, except as permitted by the regulations.

29. Sale to intoxicated person.— No person shall sell or supply liquor or permit liquor to be sold or supplied to any person who is or appears to be intoxicated.

30. (1) **Sale to person under nineteen.**— No person shall knowingly sell or supply liquor to a person under nineteen years of age.

(2) **Idem.**— No person shall sell or supply liquor to a person who appears to be under nineteen years of age.

(3) **Permitting possession or consumption.**— No licensee or employee or agent of a licensee shall knowingly permit a person under nineteen years of age to have or consume liquor in the licensee's licensed premises.

(4) **Idem.**— No licensee or employee or agent of a licensee shall permit a person who appears to be under nineteen years of age to have or consume liquor in the licensee's licensed premises.

(5) **Exception to subss. (3) and (4).**— Subsections (3) and (4) do not prohibit a licensee or employee or agent of a licensee from permitting a person eighteen years of age to be in possession of liquor during the course of the person's employment on the licensee's licensed premises.

(6) **Vendor may rely on documentation.**— A person who sells or supplies liquor to another person or permits another person to have or consume liquor in licensed premises on the basis of documentation of a prescribed type is not in contravention of subsection (2) or (4) if there is no apparent reason to doubt the authenticity of the documentation or that it was issued to the person producing it.

(7) **Court may determine apparent age.**— In a prosecution for a contravention of subsection (2) or (4), the court may determine, from the appearance of the person and from other relevant circumstances, whether a person to whom liquor was served or supplied or a person who was permitted to have or consume liquor appears to be under nineteen years of age.

(8) **Possession or consumption.**— No person under nineteen years of age shall have, consume, attempt to purchase, purchase or otherwise obtain liquor.

(9) **Exception to subs. (8).**— Subsection (8) does not prohibit a person eighteen years of age from being in possession of liquor during the course of the person's employment on premises in which the sale of liquor is authorized.

(10) **Entering premises.**— No person under nineteen years of age shall enter or remain on premises in which the sale of liquor is authorized if the person knows that a condition of the licence or permit for the premises prohibits the entry of persons under nineteen years of age.

(11) **Exception to subs. (10).**— Subsection (10) does not apply to a person eighteen years of age who is employed on premises in which the sale of liquor is authorized while the person is on the premises during the course of his or her employment.

(12) **Improper documentation.**— No person shall present as evidence of his or her age any documentation other than documentation that was lawfully issued to him or her.

O. reg. 546/90, s. 41, part; O. reg. 560/96, s. 1; O. reg. 63/98, s. 13(1)

41. (5) The following types of identification are prescribed for the purpose of subsection 30(6) of the Act:

1. A driver licence issued by the Province of Ontario with a photograph of the person to whom the licence is issued.

2. A Canadian passport.

3. A Canadian citizenship card with a photograph of the person to whom the card is issued.

4. A Canadian armed forces identification card.

> 5. A photo card issued by the board of the Alcohol and Gaming Commission of Ontario.
>
> 6. A photo card issued by the Liquor Control Board of Ontario.

(13) **Supply by parent.**— This section does not apply,

(*a*) to the supplying of liquor to a person under nineteen years of age in a residence as defined in section 31 or in a private place as defined in the regulations by a parent of the person or a person having lawful custody of the person; or

(*b*) to the consumption of liquor by a person who is supplied liquor in a manner described in clause (a), if the liquor is consumed at the place where it is supplied.

31. (1) **Definition.**— In this section, "residence" means a place that is actually occupied and used as a dwelling, whether or not in common with other persons, including all premises used in conjunction with the place to which the general public is not invited or permitted access, and, if the place occupied and used as a dwelling is a tent, includes the land immediately adjacent to and used in conjunction with the tent.

(2) **Unlawful possession or consumption.**— No person shall have or consume liquor in any place other than,

(*a*) a residence;

(*b*) premises in respect of which a licence or permit is issued; or

(*c*) a private place as defined in the regulations.

(3) **Exception.**— Subsection (2) does not apply to the possession of liquor that is in a closed container.

(4) **Intoxication.**— No person shall be in an intoxicated condition,

(*a*) in a place to which the general public is invited or permitted access; or

(*b*) in any part of a residence that is used in common by persons occupying more than one dwelling in the residence.

(5) **Arrest without warrant.**— A police officer may arrest without warrant any person whom he or she finds contravening subsection (4) if, in the opinion of the police officer, to do so is necessary for the safety of any person.

32. (1) **Conveying liquor in vehicle.**— No person shall drive or have the care or control of a motor vehicle as defined in the *Highway Traffic Act* or a motorized snow vehicle, whether it is in motion or not, while there is contained in the vehicle any liquor, except under the authority of a licence or permit.

(2) **Exception.**— Subsection (1) does not apply if the liquor in the vehicle,

(*a*) is in a container that is unopened and the seal unbroken; or

(*b*) is packed in baggage that is fastened closed or is not otherwise readily available to any person in the vehicle.

(3) **Conveying liquor in boat.**— No person shall operate or have the care or control of a boat that is underway while there is contained in the boat any liquor, except under the authority of a licence or permit.

(4) **Exception.**— Subsection (3) does not apply if the liquor in the boat,

(*a*) is in a container that is unopened and the seal unbroken; or

(*b*) is stored in a closed compartment.

(5) **Search of vehicle or boat.**— A police officer who has reasonable grounds to believe that liquor is being unlawfully kept in a vehicle or boat may at any time, without a warrant, enter and search the vehicle or boat and search any person found in it.

(6) **Definition.**— In this section, "boat" includes any ship or boat or any other description of vessel used or designed to be used in the navigation of water.

33. **Unlawful consumption or supply of alcohol.**— No person shall,

(*a*) drink alcohol in a form that is not a liquor; or

(*b*) supply alcohol in a form that is not a liquor to another person, if the person supplying the alcohol knows or ought to know that the other person intends it to be used as a drink.

34. (1) **Removing person from premises.**— The holder of a licence or permit issued in respect of premises shall ensure that a person does not remain on the premises if the holder has reasonable grounds to believe that the person,

(*a*) is unlawfully on the premises;

(*b*) is on the premises for an unlawful purpose; or

(*c*) is contravening the law on the premises.

(2) **Idem.**— The holder of a licence or permit may request a person referred to in subsection (1) to leave the premises immediately and if the request is not forthwith complied with may remove the person or cause the person to be removed by the use of no more force than is necessary.

(3) **Order to vacate premises.**— If there are reasonable grounds to believe that a disturbance or breach of the peace sufficient to constitute a threat to the public safety is being caused on premises for which a licence or permit is issued, a police officer may require that all persons vacate the premises.

(4) **Idem.**— The holder of the licence or permit for premises that are required to be vacated under subsection (3) shall take all reasonable steps to ensure that the premises are vacated.

(5) **Right to refuse entry.**— A licensee or employee of a licensee who has reason to believe that the presence of a person on the licensee's licensed premises is undesirable may,

(*a*) request the person to leave; or

(*b*) forbid the person to enter the licensed premises.

(6) **Not to remain after request to leave.**— No person shall,

(*a*) remain on licensed premises after he or she is requested to leave by the licensee or an employee of the licensee; or

(*b*) re-enter the licensed premises on the same day he or she is requested to leave.

34.1 (1) **Removing persons from premises.**— If there are reasonable grounds to believe that this Act or a prescribed provision of the regulations is being contravened on any premises, a police officer may require that all persons vacate the premises.

(2) **Same.**— Subsection (1) does not apply in respect of persons actually residing in the premises. ...

35. (3) **Unlawful possession.**— No person shall have liquor in a place designated under subsection (1).

(4) **Exception to subs. (3).**— Subsection (3) does not apply to a person in possession of liquor under the authority of a licence or permit or in possession of liquor purchased on premises in respect of which a licence or permit is issued.

(5) **Definition.**— In this section, "municipality" includes a regional, metropolitan or district municipality and the County of Oxford.

36. (1) **Taking to hospital in lieu of charge.**— A police officer who finds a person apparently in contravention of subsection 31(4) may take the person into custody and, in lieu of laying an information in respect of the contravention, may escort the person to a hospital designated by the regulations.

(2) **Protection from liability.**— No action or other proceeding for damages shall be instituted against any physician or any hospital or officer or employee of a hospital on the grounds only that the person examines or treats without consent a person who is brought to the hospital under subsection (1).

(3) **Exception.**— Subsection (2) does not apply if consent to the examination or treatment is required under the *Health Care Consent Act, 1996.*

37. (1) **Detention in institution.**— If it appears that a person in contravention of subsection 31(4) may benefit therefrom, the court making the conviction may order the person to be detained for treatment for a period of ninety days or such lesser period as the court thinks advisable in an institution designated by the regulations.

(2) **Idem.**— If, at any time during a person's period of detention ordered under subsection (1), the superintendent of the institution is of the opinion that further detention in the institution will not benefit the person, the superintendent may release the person.

(2.1) **Consent to treatment.**— An order under subsection (1) does not authorize the administration of treatment without consent, if consent to the treatment is required under the *Health Care Consent Act, 1996.* ...

39. Civil liability.— The following rules apply if a person or an agent or employee of a person sells liquor to or for a person whose condition is such that the consumption of liquor would apparently intoxicate the person or increase the person's intoxication so that he or she would be in danger of causing injury to himself or herself or injury or damage to another person or the property of another person:

1. If the person to or for whom the liquor is sold commits suicide or meets death by accident while so intoxicated, an action under Part V of the *Family Law Act* lies against the person who or whose employee or agent sold the liquor.

2. If the person to or for whom the liquor is sold causes injury or damage to another person or the property of another person while so intoxicated, the other person is entitled to recover an amount as compensation for the injury or damage from the person who or whose employee or agent sold the liquor. ...

42. Intoxicating liquor.— Liquor shall be deemed to be an intoxicating liquor for purposes of the *Importation of Intoxicating Liquors Act* (Canada).

[Handwritten margin note: CAN'T CHARGE A PERSON THAT YOU BRING TO HOSPITAL]

COMPLIANCE

43. (1) **Persons designated by chair.**— The chair of the Board may designate persons employed by the Board as persons who may carry out inspections for the purpose of determining whether there is compliance with this Act and the regulations.

(2) **Certificate of designation.**— A person designated under subsection (1) who is exercising a power under this Act shall, on request, produce his or her certificate of designation.

44. (1) **Inspections.**— For the purpose of ensuring compliance with this Act and the regulations, a person designated under subsection 43(1) may,

(*a*) enter any place at any reasonable time;

(*b*) request the production for inspection of documents or things that may be relevant to the inspection;

(*c*) inspect and, upon giving a receipt therefor, remove, for the purpose of making copies or extracts, documents or things relevant to the inspection;

(*d*) inquire into negotiations, transactions, loans or borrowings of a licensee or permit holder and into assets owned, held in trust, acquired or disposed of by a licensee or permit holder that are relevant to an inspection;

(*e*) conduct such tests as are reasonably necessary; and

(*f*) remove materials or substances for examination or test purposes subject to the licensee, permit holder or other occupant of the premises being notified thereof.

(2) **Entry to dwellings.**— Subsection (1) does not apply to confer a power of entry to a room actually used as a dwelling without the consent of the occupier.

(3) **Warrant.**— A justice of the peace may issue a warrant authorizing the person named in the warrant,

(*a*) to do anything set out in clause (1)(a), (c), (e) or (f);

(*b*) to search for and seize any document or thing relevant to the inspection; or

(*c*) to enter and search a room actually used as a dwelling.

(4) **Requirements for warrant to issue.**— A warrant may be issued under subsection (3) if the justice of the peace is satisfied on information under oath that,

(*a*) in the case of a warrant to be issued under clause (3)(a),

(i) a person designated under subsection 43(1) has been prevented from doing anything permitted under clause (1)(a), (c), (e) or (f),

(ii) there are reasonable grounds to believe that such a person may be prevented from doing any of those things, or

(iii) there are reasonable grounds to believe that there has been or is likely to be a contravention of this Act or the regulations.

(*b*) in the case of a warrant to be issued under clause (3)(b), it is necessary to search for and seize a document or thing that there are reasonable grounds to believe will afford evidence relevant to a contravention of this Act or the regulations; or (*c*) in the case of a warrant to be issued under clause (3)(c), it is necessary that a room actually used as a dwelling be entered for the purposes of carrying out an inspection or there is, in such a room, a document or thing that there are reasonable grounds to believe is relevant to an inspection under this Act.

(5) **Execution of warrant.**— A warrant issued under this section shall specify the hours and days during which it may be executed.

(6) **Expiry.**— Unless renewed, a warrant under this section expires not later than thirty days after the date on which it is made.

(7) **Notice not required.**— A warrant under this section may be issued or renewed before or after expiry upon application without notice.

(8) **Renewal of warrant.**— A warrant under this section may be renewed for any reason for which it may be issued.

(9) **Experts.**— A person carrying out an inspection under this Act is entitled to call upon such experts as are necessary to assist the person in carrying out the inspection.

(10) **Assistance.**— A person doing anything under the authority of a warrant issued under this section is authorized to call on such police officers to assist and to use such force as is necessary in the execution of the warrant.

(11) **Copies.**— A person carrying out an inspection under this Act who takes material in order to copy it shall make the copy with reasonable dispatch and shall promptly return the material taken.

(12) **Admissibility of copies.**— Copies of, or extracts from, documents and things removed under this section and certified as being true copies of, or extracts from, the originals by the person who made them are admissible in evidence to the same extent as, and have the same evidentiary value as, the documents or things of which they are copies or extracts.

(13) **Police officers.**— Every police officer has the powers set out in clauses (1)(a), (b) and (c) and subsections (2) to (12) apply with necessary modifications to police officers as if they were persons designated under subsection 43(1).

45. (1) **Obstruction.**— No person shall obstruct a person carrying out an inspection under this Act or withhold, destroy, conceal or refuse to provide any relevant information or thing required for the purpose of the inspection.

(2) **Facilitating inspection.**— It is a condition of each licence and permit issued under this Act that the licensee or permit holder facilitate an inspection relevant to the licence or permit.

46. Forfeiture of liquor.— Liquor kept for sale or offered for sale in contravention of subsection 5(1) and liquor purchased in contravention of section 27 is forfeited to the Crown.

46.1 (1) **Definition.**— In this section and in section 47, "proceeds," in relation to an offence under this Act, means,

(*a*) personal property, other than money, derived in whole or in part, directly or indirectly, from the commission of the offence; and

(*b*) money derived directly or indirectly from the commission of the offence.

(2) **Possession of proceeds.**— No person shall knowingly possess the proceeds of an offence under this Act.

47. (1) **Seizure.**— A police officer may seize any thing, including liquor, if, (*a*) he or she reasonably believes that the thing will afford evidence of an offence under this Act;

(*b*) he or she reasonably believes that,

(i) the thing was used or is being used in connection with the commission of an offence under this Act, and

(ii) unless the thing is seized it is likely that it would continue to be used or would be used again in the commission of an offence under this Act; or

(*c*) he or she reasonably believes that the thing is proceeds from the commission of an offence under this Act.

(1.1) **Same.**— If an offence appears to have been committed under this Act and a police officer reasonably believes, in view of the offence apparently committed and the presence of liquor, that a further offence is likely to be committed, the police officer may seize the liquor and the packages in which it is kept.

(2) **Order of restoration.**— The Ontario Court (Provincial Division) may, upon the application of any person made within thirty days of a seizure under subsection (1) or (1.1), order that the things seized be restored forthwith to the applicant if the court is satisfied that,

(*a*) the applicant is entitled to possession of the things seized;

(*b*) the things seized are not required as evidence in any proceeding.

(*c*) continued detention of the things seized is not necessary to prevent the commission of an offence; and

(*d*) it is unlikely that the things will be forfeited on conviction under subsection (5).

(3) **Idem.**— If the court is satisfied that an applicant under subsection (2) is entitled to possession of the things seized but is not satisfied as to all of the matters mentioned in clauses (2)(b), (c) and (d), it shall order that the things seized be restored to the applicant,

(*a*) upon the expiration of three months from the date of the seizure, if no proceeding in respect of an offence has been commenced; or

(*b*) upon the final conclusion of any such proceeding.

(4) **Forfeiture.**— If no application has been made for the return of a thing seized under subsection (1) or (1.1) or an application has been made but upon the hearing of the application no order of restoration has been made, the thing seized is forfeited to the Crown.

(5) **Same.**— If a person is convicted of an offence under this Act, the court shall order that any thing seized under subsection (1) or (1.1) in connection with the offence be forfeited to the Crown, unless the court considers that the forfeiture would be unjust in the circumstances.

(6) **Relief against forfeiture.**— Any person with an interest in a thing forfeited under this section may apply to the Ontario Court (General Division) for relief against the forfeiture and the court may make an order providing for any relief that it considers just, including, but not limited to, one or more of the following orders:

1. An order directing that the thing or any part of the thing be returned to the applicant.

2. An order directing that any interest in the thing be vested in the applicant.

3. An order directing that an amount be paid by the Crown to the applicant by way of compensation for the forfeiture.

(7) Same.— The court shall not order any relief under subsection (6) unless the court is satisfied that the applicant did not, directly or indirectly, participate in, or benefit from, any offence in connection with which the thing was seized.

48. Arrest without warrant.— If a police officer finds a person apparently in contravention of this Act or apparently in contravention of a prescribed provision of the regulations and the person refuses to give his or her name and address or there are reasonable grounds to believe that the name or address given is false, the police officer may arrest the person without warrant.

49. (1) Confidentiality.— Every person engaged in the administration of this Act shall preserve confidentiality in respect of all matters that come to his or her knowledge in the course of his or her duties and shall not communicate any such matter to any other person except,

(a) as may be required in connection with the administration of this Act and the regulations or any proceeding under this Act;

(b) to his or her counsel; or

(c) with the consent of the person to whom the matter relates.

(2) Testimony in civil proceeding.— No person engaged in the administration of this Act shall be required to give testimony in any civil proceeding with regard to information obtained by the person in the course of the person's duties except in a proceeding under this Act. ...

51. Analyst's certificate or report.— A certificate or report purporting to be signed by a federal or provincial analyst as to the composition of any liquor or any other substance is admissible in evidence in any proceeding under this Act, and in the absence of evidence to the contrary, is proof of the information set out in the certificate or report and of the authority of the person giving it or making it, without proof of the appointment or signature of the person. ...

OFFENCES

61. (1) Offences.— A person is guilty of an offence if the person,

(a) knowingly furnishes false information in any application under this Act or in any statement or return required to be furnished under this Act;

(b) knowingly fails to comply with an order under subsection 38(2); or

(c) contravenes any provision of this Act or the regulations.

(2) Derivative.— A director or officer of a corporation who caused, authorized, permitted or participated in an offence under this Act by the corporation is guilty of an offence.

(3) Penalties.— Upon conviction for an offence under this Act, other than a contravention of subsection 30(1), (2), (3) or (4),

(a) a corporation is liable to a fine of not more than $250,000; and

(b) an individual is liable to a fine of not more than $100,000 or to imprisonment for a term of not more than one year or both.

(3.0.1) Same, sale etc., to a minor.— Upon conviction for contravening subsection 30(1), (2), (3) or (4),

(a) a corporation is liable to a fine of not more than $500,000; and (*b*) an individual is liable to a fine of not more than $200,000 or to imprisonment for a term of not more than one year or both.

(3.1) **Exception.**— An individual who is convicted of an offence under subsection 31(2) or (4) is not liable to imprisonment. ...

(5) **Additional penalty.**— In addition to any other penalty or action under this Act, the licence of a licensee who contravenes subsection 30(1) or (2) shall be suspended for a period of not less than seven days.

(6) **Minimum fine.**— If a licensee contravenes subsection 30(1), (2), (3) or (4), the fine imposed under this section shall be not less than $500.

(7) **Idem.**— If a person who is not a licensee contravenes subsection 30(1), (2), (3) or (4), the fine imposed under this section shall be not less than $100.

(8) **Limitation.**— Subject to subsection (9), no proceeding under this section shall be commenced more than two years after the offence was committed.

(9) **Idem.**— No proceeding under clause (1)(a) and no proceeding under subsection (2) that relates to a matter referred to in clause (1)(a) shall be commenced more than one year after the facts upon which the proceeding is based first came to the knowledge of the Board.

REGULATIONS

62. (1) **Regulations.**— The Lieutenant Governor in Council may make regulations,

1. prescribing anything that is referred to in this Act as being prescribed;

2. governing the issuance, renewal, transfer and expiry of licences;

3. governing the issuance and expiry of permits;

4. prescribing conditions that attach to licences and permits;

5. prescribing the special occasions for which permits may be issued; ...

8. exempting any person, product or premises from any provision of this Act or the regulations;

9. requiring licensees and permit holders to provide the Board with such information and returns respecting the sale of liquor and the premises, methods and practices connected therewith as is prescribed and requiring any information provided to be verified by oath;

10. controlling the advertising of liquor or its availability for sale and requiring that advertisements be subject to the approval of the Board;

11. prescribing standards for licensed premises and premises used by permit holders for the sale and service of liquor;

12. prescribing or prohibiting methods and practices in connection with the serving of liquor;

13. prohibiting licensees and permit holders from permitting any person to engage in prescribed activities on their premises;

14. governing the sale and service of liquor by a holder of a licence to sell liquor in a place other than licensed premises;

15. prescribing classes of premises on which a person under the age of nineteen years may not enter;

16. prescribing rules for proceedings before the Board;

17. governing the issuance of documentation for proof of age;

18. prescribing hours of sale of liquor;

19. authorizing the Board to extend the hours of sale of liquor during events of municipal, provincial, national or international significance;

20. prohibiting manufacturers and employees, agents and licensed representatives of manufacturers from offering or giving inducements or engaging in prescribed practices with respect to the sale or promotion of liquor;

21. prescribing the circumstances in which a manufacturer or employee, agent or licensed representative of a manufacturer may give liquor as a gift;

22. prescribing the circumstances in which a manufacturer may obtain a licence to sell liquor despite subsection 6(4);

23. regulating and controlling the possession and delivery of liquor sold under a licence or permit;

24. authorizing the Board to approve training courses for the service or delivery of liquor;

25. authorizing the Board to approve a temporary physical extension of licensed premises;

26. authorizing the Board to exempt any person from the requirement to provide information in respect of an application for a licence or permit;

27. governing the approval by the Board of the possession, service or consumption of liquor for research or educational purposes;

28. prescribing the circumstances in which, following a prescribed change of ownership in respect of a licence, liquor may be kept for sale, offered for sale or sold or delivered for a fee under the authority of the licence despite subsection 16(1) or (2);

29. designating classes of persons for the purpose of section 19;

30. defining "private place" for purposes of sections 30 and 31;

31. designating hospitals for purposes of section 36;

32. designating institutions for purposes of section 37, governing the transfer and admission of persons to and detention of persons in such institutions and providing for the management of such institutions;

33. prescribing licences that may be issued in a municipality despite section 52;

34. prohibiting or regulating and controlling the possession of liquor in provincial parks, in a park managed or controlled by The Niagara Parks Commission, The St. Lawrence Parks Commission, The St. Clair Parkway Commission or on lands owned or controlled by a conservation authority established or continued under the *Conservation Authorities Act*.

(2) **Scope of regulations.**— A regulation may be general or particular in its application.

(3) **Conditions, qualifications, requirements.**— Any provision of a regulation may be subject to such conditions, qualifications or requirements as are specified in the regulation.

O. reg. 230/96; O. reg. 546/90, s. 43; O. reg. 346/93, s. 7

EXEMPTIONS FROM PROVISIONS OF THE ACT

9. (1) The Act does not apply with respect to a product capable of human consumption that contains 0.5 of 1 per cent or less of alcohol by volume or 0.4 of 1 per cent or less of alcohol by weight.

(2) The Act does not apply with respect to concentrated food and beverage flavouring extracts that are not palatable when consumed alone.

(3) The Act does not apply with respect to denatured cooking wine that contains 20 per cent or less alcohol by volume and 1.5 per cent or more salt by volume. ...

43. The licence holder shall ensure that the number of persons on the premises to which the licence applies, including employees of the licence holder, does not exceed the capacity of the licensed premises as stated on the licence.

LIQUOR LICENCE ACT SET FINE SCHEDULE

[The following set fine schedule is a listing of the most commonly encountered LLA offences. A complete listing of the proper wording and section numbers is found in Ontario Regulation 950 of the *Provincial Offences Act*.]

WORDING	Section	Fine
Unlawfully keeping liquor for sale	5(1)	NSF
Unlawfully offer liquor for sale	5(1)	NSF
Unlawfully sell liquor	5(1)	NSF
Purchase Liquor from other than government store	27	$105
Purchase Liquor from other than authorized person	27	$105
Sell Liquor to intoxicated person	29	NSF
Supply Liquor to intoxicated person	29	NSF
Permit Liquor to be sold to intoxicated person	29	NSF
Permit Liquor to be supplied to intoxicated person	29	NSF
Knowingly sell liquor to person under 19 years	30(1)	NSF
Knowingly supply liquor to person under 19 years	30(1)	NSF
Sell liquor to person who appears to be under 19 years	30(2)	NSF
Supply liquor to person who appears to be under 19 years	30(2)	NSF
Person under 19 years purchase	30(8)	$105
Person under 19 years obtain	30(8)	$105
Person under 19 years attempt to obtain	30(8)	$105
Person under 19 years consume	30(8)	$105
Person under 19 years have	30(8)	$105
Person under 19 years enter licenced premises	30(10)	$105
Person under 19 years remain on licenced premises	30(10)	$105
Present as evidence of age documentation not lawfully issued to person	30(12)	$105
Consume liquor in other than licenced premises, residence, or private place	31(2)	$105
Have liquor in open container in other than licenced premises, residence or private place	31(2)	$105
Consume liquor in other than licenced premises, residence or private place	31(2)	$105
Being intoxicated in public place	31(4)	$55
Being intoxicated in a common area	31(4)	$55
Drive motor vehicle with unsealed container of liquor	32(1)	$180
Have care and control of motor vehicle with unsealed container of liquor	32(1)	$180
Drive motorized snow vehicle with open container of liquor	32(1)	$180
Have care and control of motorized snow vehicle with unsealed container of liquor	32(1)	$180
Drive motor vehicle with liquor in open baggage	32(1)	$155
Have care and control of motor vehicle with liquor in open baggage	32(1)	$155

Drive motorized snow vehicle with liquor in open baggage	32(1)	$155
Have care and control of motorized snow vehicle with liquor in open baggage	32(1)	$155
Drive motor vehicle with liquor readily available	32(1)	$155
Have care and control motor vehicle with liquor readily available	32(1)	$155
Drive motorized snow vehicle with liquor readily available	32(1)	$155
Have care and control motorized snow vehicle with liquor readily available	32(1)	$155
Operating boat under way with open liquor	32(3)	$180
Have care and control of boat under way vehicle with open container of liquor	32(3)	$180
Operating boat under way with unsealed container of liquor	32(3)	$180
Operating boat under way with liquor not in closed compartment	32(3)	$180
Drink alcohol in a form that is not liquor	33(a)	$55
Supplying alcohol in a form that it is not liquor knowing it is to be used as a drink	33(b)	$105

EXERCISES

SHORT ANSWER

1. Having reference to the legislation, define the following terms:

   a. intoxication TO BE UNDER THE INFLUENCE OF ALCOHOL

   b. residence A PRIVATE PLACE

   c. liquor SPIRITS, BEER, WINE.

   d. public place A PLACE QUITE PUBLIC HAS ACCES.

   e. alcohol PRODUCT OF FERMENTATION OF FRUT, GRANS

   f. sell SUPLY FOR REMUNERATION

g. spirits _WINE , BEER , BEVERAGE CONTAINING ALCOHOL._

h. wine _DESTILATION OF FRUITS_

i. beer _DESTILATION OF MALT_ _AND MIXED WITH_

j. package or container

2. In order to arrest a person for the offence of being intoxicated in a public place, what conditions must exist?

PERSON IS INTOXICATED
FOR SAFETY OF THE PERSON

3. List the LLA offences that relate directly to persons under the age of 19 years.

4. Under certain conditions a parent is allowed to supply liquor to minors. State those conditions.

5. Describe the three forms of possession as they relate to possession offences under the *Liquor Licence Act*.

   a. SEALED, UNOPENED

   b.

   c.

6. List five examples of private places.

   a. HOUSE
   b. CAR
   c. TENT
   d. BUILDNG
   e. PARKIN LOT .

■ CASE STUDY #1

You are a police officer with your local police service and are on patrol in the downtown area. It is 8:30 p.m. on Friday, August 6. You observe three males walking out of the Brewers Retail Store on Queen St. One of the males appears to be younger than the others, so you and your partner approach them. All three are carrying cases of beer. John Smithers identifies himself by presentation of his valid Ontario driver's licence. He is 21 years old and resides at 123 North St. He is carrying a case of Molson Export. Alan Ault identifies himself with a high school ID card. It lists his age as 18 years. He lives with Smithers at 123 North St. Ault is carrying a 12-pack of Labatts Blue. The third person in the group identifies himself as George Grunt. He has no identification and states that he is a street person. He appears to be approximately 15 years of age. He is carrying a 6-pack of Budweiser.

1. Identify any offences that have been committed by the three persons.

2. List the facts in issue for each of these offences and describe how the particular elements of the offences will be proven in court.

3. Describe the proper documentation to commence proceedings against the three individuals and the information required to complete it. (Complete the documentation if your instructor provides samples.)

4. Given the information that George Grunt has provided to you, if you were not satisfied that he was who he said he was, what steps would you take to satisfy yourself of his identification?

5. At the completion of the proceedings, what will be done with the beer?

■ **CASE STUDY #2**

You are a police officer with your local police service and are on patrol in the downtown area. It is Saturday, August 7 at approximately 11:30 p.m. You observe a 1988 Pontiac 6000, Ontario plate number XTE 002. There are several occupants in the vehicle and you notice one occupant with his arm out of the window, holding a bottle of beer. You pull the vehicle over on Bay St. and you and your partner approach the vehicle. The driver identifies himself as Brady Johnson and presents you with his driver's licence and ownership and insurance for the vehicle. His date of birth is July 17, 1978. You ask him if he has had anything to drink and he says no, he is the designated driver. There is no smell of alcohol on his breath. There are three other occupants in the vehicle, one in the front and two in the back. You flash your light into the car and notice an empty beer bottle on the floor in the back. An occupant picks it up and hands it to you. There is a small quantity of what appears to be beer left in the bottle. The bottle is still quite cold.

You ask the occupants to step from the vehicle so that you can search the vehicle. You find two partly filled bottles of beer in the back seat. On the floor of the front passenger seat you find a third plastic bottle that appears to contain a mix of pop and liquor. Allison Brown had been sitting in the front seat with the driver. She has a large brown purse in her possession. Allison identifies herself with a college photo ID card that states that she is 21 years old. The two occupants in the back seat identify themselves orally as Robert Jones, age 20, of 49 Cedar St. and Angela Cartelli, age 18, of 429 Wellington St. Brown and Johnson live at the college residence at 444 Northern Ave. In conducting a search of the trunk of the vehicle you find a cooler containing 21 full bottles of Labatts Blue.

1. Identify the offences committed and list the facts in issue for these offences and describe how the elements will be proven in court.

2. Describe the required documentation to commence proceedings, and the information required to complete it. (Complete the documentation if your instructor provides samples.)

3. What is the legal authority authorizing a search of the vehicle for liquor? Given the circumstances, does that authority extend to Allison's purse and to the trunk of the vehicle? Explain.

4. Describe and/or complete the required documentation with respect to the seizure of the beer.

■ CASE STUDY #3

You are a police officer with your local police service and are on patrol in the downtown area. It is 11:00 p.m. on Saturday, February 20. You observe an elderly man staggering along the sidewalk on Queen St. You approach this individual and immediately notice that he is heavily intoxicated. As you are speaking to him he falls to the ground and is unable to get up without your assistance. This man is known to you as David Daglish, age 53, of no fixed address.

1. There are several methods of dealing with this individual. Explain these methods and describe or complete any required documentation.

■ CASE STUDY #4

You are a police officer with your local police service and are on patrol in the downtown area. At 12:45 a.m. on Friday, July 9, you and your partner are dispatched to the Horn of Plenty Tavern, 531 Bay St., regarding a disturbance. On arrival you are met by the bartender, Alphie Bishop. He points to a table at the back of the bar and indicates that he wants all four people sitting there removed from the premises. You, your partner, and Alphie approach the table and immediately notice that all four men are intoxicated to the point of being obnoxious. While you are attempting to determine what's going on, they continue to make rude comments to the people at the next table.

1. What offence or offences have the four intoxicated individuals committed? Explain.

2. List the elements of those offences and describe how you would prove each of them.

3. What offence could Alphie be charged with? Explain how you would prove the facts in issue for that offence. Describe or complete the required documentation.

4. Explain the process for removing the four individuals from the tavern.

5. If the four individuals refuse to leave, what options are available to you and your partner?

CHAPTER 4
The Tenant Protection Act

CHAPTER OBJECTIVES

After completing this chapter, you should be able to:

◆ Understand key terms defined in the *Tenant Protection Act.*

◆ Identify common problems related to the Act.

◆ Explain the major role of police officers with respect to enforcement of the Act.

◆ Be prepared to apply the provisions of the Act in a hypothetical fact situation, to determine whether any charges are appropriate for the situation, and to complete the required documentation.

INTRODUCTION

The *Tenant Protection Act,* which has replaced the *Landlord and Tenant Act,* applies to rental units and residential rental complexes. It deals with tenancy agreements and, specifically, the rights of tenants and landlords and the protections afforded to them. This Act affects a great number of people, since most individuals at some time in their lives either rent a place to live or rent out a place they own.

The Act places restrictions on assignment, subletting, and entry into rental units or residential complexes. It requires landlords to provide and maintain residential complexes and the rental units within them in a good state of repair and fit for habitation, and to comply with health, safety, housing, and maintenance standards. It prohibits landlords from withholding the reasonable supply of any vital service, care service, or food that is the landlord's obligation to supply under the tenancy agreement. It also prohibits landlords from harassing, obstructing, coercing, threatening, or interfering with a tenant. Section 58 of the Act sets out a mechanism for landlords to evict their tenants for non-payment of rent.

TENANT PROTECTION ACT, 1997

SO 1997, Chapter 24

**An Act to Consolidate and Revise the Law with respect to
Residential Tenancies**

*Her Majesty, by and with the advice and consent of the Legislative
Assembly of the Province of Ontario, enacts as follows:*

PART I
INTRODUCTION

1. (1) **Definitions.**— In this Act, ...
"landlord" includes,

> (a) the owner or other person permitting occupancy of a rental unit,

> (b) the heirs, assigns, personal representatives and successors in title of a person referred to in clause (a), and

> (c) a person, other than a tenant occupying a rental unit in a residential complex, who is entitled to possession of the residential complex and who attempts to enforce any of the rights of a landlord under a tenancy agreement or this Act, including the right to collect rent;

"Minister" means the *Minister of Municipal Affairs and Housing*;

"Ministry" means the Ministry of Municipal Affairs and Housing;

"mobile home" means a dwelling that is designed to be made mobile and that is being used as a permanent residence;

"mobile home park" means the land on which one or more occupied mobile homes are located and includes the rental units and the land, structures, services and facilities of which the landlord retains possession and that are intended for the common use and enjoyment of the tenants of the landlord; ...

"regulations" means the regulations made under this Act;

"rent" includes the amount of any consideration paid or given or required to be paid or given by or on behalf of a tenant to a landlord or the landlord's agent for the right to occupy a rental unit and for any services and facilities and any privilege, accommodation or thing that the landlord provides for the tenant in respect of the occupancy of the rental unit, whether or not a separate charge is made for services and facilities or for the privilege, accommodation or thing, but "rent" does not include,

> (a) an amount paid by a tenant to a landlord to reimburse the landlord for property taxes paid by the landlord with respect to a mobile home or a land lease home owned by a tenant, or

> (b) an amount that a landlord charges a tenant of a rental unit in a care home for care services or meals;

"rental unit" means any living accommodation used or intended for use as rented residential premises, and "rental unit" includes,

> (a) a site for a mobile home or site on which there is a land lease home used or intended for use as rented residential premises, and

(b) a room in a boarding house, rooming house or lodging house and a unit in a care home;

"residential complex" means,

(a) a building or related group of buildings in which one or more rental units are located,

(b) a mobile home park or land lease community,

(c) a site that is a rental unit,

(d) a care home, and

"residential complex" includes all common areas and services and facilities available for the use of its residents;

"residential unit" means any living accommodation used or intended for use as residential premises, and "residential unit" includes,

(a) a site for a mobile home or on which there is a land lease home used or intended for use as a residential premises, and

(b) a room in a boarding house, rooming house or lodging house and a unit in a care home;

"Rules" means the rules of practice and procedure made by the Tribunal or the Minister under section 164 of this Act and section 25.1 of the *Statutory Powers Procedure Act*;

"services and facilities" includes,

(a) furniture, appliances and furnishings,

(b) parking and related facilities,

(c) laundry facilities,

(d) elevator facilities,

(e) common recreational facilities,

(f) garbage facilities and related services,

(g) cleaning and maintenance services,

(h) storage facilities,

(i) intercom systems,

(j) cable television facilities,

(k) heating facilities and services,

(l) air-conditioning facilities,

(m) utilities and related services, and

(n) security services and facilities;

"subtenant" means the person to whom a tenant gives the right under section 18 to occupy a rental unit;

"superintendent's premises" means a rental unit used by a person employed as a janitor, manager, security guard or superintendent and located in the residential complex with respect to which the person is so employed;

"tenancy agreement" means a written, oral or implied agreement between a tenant and a landlord for occupancy of a rental unit and includes a licence to occupy a rental unit;

"tenant" includes a person who pays rent in return for the right to occupy a rental unit and includes the tenant's heirs, assigns and personal representatives, but "tenant" does not include a person who has the right to occupy a rental unit by virtue of being,

> (a) a co-owner of the residential complex in which the rental unit is located, or
>
> (b) a shareholder of a corporation that owns the residential complex;

"Tribunal" means the Ontario Rental Housing Tribunal;

"utilities" means heat, hydro and water;

"vital service" means fuel, hydro, gas or hot or cold water.

(2) **Rental unit, classification.**— A rented site for a mobile home or a land lease home is a rental unit for the purposes of this Act even if the mobile home or the land lease home on the site is owned by the tenant of the site.

2. (1) **Application of Act.**— This Act applies with respect to rental units in residential complexes, despite any other Act and despite any agreement or waiver to the contrary. ...

(4) **Conflict with other Acts.**— If a provision of this Act conflicts with a provision of another Act, other than the *Human Rights Code*, the provision of this Act applies.

3. Exemptions from Act.— This Act does not apply with respect to,

> (*a*) living accommodation intended to be provided to the travelling or vacationing public or occupied for a seasonal or temporary period in a hotel, motel or motor hotel, resort, lodge, tourist camp, cottage or cabin establishment, inn, campground, trailer park, tourist home, bed and breakfast vacation establishment or vacation home;
>
> (*b*) living accommodation whose occupancy is conditional upon the occupant continuing to be employed on a farm, whether or not the accommodation is located on that farm;
>
> (*c*) living accommodation provided by a non-profit housing co-operative to tenants in member units;
>
> (*d*) living accommodation occupied by a person for penal or correctional purposes;
>
> (*e*) living accommodation that is subject to the *Public Hospitals Act*, the *Private Hospitals Act*, the *Community Psychiatric Hospitals Act*, the *Mental Hospitals Act*, the *Homes for the Aged and Rest Homes Act*, the *Nursing Homes Act*, the *Ministry of Correctional Services Act*, the *Charitable Institutions Act*, the *Child and Family Services Act* or Schedule I, II or III of Regulation 272 of the Revised Regulations of Ontario, 1990, made under the *Developmental Services Act*;
>
> (*f*) short term living accommodation provided as emergency shelter;
>
> (*g*) living accommodation provided by an educational institution to its students or staff where,
>
>> (i) the living accommodation is provided primarily to persons under the age of majority, or all major questions related to the living accommodation are decided after consultation with a council or association representing the residents, and
>>
>> (ii) the living accommodation does not have its own self-contained bathroom and kitchen facilities or is not intended for year-round oc-

cupancy by full-time students or staff and members of their house-holds;

(*h*) living accommodation located in a building or project used in whole or in part for non-residential purposes if the occupancy of the living accommodation is conditional upon the occupant continuing to be an employee of or perform services related to a business or enterprise carried out in the building or project;

(*i*) living accommodation whose occupant or occupants are required to share a bathroom or kitchen facility with the owner, the owner's spouse, child or parent or the spouse's child or parent, and where the owner, spouse, child or parent lives in the building in which the living accommodation is located;

(*j*) premises occupied for business or agricultural purposes with living accommodation attached if the occupancy for both purposes is under a single lease and the same person occupies the premises and the living accommodation;

(*k*) living accommodation occupied by a person for the purpose of receiving rehabilitative or therapeutic services agreed upon by the person and the provider of the living accommodation, where,

(i) the parties have agreed that,

(A) the period of occupancy will be of a specified duration. ...

5. (1) Exemptions related to social, etc., housing.— Sections 17 and 18, paragraph 1 of subsection 32(1), sections 33, 54, 55, 57, 58 and 59, subsection 81(2) and sections 82, 89, 90, 92, 95, 100 to 102, 108, 114, 116, 121, 123 to 125, 129 to 139, 142 and 143 do not apply with respect to a rental unit described below:

1. A rental unit located in a residential complex owned, operated or administered by or on behalf of the Ontario Housing Corporation, the Government of Canada or an agency of either of them.

2. A rental unit located in a non-profit housing project that is developed under a prescribed federal or provincial program.

3. A rental unit provided by a non-profit housing co-operative to tenants in non-member units.

4. A rental unit provided by an educational institution to a student or member of its staff and that is not exempt from this Act under clause 3(g).

5. A rental unit located in a residential complex owned, operated or administered by a religious institution for a charitable use on a non-profit basis. ...

7. (1) Application to determine issues.— A landlord or a tenant may apply to the Tribunal for an order determining,

(*a*) whether this Act or any provision of it applies to a particular rental unit or residential complex;

(*b*) any other prescribed matter. ...

PART II
RIGHTS AND DUTIES OF LANDLORDS AND TENANTS

TENANCY AGREEMENTS

8. (1) **Name and address in written agreement.**— Every written tenancy agreement entered into on or after the day this section comes into force shall set out the legal name and address of the landlord to be used for the purpose of giving notices or other documents under this Act.

(2) **Copy of tenancy agreement.**— If a tenancy agreement entered into on or after the day this section comes into force is in writing, the landlord shall give a copy of the agreement, signed by the landlord and the tenant, to the tenant within 21 days after the tenant signs it and gives it to the landlord.

(3) **Notice of agreement not in writing.**— If a tenancy agreement entered into on or after the day this section comes into force is not in writing, the landlord shall, within 21 days after the tenancy begins, give to the tenant written notice of the legal name and address of the landlord to be used for giving notices and other documents under this Act.

(4) **Failure to comply.**— Until a landlord has complied with subsections (1) and (2) or subsection (3), as the case may be,

(*a*) the tenant's obligation to pay rent is suspended; and

(*b*) the landlord shall not require the tenant to pay rent.

(5) **After compliance.**— After the landlord has complied with subsections (1) and (2), or subsection (3), as the case may be, the landlord may require the tenant to pay any rent withheld by the tenant under subsection (4).

9. (1) **Commencement of tenancy.**— The term or period of a tenancy begins on the day the tenant is entitled to occupy the rental unit under the tenancy agreement.

(2) **Actual entry not required.**— A tenancy agreement takes effect when the tenant is entitled to occupy the rental unit, whether or not the tenant actually occupies it. …

13. Minimize losses.— When a landlord or a tenant becomes liable to pay any amount as a result of a breach of a tenancy agreement, the person entitled to claim the amount has a duty to take reasonable steps to minimize the person's losses. …

15. "No pet" provisions void.— A provision in a tenancy agreement prohibiting the presence of animals in or about the residential complex is void. …

ASSIGNMENT AND SUBLETTING

17. (1) **Assignment of tenancy.**— Subject to subsections (2), (3) and (6), and with the consent of the landlord, a tenant may assign a rental unit to another person.

(2) **Landlord's options, general request.**— If a tenant asks a landlord to consent to an assignment of a rental unit, the landlord may,

(*a*) consent to the assignment of the rental unit; or

(*b*) refuse consent to the assignment of the rental unit.

(3) **Landlord's options, specific request.**— If a tenant asks a landlord to consent to the assignment of the rental unit to a potential assignee, the landlord may,

(*a*) consent to the assignment of the rental unit to the potential assignee;

(*b*) refuse consent to the assignment of the rental unit to the potential assignee; or

(*c*) refuse consent to the assignment of the rental unit.

(4) **Refusal or non-response.**— A tenant may give the landlord a notice of termination under section 48 within 30 days after the date a request is made if,

(*a*) the tenant asks the landlord to consent to an assignment of the rental unit and the landlord refuses consent;

(*b*) the tenant asks the landlord to consent to an assignment of the rental unit and the landlord does not respond within seven days after the request is made;

(*c*) the tenant asks the landlord to consent to an assignment of the rental unit to a potential assignee and the landlord refuses consent to the assignment under clause (3)(c); or

(*d*) the tenant asks the landlord to consent to an assignment of the rental unit to a potential assignee and the landlord does not respond within seven days after the request is made.

(5) **Same.**— A landlord shall not arbitrarily or unreasonably refuse consent to an assignment of a rental unit to a potential assignee under clause (3)(b).

(6) **Same.**— Subject to subsection (5), a landlord who has given consent to an assignment of a rental unit under clause (2)(a) may subsequently refuse consent to an assignment of the rental unit to a potential assignee under clause (3)(b).

(7) **Charges.**— A landlord may charge a tenant only for the landlord's reasonable out of pocket expenses incurred in giving consent to an assignment to a potential assignee.

(8) **Consequences of assignment.**— If a tenant has assigned a rental unit to another person, the tenancy agreement continues to apply on the same terms and conditions and,

(*a*) the assignee is liable to the landlord for any breach of the tenant's obligations and may enforce against the landlord any of the landlord's obligations under the tenancy agreement or this Act, if the breach or obligation relates to the period after the assignment, whether or not the breach or obligation also related to a period before the assignment;

(*b*) the former tenant is liable to the landlord for any breach of the tenant's obligations and may enforce against the landlord any of the landlord's obligations under the tenancy agreement or this Act, if the breach or obligation relates to the period before the assignment;

(*c*) if the former tenant has started a proceeding under this Act before the assignment and the benefits or obligations of the new tenant may be affected, the new tenant may join in or continue the proceeding.

(9) **Application of section.**— This section applies with respect to all tenants, regardless of whether their tenancies are periodic, fixed, contractual or statutory, but does not apply with respect to a tenant of superintendent's premises.

18. (1) **Subletting rental unit.**— With the consent of the landlord, a tenant may sublet a rental unit to another person, thus giving the other person the right to occupy the rental unit for a term ending on a specified date before the end of the tenant's term or period and giving the tenant the right to resume occupancy on that date.

(2) **Same.**— A landlord shall not arbitrarily or unreasonably withhold consent to the sublet of a rental unit to a potential subtenant.

(3) **Charges.**— A landlord may charge a tenant only for the landlord's reasonable out of pocket expenses incurred in giving consent to a subletting.

(4) **Consequences of subletting.**— If a tenant has sublet a rental unit to another person,

(*a*) the tenant remains entitled to the benefits, and is liable to the landlord for the breaches, of the tenant's obligations under the tenancy agreement or this Act during the subtenancy; and

(*b*) the subtenant is entitled to the benefits, and is liable to the tenant for the breaches, of the subtenant's obligations under the subletting agreement or this Act during the subtenancy.

(5) **Overholding subtenant.**— A subtenant has no right to occupy the rental unit after the end of the subtenancy.

(6) **Application of section.**— This section applies with respect to all tenants, regardless of whether their tenancies are periodic, fixed, contractual or statutory, but does not apply with respect to a tenant of superintendent's premises.

ENTRY INTO RENTAL UNIT OR RESIDENTIAL COMPLEX

19. Privacy.— A landlord may enter a rental unit only in accordance with section 20 or 21.

20. (1) **Entry without notice, emergency, consent.**— A landlord may enter a rental unit at any time without written notice,

(*a*) in cases of emergency; or

(*b*) if the tenant consents to the entry at the time of entry.

(2) **Same, housekeeping.**— A landlord may enter a rental unit without written notice to clean it if the tenancy agreement requires the landlord to clean the rental unit at regular intervals and,

(*a*) the landlord enters the unit at the times specified in the tenancy agreement; or

(*b*) if no times are specified, the landlord enters the unit between the hours of 8 a.m. and 8 p.m.

(3) **Entry to show rental unit.**— A landlord may enter the rental unit without written notice to show the unit to prospective tenants if,

(*a*) the landlord and tenant have agreed that the tenancy will be terminated or one of them has given notice of termination to the other;

(*b*) the landlord enters the unit between the hours of 8 a.m. and 8 p.m.; and

(*c*) before entering, the landlord informs or makes a reasonable effort to inform the tenant of the intention to do so.

21. (1) **Entry with notice.**— A landlord may enter a rental unit in accordance with written notice given to the tenant at least 24 hours before the time of entry under the following circumstances:

1. To carry out a repair or do work in the rental unit.

2. To allow a potential mortgagee or insurer of the residential complex to view the rental unit.

3. To allow a potential purchaser to view the rental unit.

4. For any other reasonable reason for entry specified in the tenancy agreement.

(2) **Same.**— The written notice under subsection (1) shall specify the reason for entry, the day of entry and a time of entry between the hours of 8 a.m. and 8 p.m.

22. Entry by canvassers.— No landlord shall restrict reasonable access to a residential complex by candidates for election to any office at the federal, provincial or municipal level, or their authorized representatives, if they are seeking access for the propose of canvassing or distributing election material.

23. (1) Changing locks.— A landlord shall not alter the locking system on a door giving entry to a rental unit or residential complex or cause the locking system to be altered during the tenant's occupancy of the rental unit without giving the tenant replacement keys.

(2) **Same.**— A tenant shall not alter the locking system on a door giving entry to a rental unit or residential complex or cause the locking system to be altered during the tenant's occupancy of the rental unit without the consent of the landlord.

ADDITIONAL RESPONSIBILITIES OF LANDLORD

24. (1) Landlord's responsibility to repair.— A landlord is responsible for providing and maintaining a residential complex, including the rental units in it, in a good state of repair and fit for habitation and for complying with health, safety, housing and maintenance standards.

(2) **Same.**— Subsection (1) applies even if the tenant was aware of a state of non-repair or a contravention of a standard before entering into the tenancy agreement.

25. Landlord's responsibility re services.— A landlord shall not at any time during a tenant's occupancy of a rental unit and before the day on which an order evicting the tenant is executed, withhold reasonable supply of any vital service, care service or food that it is the landlord's obligation to supply under the tenancy agreement or deliberately interfere with the reasonable supply of any vital service, care service or food.

26. Landlord not to interfere with reasonable enjoyment.— A landlord shall not at any time during a tenant's occupancy of a rental unit and before the day on which an order evicting the tenant is executed substantially interfere with the reasonable enjoyment of the rental unit or the residential complex in which it is located for all usual purposes by a tenant or members of his or her household.

27. Landlord not to harass, etc.— A landlord shall not harass, obstruct, coerce, threaten or interfere with a tenant.

ADDITIONAL RESPONSIBILITIES OF TENANT

28. Tenant not to harass, etc.— A tenant shall not harass, obstruct, coerce, threaten or interfere with a landlord.

29. Cleanliness.— The tenant is responsible for ordinary cleanliness of the rental unit, except to the extent that the tenancy agreement requires the landlord to clean it.

30. Tenant's responsibility for damage.— The tenant is responsible for the repair of damage to the rental unit or residential complex caused by the wilful or negligent conduct of the tenant, other occupants of the rental unit or persons who are permitted in the residential complex by the tenant.

ENFORCEMENT OF RIGHTS UNDER THIS PART

31. Distress abolished.— No landlord shall, without legal process, seize a tenant's property for default in the payment of rent or for the breach of any other obligation of the tenant.

32. (1) Tenant applications.— A tenant or former tenant of a rental unit may apply to the Tribunal for any of the following orders:

1. An order determining that the landlord has arbitrarily or unreasonably withheld consent to the assignment or sublet of a rental unit to a potential assignee or subtenant.

2. An order determining that the landlord breached the obligations under subsection 24(1).

3. An order determining that the landlord, superintendent or agent of the landlord has illegally entered the rental unit.

4. An order determining that the landlord, superintendent or agent of the landlord has altered the locking system on a door giving entry to the rental unit or the residential complex or caused the locking system to be altered during the tenant's occupancy of the rental unit without giving the tenant replacement keys.

5. An order determining that the landlord, superintendent or agent of the landlord has withheld the reasonable supply of any vital service, care service or food that it is the landlord's obligation to supply under the tenancy agreement or deliberately interfered with the reasonable supply of any vital service, care service or food.

6. An order determining that the landlord, superintendent or agent of the landlord has substantially interfered with the reasonable enjoyment of the rental unit or residential complex for all usual purposes by the tenant or a member of his or her household.

7. An order determining that the landlord, superintendent or agent of the landlord has harassed, obstructed, coerced, threatened or interfered with the tenant during the tenant's occupancy of the rental unit. ...

(2) **Time limitation.—** No application may be made under subsection (1) more than one year after the day the alleged conduct giving rise to the application occurred. ...

PART III
SECURITY OF TENURE AND TERMINATION OF TENANCIES

SECURITY OF TENURE

39. (1) **Tenancy terminated.**— A tenancy may be terminated only in accordance with this Act.

(2) **Same.**— A notice of termination need not be given if a landlord and a tenant have agreed to terminate a tenancy.

(3) **When agreement void.**— An agreement between a landlord and tenant to terminate a tenancy is void if it is entered into,

(*a*) at the time the tenancy agreement is entered into; or

(*b*) as a condition of entering into the tenancy agreement.

41. Restriction on recovery of possession.— A landlord shall not recover possession of a rental unit subject to a tenancy unless,

(*a*) the tenant has vacated or abandoned the unit; or

(*b*) an order of the Tribunal evicting the tenant has authorized the possession.

42. (1) **Disposal of abandoned property, unit vacated.**— A landlord may sell, retain for the landlord's own use or otherwise dispose of property in a rental unit or the residential complex if the rental unit has been vacated in accordance with,

(*a*) a notice of termination of the landlord or the tenant;

(*b*) an agreement between the landlord and the tenant to terminate the tenancy;

(*c*) subsection 68(2); or

(*d*) an order of the Tribunal terminating the tenancy or evicting the tenant.

(2) **Where eviction order enforced.**— Despite subsection (1), where an order is made to evict a tenant, the landlord shall not sell, retain or otherwise dispose of the tenant's property before 48 hours have elapsed after the enforcement of the eviction order.

(3) **Same.**— A landlord shall make an evicted tenant's property available to be retrieved at a location proximate to the rental unit for 48 hours after the enforcement of an eviction order.

(4) **Liability of landlord.**— A landlord is not liable to any person for selling, retaining or otherwise disposing of a tenant's property in accordance with this section.

(5) **Agreement.**— A landlord and a tenant may agree to terms other than those set out in this section with regard to the disposal of the tenant's property.

NOTICE OF TERMINATION—GENERAL PROVISIONS

43. (1) **Notice of termination.**— Where this Act permits a landlord or tenant to terminate a tenancy by notice, the notice shall be in a form approved by the Tribunal and shall,

(*a*) identify the rental unit for which the notice is given;

(*b*) state the date on which the tenancy is to terminate; and

(*c*) be signed by the person giving the notice, or the person's agent.

(2) **Same.**— If the notice is given by a landlord, it shall also set out the reasons and details respecting the termination and inform the tenant that,

(*a*) if the tenant does not vacate the rental unit, the landlord may apply to the Tribunal for an order terminating the tenancy and evicting the tenant; and

(*b*) if the landlord applies for an order, the tenant is entitled to dispute the application.

44. (1) **Where notice void.**— A notice of termination becomes void 30 days after the termination date specified in the notice unless,

(*a*) the tenant vacates the rental unit before that time; or

(*b*) the landlord applies for an order terminating the tenancy and evicting the tenant before that time.

(2) **Exception.**— Subsection (1) does not apply with respect to a notice based on a tenant's failure to pay rent.

45. (1) **Compensation when rental unit not vacated.**— A landlord is entitled to compensation for the use and occupation of a rental unit by any unauthorized occupant or after the tenancy has been terminated by notice.

(2) **Effect of payment of arrears.**— Unless a landlord and tenant agree otherwise, the landlord does not waive a notice of termination, reinstate a tenancy or create a new tenancy,

(*a*) by accepting arrears of rent or compensation for use or occupation of a rental unit after notice of termination of the tenancy has been given; or

(*b*) by giving the tenant a notice of rent increase.

NOTICE OF TERMINATION—END OF PERIOD OR TERM OF TENANCY

46. Tenant's notice to terminate tenancy, end of period or term.— A tenant may terminate a tenancy at the end of a period of the tenancy or at the end of the term of a tenancy for a fixed term by giving notice of termination to the landlord in accordance with section 47.

47. (1) **Period of notice, daily or weekly tenancy.**— A notice under section 46, 60 or 96 to terminate a daily or weekly tenancy shall be given at least 28 days before the date the termination is specified to be effective and that date shall be on the last day of a rental period.

(2) **Period of notice, monthly tenancy.**— A notice under section 46, 60 or 96 to terminate a monthly tenancy shall be given at least 60 days before the date the termination is specified to be effective and that date shall be on the last day of a rental period.

(3) **Period of notice, yearly tenancy.**— A notice under section 46, 60 or 96 to terminate a yearly tenancy shall be given at least 60 days before the date the termination is specified to be effective and that date shall be on the last day of a yearly period on which the tenancy is based.

(4) **Period of notice, tenancy for fixed term.**— A notice under section 46, 60 or 96 to terminate a tenancy for a fixed term shall be given at least 60 days before the expiration date specified in the tenancy agreement, to be effective on that expiration date. ...

NOTICE BY TENANT FOR TERMINATION ASSIGNMENT OF TENANCY REFUSED

48. (1) **Notice by tenant.**— A tenant may give notice of termination of a tenancy if the circumstances set out in subsection 17(4) apply.

(2) **Same.**— The date for termination specified in the notice shall be at least a number of days after the date of the notice that is the lesser of the notice period otherwise required under this Act and 30 days.

DEATH OF TENANT

49. (1) **Death of tenant.**— If a tenant of a rental unit dies and there are no other tenants of the rental unit, the tenancy shall be deemed to be terminated 30 days after the death of the tenant.

(2) **Reasonable access.**— The landlord shall, until the tenancy is terminated under subsection (1),

    (*a*) preserve any property of a tenant who has died that is in the rental unit or the residential complex other than property that is unsafe or unhygienic; and

    (*b*) afford the executor or administrator of the tenant's estate, or if there is no executor or administrator, a member of the tenant's family reasonable access to the rental unit and the residential complex for the purpose of removing the tenant's property.

50. (1) **Landlord may dispose of property.**— The landlord may sell, retain for the landlord's own use or otherwise dispose of property of a tenant who has died that is in a rental unit and in the residential complex in which the rental unit is located,

    (*a*) if the property is unsafe or unhygienic, immediately; and

    (*b*) otherwise, after the tenancy is terminated under section 49.

(2) **Same.**— Subject to subsections (3) and (4), a landlord is not liable to any person for selling, retaining or otherwise disposing of the property of a tenant in accordance with subsection (1).

(3) **Same.**— If, within six months after the tenant's death, the executor or administrator of the estate of the tenant, or if there is no executor or administrator, a member of the tenant's family claims any property of the tenant that the landlord has sold, the landlord shall pay to the estate the amount by which the proceeds of sale exceed the sum of,

    (*a*) the landlord's reasonable out of pocket expenses for moving, storing, securing or selling the property; and

    (*b*) any arrears of rent.

(4) **Same.**— If, within the six month period after the tenant's death, the executor or administrator of the estate of the tenant, or if there is no executor or administrator, a member of the tenant's family claims any property of the tenant that the landlord has retained for the landlord's own use, the landlord shall return the property to the tenant's estate. ...

NOTICE BY LANDLORD FOR TERMINATION AT END OF PERIOD OR TERM

51. (1) **Notice, landlord personally, etc., requires unit.**— A landlord may, by notice, terminate a tenancy if the landlord in good faith requires possession of the rental unit for the purpose of residential occupation by the landlord, the landlord's spouse or a child or parent of one of them.

(2) **Same.**— The date for termination specified in the notice shall be at least 60 days after the notice is given and shall be the day a period of the tenancy ends or, where the tenancy is for a fixed term, the end of the term. ...

52. (1) **Where purchasing landlord personally requires unit.**— A landlord of a residential complex that contains no more than three residential units and that is subject to a tenancy agreement may give notice to the tenant on behalf of a purchaser of the residential complex to terminate the tenancy if,

(a) the landlord has entered into an agreement of purchase and sale to sell the residential complex; and

(b) the purchaser in good faith requires possession of the residential complex or a unit in it for the purpose of residential occupation by the purchaser, the purchaser's spouse or a child or parent of one of them.

(2) **Period of notice.**— The date for termination specified in the notice shall be at least 60 days after the notice is given and shall be the day a period of the tenancy ends or, where the tenancy is for a fixed term, the end of the term. ...

60. (1) **Notice end of term, additional grounds.**— A landlord may give a tenant notice of termination of their tenancy on any of the following grounds:

1. The tenant has persistently failed to pay rent on the date it becomes due and payable.

2. The rental unit that is the subject of the tenancy agreement is a rental unit as described in paragraph 1, 2 or 3 of subsection 5(1) and the tenant has ceased to meet the qualifications required for occupancy of the rental unit.

3. The tenant was an employee of an employer who provided the tenant with the rental unit during the tenant's employment and the employment has terminated.

4. The tenancy arose by virtue of or collateral to an agreement of purchase and sale of a proposed unit within the meaning of the *Condominium Act* in good faith and the agreement of purchase and sale has been terminated.

(2) **Period of notice.**— The date for termination specified in the notice shall be at least the number of days after the date the notice is given that is set out in section 47 and shall be the day a period of the tenancy ends or, where the tenancy is for a fixed term, the end of the term.

NOTICE BY LANDLORD FOR TERMINATION BEFORE END OF PERIOD OR TERM

61. (1) **Non-payment of rent.**— if a tenant fails to pay rent lawfully owing under a tenancy agreement, the landlord may give the tenant notice of termination of the tenancy effective not earlier than, (*a*) the 7th day after the notice is given, in the case of a daily or weekly tenancy; and

(*b*) the 14th day after the notice is given, in all other cases.

(2) **Contents of notice.**— The notice shall set out the amount of rent due and shall specify that the tenant may avoid the termination of the tenancy by paying that rent and any other rent that has become owing under the tenancy agreement before the notice of termination becomes effective.

(3) **Notice void if rent paid.**— The notice of termination under this section is void if the tenant pays the rent that is due in accordance with the tenancy agreement before the day the landlord applies to the Tribunal to terminate the tenancy.

62. (1) **Termination for cause, illegal act.**— A landlord may give a tenant notice of termination of the tenancy if the tenant commits an illegal act or carries on an illegal trade, business or occupation or permits a person to do so in the rental unit or the residential complex.

(2) **Termination for cause, misrepresentation of income.**— A landlord may give a tenant notice of termination of the tenancy if the rental unit is a rental unit described in paragraph 1, 2 or 3 of subsection 5(1) and the tenant has knowingly and materially misrepresented his or her income or that of other members of his or her family occupying the rental unit.

(3) **Notice.**— A notice of termination under this section shall,

(*a*) provide a termination date not earlier than the 20th day after the notice is given; and

(*b*) set out the grounds for termination.

63. (1) **Termination for cause, damage.**— A landlord may give a tenant notice of termination of the tenancy if the tenant or a person whom the tenant permits in the residential complex wilfully or negligently causes undue damage to the rental unit or the residential complex.

(2) **Notice.**— A notice of termination under this section shall,

(*a*) provide a termination date not earlier than the 20th day after the notice is given;

(*b*) set out the grounds for termination; and

(*c*) require the tenant, within seven days, to pay to the landlord the reasonable costs of repair or to make the repairs.

(3) **Notice void if tenant complies.**— The notice of termination under this section is void if the tenant, within seven days after receiving the notice, makes the repair, pays the reasonable costs of repair or makes arrangements satisfactory to the landlord to pay the costs or to make the repairs.

64. (1) **Termination for cause, reasonable enjoyment.**— A landlord may give a tenant notice of termination of the tenancy if the conduct of the tenant, another occupant of the rental unit or a person permitted in the residential complex by the tenant is such that it substantially interferes with the reasonable enjoyment of the residential complex for all usual purposes by the landlord or another tenant or substantially interferes with another lawful right, privilege or interest of the landlord or another tenant.

(2) **Notice.**— A notice of termination under subsection (3) shall,

(*a*) provide a termination date not earlier than the 20th day after the notice is given;

(*b*) set out the grounds for termination; and

(*c*) require the tenant, within seven days, to stop the conduct or activity or correct the omission set out in the notice.

(3) **Notice void if tenant complies.**— The notice of termination under subsection (1) is void if the tenant, within seven days after receiving the notice, stops the conduct or activity or corrects the omission.

65. (1) **Termination for cause, act impairs safety.**— A landlord may give a tenant notice of termination of the tenancy if,

(*a*) an act or omission of the tenant, another occupant of the rental unit or a person permitted in the residential complex by the tenant seriously impairs or has seriously impaired the safety of any person; and

(*b*) the act or omission occurs in the residential complex.

(2) **Same.**— A notice of termination under this section shall provide a termination date not earlier than the 10th day after the notice is given and set out the grounds for termination.

66. (1) **Termination for cause, too many persons.**— A landlord may give a tenant notice of termination of the tenancy if the number of persons occupying the rental unit on a continuing basis results in a contravention of health, safety or housing standards required by law.

(2) **Notice.**— A notice of termination under this section shall,

(*a*) provide a termination date not earlier than the 20th day after the notice is given;

(*b*) set out the details of the grounds for termination; and

(*c*) require the tenant, within seven days, to reduce the number of persons occupying the rental unit to comply with health, safety or housing standards required by law.

(3) **Notice void if tenant complies.**— The notice of termination under this section is void if the tenant, within seven days after receiving the notice, sufficiently reduces the number of persons occupying the rental unit.

67. (1) **Notice of termination, further contravention.**— A landlord may give a tenant notice of termination of the tenancy if,

(*a*) a notice of termination under section 63, 64 or 66 or under an equivalent provision of Part IV of the *Landlord and Tenant Act* has become void as a result of the tenant's compliance with the terms of the notice; and

(*b*) the tenant contravenes any of section 62, 63, 64 or 66 within six months after the first notice became void.

(2) **Same.**— The notice under this section shall set out the date it is to be effective and that date shall not be earlier than the 14th day after the notice is given. …

APPLICATION TO TRIBUNAL BY LANDLORD—LANDLORD HAS GIVEN NOTICE OF TERMINATION

69. (1) **Application by landlord.**— A landlord may apply to the Tribunal for an order terminating a tenancy and evicting the tenant if the landlord has given notice to terminate the tenancy under this Act or under the former Part IV of the *Landlord and Tenant Act*.

(2) **Same.**— An application under subsection (1) may not be made later than 30 days after the termination date specified in the notice.

(3) **Exception.**— Subsection (2) does not apply with respect to an application based on the tenant's failure to pay rent. ...

72. (1) **Non-payment of rent.**— A landlord may not apply to the Tribunal for an order terminating a tenancy and evicting the tenant based on a notice of termination under section 61 before the notice of termination becomes effective. ...

APPLICATION TO TRIBUNAL BY LANDLORD—LANDLORD HAS NOT
GIVEN NOTICE OF TERMINATION

• • •

78. Abandonment of rental unit.— If a landlord believes that a tenant has abandoned a rental unit, the landlord may apply to the Tribunal for an order terminating the tenancy.

79. (1) **Landlord may dispose of property, abandoned unit.**— A landlord may dispose of property in a rental unit that a tenant has abandoned and property of persons occupying the rental unit that is in the residential complex in which the rental unit is located in accordance with subsections (2) and (3) if,

　　(a) the landlord obtains an order terminating the tenancy under section 78; or

　　(b) the landlord gives notice to the tenant of the rental unit and to the Tribunal of the landlord's intention to dispose of the property. ...

(4) **Tenant's claim to property.**— If, before the 30 days have passed, the tenant notifies the landlord that he or she intends to remove property referred to in subsection (3), the tenant may remove the property within that 30 day period.

(5) **Same.**— If the tenant notifies the landlord in accordance with subsection (4) that he or she intends to remove the property, the landlord shall make the property available to the tenant at a reasonable time and within a reasonable proximity to the rental unit.

(6) **Same.**— The landlord may require the tenant to pay the landlord for arrears of rent and any reasonable out of pocket expenses incurred by the landlord in moving, storing or securing the tenant's property before allowing the tenant to remove the property.

(7) **Same.**— If, within six months after the date the notice referred to in clause (1)(b) is given to the tenant and the Tribunal or the order terminating the tenancy is issued, the tenant claims any of his or her property that the landlord has sold, the landlord shall pay to the tenant the amount by which the proceeds of sale exceed the sum of,

　　(a) the landlord's reasonable out of pocket expenses for moving, storing, securing or selling the property; and

　　(b) any arrears of rent.

(8) **No liability.**— Subject to subsections (5) and (7), a landlord is not liable to any person for selling, retaining or otherwise disposing of the property of a tenant in accordance with this section. ...

81. (1) **Unauthorized occupancy.**— If a tenant transfers the occupancy of a rental unit to a person in a manner other than by an assignment authorized under section 17 or a subletting authorized under section 18, the landlord may apply to the Tribunal for an order evicting the person to whom occupancy of the rental unit was transferred.

(2) **Time limitation.**— An application under this section must be made no later than 60 days after the landlord discovers the unauthorized occupancy. ...

EVICTION ORDERS

• • •

85. Effect of eviction order.— An order evicting a person shall have the same effect, and shall be enforced in the same manner, as a writ of possession.

86. (1) **Arrears of rent.**— A landlord may apply to the Tribunal for an order for the payment of arrears of rent if,

(*a*) the tenant has not paid rent lawfully required under the tenancy agreement; and

(*b*) the tenant is in possession of the rental unit. ...

87. Compensation for damage.— A landlord may apply to the Tribunal for an order for compensation if the tenant or a person whom the tenant permits in the residential complex wilfully or negligently causes undue damage to the rental unit or the residential complex and the tenant is in possession of the rental unit.

88. Compensation, misrepresentation of income.— If a landlord has a right to give a notice of termination under subsection 62(2), the landlord may apply to the Tribunal for an order for the payment of money the tenant would have been required to pay if the tenant had not misrepresented his or her income or that of other members of his or her family, so long as the application is made while the tenant is in possession of the rental unit. ...

PART VI
RULES RELATING TO RENT

GENERAL RULES

117. (1) **Security deposits, limitation.**— The only security deposit that a landlord may collect is a rent deposit collected in accordance with section 118.

(2) **Definition.**— In this section and section 118,
"security deposit" means money, property or a right paid or given by, or on behalf of, a tenant of a rental unit to a landlord or to anyone on the landlord's behalf to be held by or for the account of the landlord as security for the performance of an obligation or the payment of a liability of the tenant or to be returned to the tenant upon the happening of a condition.

118. (1) **Rent deposit may be required.**— A landlord may require a tenant to pay a rent deposit with respect to a tenancy if the landlord does so on or before entering into the tenancy agreement.

(2) **Amount of rent deposit.**— The amount of a rent deposit shall not be more than the lesser of the amount of rent for one rent period and the amount of rent for one month.

(3) **Same.**— If the lawful rent increases after a tenant has paid a rent deposit, the landlord may require the tenant to pay an additional amount to increase the rent deposit up to the amount permitted by subsection (2). ...

(6) **Interest.**— A landlord of a rental unit shall pay interest to the tenant annually on the amount of the rent deposit at the rate of 6 per cent per year.

(7) **Same.**— Where the landlord has failed to make the payment required by subsection (6) when it comes due, the tenant may deduct the amount of the payment from a subsequent rent payment.

(8) **Rent deposit applied to last rent.**— A landlord shall apply a rent deposit that a tenant has paid to the landlord or to a former landlord in payment of the rent for the last rent period before the tenancy terminates. …

LAWFUL RENT

• • •

124. New tenant.— Subject to section 121, the lawful rent for the first rental period for a new tenant under a new tenancy agreement is the rent first charged to the tenant. …

126. (1) 12-month rule.— A landlord who is lawfully entitled to increase the rent charged to a tenant for a rental unit may do so only if at least 12 months have elapsed,

> (*a*) since the day of the last rent increase for that tenant in that rental unit, if there has been a previous increase; or

> (*b*) since the day the rental unit was first rented to that tenant, otherwise.

(2) **Exception.**— An increase in rent under section 132 shall be deemed not to be an increase in rent for the purposes of this section.

127. (1) Notice of rent increase required.— A landlord shall not increase the rent charged to a tenant for a rental unit without first giving the tenant at least 90 days written notice of the landlord's intention to do so. …

ILLEGAL ADDITIONAL CHARGES

140. (1) Additional charges prohibited.— Unless otherwise prescribed, no landlord shall, directly or indirectly, with respect to any rental unit,

> (*a*) collect or require or attempt to collect or require from a tenant or prospective tenant of the rental unit a fee, premium, commission, bonus, penalty, key deposit or other like amount of money whether or not the money is refundable;

> (*b*) require or attempt to require a tenant or prospective tenant to pay any consideration for goods or services as a condition for granting the tenancy or continuing to permit occupancy of a rental unit if that consideration is in addition to the rent the tenant is lawfully required to pay to the landlord; or

> (*c*) rent any portion of the rental unit for a rent which, together with all other rents payable for all other portions of the rental unit, is a sum that is greater than the rent the landlord lawfully may charge for the rental unit.

(2) **Same.**— No superintendent, property manager or other person who acts on behalf of a landlord with respect to a rental unit shall, directly or indirectly, with or without the authority of the landlord, do any of the things mentioned in clause (1)(a), (b) or (c) with respect to that rental unit.

(3) **Same.**— Unless otherwise prescribed, no tenant and no person acting on behalf of the tenant shall, directly or indirectly,

(*a*) sublet a rental unit for a rent that is greater than the rent that is lawfully charged by the landlord for the rental unit;

(*b*) sublet any portion of the rental unit for a rent which, together with all other rents payable for all other portions of the rental unit, is a sum that is greater than the rent that is lawfully charged by the landlord for the rental unit;

(*c*) collect or require or attempt to collect or require from any person any fee, premium, commission, bonus, penalty, key deposit or other like amount of money, for subletting a rental unit or any portion of it, for surrendering occupancy of a rental unit or for otherwise parting with possession of a rental unit; or

(*d*) require or attempt to require a person to pay any consideration for goods or services as a condition for the subletting, assignment or surrender of occupancy or possession in addition to the rent the person is lawfully required to pay to the tenant or landlord. ...

PART VII
VITAL SERVICES AND MAINTENANCE STANDARDS

VITAL SERVICES

145. Definitions.— In this section and sections 146 to 153,
"local municipality" has the same meaning as in the *Municipal Act*;
"vital services by-law" means a by-law passed under section 146.

146. (1) **By-laws respecting vital services.**— The council of a local municipality may pass by-laws,

(*a*) requiring every landlord to provide adequate and suitable vital services to each of the landlord's rental units;

(*b*) prohibiting a supplier from ceasing to provide the vital service until a notice has been given under subsection 147(1);

(*c*) requiring a supplier to promptly restore the vital service when directed to do so by an official named in the by-law;

(*d*) prohibiting a person from hindering, obstructing or interfering with or attempting to hinder, obstruct or interfere with the official or person referred to in subsection 148(1) in the exercise of a power or performance of a duty under this section or sections 147 to 153;

(*e*) providing that a person who contravenes or fails to comply with a by-law is guilty of an offence for each day or part of a day on which the offence occurs or continues;

(*f*) providing that every director or officer of a corporation that is convicted of an offence who knowingly concurs in the commission of the offence is guilty of an offence;

(*g*) authorizing an official named in the by-law to enter into agreements on behalf of a local municipality with suppliers of vital services to ensure that adequate and suitable vital services are provided for rental units.

(2) **Exception.**— A vital services by-law does not apply to a landlord with respect to a rental unit to the extent that the tenant has expressly agreed to obtain and maintain the vital services. ...

149. (1) **Services by municipality.**— If a landlord does not provide a vital service for a rental unit in accordance with a vital services by-law, the local municipality may arrange for the service to be provided. ...

PART X
GENERAL

ADMINISTRATION AND ENFORCEMENT

• • •

204. (1) **Warrant.**— A provincial judge or justice of the peace may at any time issue a warrant in the prescribed form authorizing a person named in the warrant to enter and search a building, receptacle or place if the provincial judge or justice of the peace is satisfied by information on oath that there are reasonable grounds to believe that an offence has been committed under this Act and the entry and search will afford evidence relevant to the commission of the offence.

(2) **Seizure.**— In a warrant, the provincial judge or justice of the peace may authorize the person named in the warrant to seize anything that, based on reasonable grounds, will afford evidence relevant to the commission of the offence.

(3) **Receipt and removal.**— Anyone who seizes something under a warrant shall,

    (*a*) give a receipt for the thing seized to the person from whom it was seized; and

    (*b*) bring the thing seized before the provincial judge or justice of the peace issuing the warrant or another provincial judge or justice to be dealt with according to law.

(4) **Expiry.**— A warrant shall name the date upon which it expires, which shall be not later than 15 days after the warrant is issued.

(5) **Time of execution.**— A warrant shall be executed between 6 a.m. and 9 p.m. unless it provides otherwise.

(6) **Other matters.**— Sections 159 and 160 of the *Provincial Offences Act* apply with necessary modifications with respect to any thing seized under this section. ...

OFFENCES

206. (1) **Offences.**— Any person who knowingly does any of the following is guilty of an offence:

    1. Restrict reasonable access to the residential complex by political candidates or their authorized representatives in contravention of section 22.

    2. Alter or cause to be altered the locking system on any door giving entry to a rental unit or the residential complex in a manner that contravenes section 23.

3. Withhold reasonable supply of a vital service, care service or food or deliberately interfere with the supply in contravention of section 25.

4. Harass, hinder, obstruct or interfere with a tenant in the exercise of,

   i. securing a right or seeking relief under this Act or in the court,

   ii. participating in a proceeding under this Act, or

   iii. participating in a tenants' association or attempting to organize a tenants' association.

5. Harass, coerce, threaten or interfere with a tenant in such a manner that the tenant is induced to vacate the rental unit.

6. Harass, hinder, obstruct or interfere with a landlord in the exercise of,

   i. securing a right or seeking relief under this Act or in the court, or

   ii. participating in a proceeding under this Act.

7. Seize any property of the tenant in contravention of section 31.

8. Obtain possession of a rental unit improperly by giving a notice to terminate in bad faith.

9. Fail to afford a tenant a right of first refusal in contravention of section 54 or 56.

10. Recover possession of a rental unit without complying with the requirements of sections 55, 57 and 58.

11. Coerce a tenant of a mobile home park or land lease community to enter into an agency agreement for the sale or lease of their mobile home or land lease home or to require an agency agreement as a condition of entering into a tenancy agreement.

12. Coerce a tenant to sign an agreement referred to in section 130.

(2) **Same.**— Any person who does any of the following is guilty of an offence:

1. Furnish false or misleading information in any document filed in any proceeding under this Act or provided to an inspector, investigator, the Minister, a delegate of the Minister or any employee or official of the Tribunal.

2. Enter a rental unit where such entry is not permitted by section 20, 21 or 94 or enter without first complying with the requirements of section 20, 21 or 94.

3. Contravene an order of the Tribunal under paragraph 4 of subsection 34(1) or clause 35(1)(a).

4. Unlawfully recover possession of a rental unit.

5. Give a notice to terminate a tenancy under section 51 or 52 in contravention of section 54.

6. Give a notice of rent increase or a notice of increase of a charge in a care home without first giving an information package contrary to section 92.

7. Increase a charge for providing a care service or meals to a tenant in a care home in contravention of section 101.

8. Interfere with a tenant's right under section 105 to sell or lease his or her mobile home.

9. Restrict the right of a tenant of a mobile home park or land lease community to purchase goods or services from the person of his or her choice in contravention of section 109.

10. Require or receive a security deposit from a tenant contrary to section 117.

11. Fail to pay to the tenant annually interest on the rent deposit held in respect of their tenancy in accordance with subsection 118(6).

12. Fail to apply the rent deposit held in respect of a tenancy to the rent for the last month of the tenancy in contravention of subsection 118(8).

13. Fail to provide a tenant with a receipt in accordance with section 120.

14. Charge rent in all amount greater than permitted under the Act.

15. Require a tenant to pay rent proposed in an application in contravention of subsection 138(4).

16. Charge or collect amounts from a tenant, a prospective tenant, a subtenant, a potential subtenant, an assignee or a potential assignee in contravention of section 140.

17. Fail to comply with any or all of the items contained in a work order issued under section 155.

18. Charge an illegal contingency fee in contravention of subsection 199(1).

19. Obstruct or interfere with an inspector or investigator exercising a power of entry under section 203.

(3) **Same.**— Any landlord or superintendent, agent or employee of the landlord who knowingly harasses a tenant or interferes with a tenant's reasonable enjoyment of a rental unit or the residential complex in which it is located is guilty of an offence.

(4) **Same.**— Any person who knowingly attempts to commit any offence referred to in subsection (1), (2) or (3) is guilty of an offence.

(5) **Same.**— Every director or officer of a corporation who knowingly concurs in an offence is guilty of an offence.

(6) **Same.**— A person, other than a corporation, who is guilty of an offence under this section is liable on conviction to a fine of not more than $10,000.

(7) **Same.**— A corporation that is guilty of an offence under this section is liable on conviction to a fine of not more than $50,000.

(8) **Limitation.**— No proceeding shall be commenced respecting an offence under paragraph 1 of subsection (2) more than two years after the date on which the facts giving rise to the offence came to the attention of the Minister.

(9) **Same.**— No proceeding shall be commenced respecting any other offence under this section more than two years after the date on which the offence was, or is alleged to have been, committed. ...

REGULATIONS

208. (1) **Regulations.**— The Lieutenant Governor in Council may make regulations,

1. prescribing services that are to be included or not included in the definition of care services in subsection 1(1);

2. prescribing charges not to be included in the definition of "municipal taxes and charges" in subsection 1(1);

3. prescribing circumstances under which one or more rental units that form part of a residential complex, rather than the entire residential complex, are care homes for the purposes of the definition of "care home" in subsection 1(1);

4. providing that specified provisions of this Act do not apply with respect to specified classes of accommodation;

5. prescribing classes of accommodation for the purposes of clause 3(m);

6. prescribing grounds of an application for the purposes of clause 7(1)(b);

7. respecting the rules for making findings for the purposes of subsection 7(2);

8. prescribing the information that shall be contained in an information package for the purposes of section 92;

9. prescribing rules for determining the amount by which rent charged to a new tenant may exceed the last lawful rent charged for the purposes of section 114;

10. prescribing services and things for the purposes of section 116;

11. prescribing rules for calculating the lawful rent which may be charged where a landlord provides a tenant with a discount in rent at the beginning of, or during, a tenancy and the rules may differ for different types of discounts;

12. prescribing rules for the calculation of lawful rent where the rent a landlord charges for the first rental period of a tenancy is greater than the rent the landlord charges for any subsequent rental period;

13. prescribing the circumstances under which lawful rent for the purposes of section 123 will be other than that provided for in section 123 and providing the lawful rent under those circumstances;

14. prescribing the Table setting out the weights and operating costs categories needed to calculate the guideline;

15. respecting rules for increasing or decreasing rent charged for the purposes of sections 132 and 134;

16. prescribing services, facilities, privileges, accommodations and things for the purposes of paragraph 2 of subsection 132(1);

17. prescribing rules with respect to making findings in an order under section 138 and prescribing time periods during which rent increases may be taken;

18. prescribing the rules for phasing in of an increase in rent for the purposes of subsection 138(10);

19. prescribing rules for the purposes of section 139;

20. exempting specified payments from the operation of section 140;

21. prescribing the rules for making findings for the purposes of subsection 142(3);

22. prescribing the rules for making findings for the purposes of subsection 143(2) and for determining the effective date for an order under section 143;

23. prescribing maintenance standards for the purposes of section 154;

24. prescribing other criteria for determining areas in which maintenance standards apply for the purposes of subsection 154(1);

25. respecting the amount or the determination of the amount the Minister may charge a municipality for the purposes of subsection 154(4), including payments to inspectors, overhead costs related to inspections and interest on overdue accounts;

26. prescribing information to be filed with an application to the Tribunal;

27. respecting the appointment, including the status, duties and benefits, of employees of the Tribunal for the purposes of section 166;

28. restricting the circumstances in which the Tribunal may under section 182, require a respondent to make a payment into the Tribunal;

29. governing the management and investment of money paid into the Tribunal providing for the payment of interest on money paid into the Tribunal and fixing the rate of interest so paid;

30. prescribing an amount for the purposes of subsection 199(1);

31. prescribing the form of a search warrant for the purposes of section 204;

32. prescribing any matter required or permitted by this Act to be prescribed;

33. defining any word or expression used in this Act that has not already been expressly defined in this Act.

EXERCISES

■ SHORT ANSWER

1. Who is included in the definition of landlord?

   THE PERSON WHO RENTS TO & THE TENANT.

2. Define the term "tenancy agreement."

   ORAL, WRITEN OR IMPLIED AGREEMEN TO OCCUPY A RENTAL UNIT.

3. What do "facilities and services" under the *Tenant Protection Act* include?

   a. HYDRO
   b. WATTER
   c. FUEL
   d. GAS
   e. FOOD
   f. PARKING
   g. REPCARING
   h.
   i.
   j.

4. List 10 accommodations that are not covered by the *Tenant Protection Act*.

   a.
   b.
   c.
   d.
   e.
   f.
   g.
   h.
   i.
   j.

5. You are dispatched to a landlord–tenant dispute at 106 Pine St. The
    tenant refuses to pay his rent because the landlord has not provided
    a written tenancy agreement. What advice would you provide to the
    tenant and the landlord?

6. The superintendent at 696 Pine St. has called you because the tenant
    in room 306 has a large dog in his apartment. His lease states that he
    is not allowed to bring any pets into his apartment. How would you
    resolve this dispute?

7. Explain in your own words the provisions of the *Tenant Protection
    Act* as they relate to the subletting of premises.

    IT'S AN ACT THAT WILL PROTECT
    TENANTS TO

8. A landlord suspects that two persons not named in the rental
    agreement are living in an apartment. While the tenant is away at
    school, the landlord enters the apartment to check for signs of
    unlawful guests. Has the landlord committed any offence? Explain.

    NO THAT COULD BE TAKEN
    AS AN EMERGENCY

9. What does the *Tenant Protection Act* say with respect to "who shall live in a residence that is under a tenancy agreement"?

10. Under what conditions is a landlord authorized to gain entry into a rental unit with notice?

11. Members of a religious group have been denied entry into an apartment complex. They have called the police and want you to straighten this problem out with the landlord. What would you tell the members of this group and the landlord?

12. A landlord who has been having trouble with a tenant padlocks the tenant's door. The tenant calls the police and wants the police to force the landlord to remove the padlock. What is your response to the landlord and the tenant?

13. Jim Smale is a local college student. Because his resources are limited, he has taken up residence in an old six-unit apartment building in the west end of town. The landlord, Jack Walters, demanded three months' rent in advance and told Smale that he is not to have any female visitors after 9:00 p.m. Three days into the rental agreement, the heaters break down in Smale's apartment and the hot water is not working. Smale calls the landlord to complain and is told, "if you don't like it, move out." Smale calls the police and you arrive. You find garbage piled up in the hallways and discover that the breaker for the heaters and the hot water has been turned off. Smale complains to the officers. Smale is questioned further and the officers discover that Walters has also taken three months' rent in advance. What offences under the *Tenant Protection Act* has the landlord committed?

CHAPTER 5
The Trespass to Property Act

CHAPTER OBJECTIVES

After completing this chapter, you should be able to:

◆ Understand key terms defined in the *Trespass to Property Act*.

◆ State the offences related to trespass to property.

◆ List the methods of notice that prohibit or limit entry and/or use of property.

◆ Identify premises that prohibit entry without notice.

◆ Describe owner liability with respect to the offence of trespass onto property with a motor vehicle.

◆ State the arrest authorities, on and off premises, by an occupier and a police officer.

INTRODUCTION

The *Trespass to Property Act* is fairly self-explanatory. It makes trespassing without the express permission of the occupier, the proof of which rests on the defendant, an offence, unless an individual is acting under a legal right. It prohibits trespassing on premises when entry is prohibited. It also prohibits the engaging of an activity on premises when the activity is prohibited under the Act. It also creates an offence of failing to leave premises immediately after being directed to do so by the occupier or by a person authorized by the occupier.

An occupier is defined as someone who either is in physical possession of the premises or has responsibility for and control over the condition of the premises or the activities that are carried on in the premises. Most often, offences under the *Trespass to Property Act* arise in the context of businesses and homes. However, school boards also have all the rights and duties of occupiers in relation to their school sites. One can easily imagine why it is important to have school boards included as occupiers. It can be dangerous to have adults who have no business on school property loitering in the presence of young, vulnerable children.

The *Trespass to Property Act* creates authority for police and occupiers to remove trespassers from designated premises. It also allows for the prosecution of trespassers, and it allows for the compensation of victims of trespass in limited circumstances (for example, where the trespasser committed an offence with a motor vehicle and caused damage to property).

TRESPASS TO PROPERTY ACT

RSO 1990, Chapter T.21

1. (1) **Definitions.**— In this Act,
"occupier" includes,

(a) a person who is in physical possession of premises, or

(b) a person who has responsibility for and control over the condition of premises or the activities there carried on, or control over persons allowed to enter the premises,

even if there is more than one occupier of the same premises;

"premises" means lands and structures, or either of them, and includes,

(a) water,

(b) ships and vessels,

(c) trailers and portable structures designed or used for residence, business or shelter,

(d) trains, railway cars, vehicles and aircraft, except while in operation.

(2) **School boards.**— A school board has all the rights and duties of an occupier in respect of its school sites as defined in the *Education Act*.

2. (1) **Trespass an offence.**— Every person who is not acting under a right or authority conferred by law and who,

(*a*) without the express permission of the occupier, the proof of which rests on the defendant,

(i) enters on premises when entry is prohibited under this Act, or

(ii) engages in an activity on premises when the activity is prohibited under this Act; or

(*b*) does not leave the premises immediately after he or she is directed to do so by the occupier of the premises or a person authorized by the occupier,

is guilty of an offence and on conviction is liable to a fine of not more than $2,000.

(2) **Colour of right as a defence.**— It is a defence to a charge under subsection (1) in respect of premises that is land that the person charged reasonably believed that he or she had title to or an interest in the land that entitled him or her to do the act complained of.

3. (1) **Prohibition of entry.**— Entry on premises may be prohibited by notice to that effect and entry is prohibited without any notice on premises,

(*a*) that is a garden, field or other land that is under cultivation, including a lawn, orchard, vineyard and premises on which trees have been planted and have not attained an average height of more than two metres and woodlots on land used primarily for agricultural purposes; or

(*b*) that is enclosed in a manner that indicates the occupier's intention to keep persons off the premises or to keep animals on the premises.

(2) **Implied permission to use approach to door.**— There is a presumption that access for lawful purposes to the door of a building on premises by a means apparently provided and used for the purpose of access is not prohibited.

4. (1) **Limited permission.**— Where notice is given that one or more particular activities are permitted, all other activities and entry for the purpose are prohibited and any additional notice that entry is prohibited or a particular activity is prohibited on the same premises shall be construed to be for greater certainty only.

(2) **Limited prohibition.**— Where entry on premises is not prohibited under section 3 or by notice that one or more particular activities are permitted under subsection (1), and notice is given that a particular activity is prohibited, that activity and entry for the purpose is prohibited and all other activities and entry for the purpose are not prohibited.

5. (1) **Method of giving notice.**— A notice under this Act may be given,

(a) orally or in writing;

(b) by means of signs posted so that a sign is clearly visible in daylight under normal conditions from the approach to each ordinary point of access to the premises to which it applies; or

(c) by means of the marking system set out in section 7.

(2) **Substantial compliance.**— Substantial compliance with clause (1)(b) or (c) is sufficient notice.

6. (1) **Form of sign.**— A sign naming an activity or showing a graphic representation of an activity is sufficient for the purpose of giving notice that the activity is permitted.

(2) **Idem.**— A sign naming an activity with an oblique line drawn through the name or showing a graphic representation of an activity with an oblique line drawn through the representation is sufficient for the purpose of giving notice that the activity is prohibited.

7. (1) **Red marking.**— Red markings made and posted in accordance with subsections (3) and (4) are sufficient for the purpose of giving notice that entry on the premises is prohibited.

(2) **Yellow markings.**— Yellow markings made and posted in accordance with subsections (3) and (4) are sufficient for the purpose of giving notice that entry is prohibited except for the purpose of certain activities and shall be deemed to be notice of the activities permitted.

(3) **Size.**— A marking under this section shall be of such a size that a circle ten centimetres in diameter can be contained wholly within it.

(4) **Posting.**— Markings under this section shall be so placed that a marking is clearly visible in daylight under normal conditions from the approach to each ordinary point of access to the premises to which it applies.

8. **Notice applicable to part of premises.**— A notice or permission under this Act may be given in respect of any part of the premises of an occupier.

9. (1) **Arrest without warrant on premises.**— A police officer, or the occupier of premises, or a person authorized by the occupier may arrest without warrant any person he or she believes on reasonable and probable grounds to be on the premises in contravention of section 2.

(2) **Delivery to police officer.**— Where the person who makes an arrest under subsection (1) is not a police officer, he or she shall promptly call for the assistance of a police officer and give the person arrested into the custody of the police officer.

(3) **Deemed arrest.**— A police officer to whom the custody of a person is given under subsection (2) shall be deemed to have arrested the person for the purposes of the provisions of the *Provincial Offences Act* applying to his or her release or continued detention and bail.

10. Arrest without warrant off premises.— Where a police officer believes on reasonable and probable grounds that a person has been in contravention of section 2 and has made fresh departure from the premises, and the person refuses to give his or her name and address, or there are reasonable and probable grounds to believe that the name or address given is false, the police officer may arrest the person without warrant.

11. Motor vehicles.— Where an offence under this Act is committed by means of a motor vehicle, as defined in the *Highway Traffic Act*, the driver of the motor vehicle is liable to the fine provided under this Act and, where the driver is not the owner, the owner of the motor vehicle is liable to the fine provided under this Act unless the driver is convicted of the offence or, at the time the offence was committed, the motor vehicle was in the possession of a person other than the owner without the owner's consent.

12. (1) **Damage award.**— Where a person is convicted of an offence under section 2, and a person has suffered damage caused by the person convicted during the commission of the offence, the court shall, on the request of the prosecutor and with the consent of the person who suffered the damage, determine the damages and shall make a judgment for damages against the person convicted in favour of the person who suffered the damage, but no judgment shall be for an amount in excess of $1,000.

(2) **Costs of prosecution.**— Where a prosecution under section 2 is conducted by a private prosecutor, and the defendant is convicted, unless the court is of the opinion that the prosecution was not necessary for the protection of the occupier or the occupier's interests, the court shall determine the actual costs reasonably incurred in conducting the prosecution and, despite section 60 of the *Provincial Offences Act*, shall order those costs to be paid by the defendant to the prosecutor.

(3) **Damages and costs in addition to fine.**— A judgment for damages under subsection (1), or an award of costs under subsection (2), shall be in addition to any fine that is imposed under this Act.

(4) **Civil action.**— A judgment for damages under subsection (1) extinguishes the right of the person in whose favour the judgment is made to bring a civil action for damages against the person convicted arising out of the same facts.

(5) **Idem.**— The failure to request or refusal to grant a judgment for damages under subsection (1) does not affect a right to bring a civil action for damages arising out of the same facts.

(6) **Enforcement.**— The judgment for damages under subsection (1), and the award for costs under subsection (2), may be filed in the Small Claims Court and shall be deemed to be a judgment or order of that court for the purposes of enforcement.

EXERCISES

■ MULTIPLE CHOICE

1. Indicate which of the following locations requires the posting of a notice to prohibit trespassing:

   a. a school yard

   b. a backyard garden

   c. a fenced-in industrial site

   d. a lawn

   e. property that has trees suitable for logging purposes

   f. a government building

■ SHORT ANSWER

1. Adam Shelhorne has just purchased a 200 acre farm. He has livestock in the form of cattle and sheep and has fenced in all of the property. He wants to make certain that no one trespasses on his property. What type of notices can he use to notify people that they are not welcome on his property?

2. Shelhorne's neighbour also has 200 acres of land. He has a stream and a pond on his property. He does not mind people using his property to ski or snow shoe, however, he does not want anybody fishing or snowmobiling on the land. What type(s) of notice would be appropriate on his property?

3. On Monday, July 12, Shelhorne notices that his cattle are rampaging through the field. He then notices a 4 × 4 truck, licence number AB1 234, chasing the cattle and tearing up the soil. He calls the OPP and the trucker is stopped five minutes later on the highway. Evan Nuxey is the driver and owner of the 4 × 4. The truck is full of dirt and grass. When questioned about the activity on Shelhorne's farm, he denies any involvement. Shelhorne arrives and points out Nuxey to the officer as the person who spooked his cattle and tore up his land. One cow has suffered a broken leg and may have to be destroyed. The officer decides to charge Nuxey.

    Complete the required documentation for the charge.

    Is there a responsibility placed on the owner of the truck for damage to Shelhorne's property? Explain.

4. You are called to the Central Hotel on King Street at 11:30 p.m. on Monday, February 15. On arrival, you are met by the bartender. He informs you that John Allison, sitting at a table near the stage, has been rude to the customers as they passed his table. He was asked to leave and he refused. Describe the process to be followed to give Allison notice.

5. Allison refuses to leave. Describe your next step as a police officer. Complete the required documentation.

6. One hour later you are again called by the bartender at the Central Hotel. Allison, age 53, has returned and refuses to leave. The bartender is holding him on the floor when you arrive. What is the bartender's authority for holding Allison?

CHAPTER 6
Blind Persons' Rights Act

CHAPTER OBJECTIVES

After completing this chapter, you should be able to:

◆ Understand key terms defined in the *Blind Persons' Rights Act*.

◆ List the charges that can be laid for denying access to or discriminating against a blind person because he or she is a blind person accompanied by a guide dog.

◆ Be prepared to apply the provisions of the Act in a hypothetical fact situation.

INTRODUCTION

The purpose of the *Blind Person's Rights Act* is self-explanatory. Charges under the *Blind Person's Rights Act* are rarely prosecuted, probably because most people are sensitive to and aware of the needs of blind persons and the special allowances they require. However, without this statute, the rights of blind persons to have guide dogs accompany them in any facility and their right to have their guide dogs live with them in their self-contained dwelling units would not be enshrined in legislation, and therefore could not be enforced. As a result of this statute, even where dogs are otherwise prohibited by law, guide dogs are allowed to be present.

BLIND PERSONS' RIGHTS ACT

RSO 1990, Chapter B.7

1. (1) Definitions.— In this Act,

"blind person" means a person who because of blindness is dependent on a guide dog or white cane;

"guide dog" means a dog trained as a guide for a blind person and having the qualifications prescribed by the regulations.

(2) **Application.—** This Act applies despite any other Act or any regulation, by-law or rule made thereunder. ...

2. (1) Guide dogs permitted in places to which public admitted.— No person, directly or indirectly, alone or with another, by himself, herself or itself or by the interposition of another, shall,

　　(*a*) deny to any person the accommodation, services or facilities available in any place to which the public is customarily admitted; or

　　(*b*) discriminate against any person with respect to the accommodation, services or facilities available in any place to which the public is customarily admitted, or the charges for the use thereof,

for the reason that he or she is a blind person accompanied by a guide dog.

(2) **Guide dogs permitted in self-contained dwelling unit.—** No person, directly or indirectly, alone or with another, by himself, herself or itself or by the interposition of another, shall,

　　(*a*) deny to any person occupancy of any self-contained dwelling unit; or

　　(*b*) discriminate against any person with respect to any term or condition of occupancy of any self-contained dwelling unit,

for the reason that he or she is a blind person keeping or customarily accompanied by a guide dog.

(3) **Other facilities.—** Nothing in this section shall be construed to entitle a blind person to require any service, facility or accommodation in respect of a guide dog other than the right to be accompanied by the guide dog.

3. Restriction on use of white cane.— No person, other than a blind person, shall carry or use a cane or walking stick, the major part of which is white, in any public place, public thoroughfare or public conveyance.

4. (1) Identification cards.— The Attorney General or an officer of his or her Ministry designated by the Attorney General in writing may, upon application therefor, issue to a blind person an identification card identifying the blind person and his or her guide dog.

(2) **Cards as proof of qualification.—** An identification card issued under subsection (1) is proof, in the absence of evidence to the contrary, that the blind person and the guide dog identified therein are qualified for the purposes of this Act.

(3) **Surrender of cards.—** Any person to whom an identification card is issued under subsection (1) shall, upon the request of the Attorney General or an officer designated under subsection (1), surrender the identification card for amendment or cancellation.

5. Regulations.— The Lieutenant Governor in Council may make regulations prescribing qualifications for guide dogs.

6. (1) **Penalty.—** Every person who is in contravention of section 2 is guilty of an offence and on conviction is liable to a fine not exceeding $5,000.

(2) **Idem.—** Every person who is in contravention of section 3 or of subsection 4 (3) or who, not being a blind person, purports to be a blind person for the purpose of claiming the benefit of this Act is guilty of an offence and on conviction is liable to a fine not exceeding $500.

EXERCISES

■ SHORT ANSWER

1. Define the following terms:

    a. blind person

    b. guide dog

■ MULTIPLE CHOICE

Circle the correct response(s).

1. A blind person, accompanied by a guide dog, must be admitted into the following facilities:

    a. restaurants

    b. hotels

    c. baseball fields

    d. all of the above

    e. a and b

■ TRUE OR FALSE

_____ 1. A blind person, accompanied by a guide dog, may be refused the right to purchase a condominium solely on the grounds that pets are not permitted in the building.

_____ 2. A blind person, accompanied by a guide dog, who registers in any hotel or motel may require the manager of a hotel to provide special facilities for the dog.

■ **CASE STUDY**

Jason Alexander is a blind person visiting the city of Toronto. His guide dog, Rover, accompanies him wherever he goes. One day he walks into Chez Hélène, an exclusive, four-star restaurant in downtown Toronto. He is met at the door by a hostess and advised that the dog is not permitted in the facility. Alexander refuses to leave and the police are called. Alexander meets the police and claims that the restaurant is discriminating against him by refusing him admittance into the restaurant, solely because he has a dog with him. You are the police officer responding to this call.

1. What documentation could Alexander provide to prove that he is in fact blind and that Rover is a guide dog by definition under the *Blind Persons' Rights Act*?

2. How would you resolve this situation?

CHAPTER 7

The Coroners Act

CHAPTER OBJECTIVES

After completing this chapter, you should be able to:

◆ Understand key terms defined in the *Coroners Act*.

◆ List the five purposes of an inquest.

◆ List the situations in which police officers are required to notify the coroner that a death has occurred.

◆ Identify the locations of death that require police officers to notify the coroner.

◆ Describe the duties of a coroner's constable in preparation for an inquest.

◆ State the methods of delivering a summons to a juror or witness for an inquest.

◆ Locate and interpret the offence of knowingly obstructing a coroner or person authorized by a coroner.

◆ Be prepared to apply the provisions of the Act in a hypothetical fact situation.

INTRODUCTION

The *Coroners Act* is an interesting statute with a wider range than might be thought at first glance. Coroners are appointed by the lieutenant governor in council and continue to hold office until they attain the age of 70 years. There may be more than one coroner appointed for a particular region.

The *Coroners Act* imposes duties on members of the public to immediately notify a coroner or a police officer of the facts and circumstances relating to any death that occurs in any of the scenarios set out in s. 10 of the Act. For example, the coroner or a police officer must be called where an individual dies as a result of disease or sickness for which the deceased was not treated by a legally qualified medical practitioner, or where the death was sudden or unusual or as the result of an accident.

The *Coroners Act* establishes procedures for inquests and determines when an inquest may be held. If a coroner is of the view that an inquest is necessary, it will be held. If the coroner determines an inquest is unnecessary, a close relative or personal representative of the deceased may request the coroner in writing to hold an inquest. If an inquest is directed pursuant to a criminal charge, the person charged shall not be a compellable witness. An inquest, like a criminal or civil jury trial, involves a jury. It is quite different from a criminal or civil trial, however, in that the jurors take notes throughout the proceedings, and at the conclusion of the inquest the jurors deliver specific recommendations rather than delivering a verdict.

CORONERS ACT

R.S.O. 1990, Chapter C.37

1. Definitions.— In this Act,

"Chief Coroner" means the Chief Coroner for Ontario;

"mine" means a mine as defined in the *Occupational Health and Safety Act*;

"mining plant" means a mining plant as defined in the *Occupational Health and Safety Act*;

"Minister" means the *Solicitor General*;

"spouse" means a person of the opposite sex,

> (a) to whom the deceased was married immediately before his or her death,

> (b) with whom the deceased was living in a conjugal relationship outside marriage immediately before his or her death, if the deceased and the other person,

>> (i) had cohabited for at least one year,

>> (ii) were together the parents of a child, or

>> (iii) had together entered into a cohabitation agreement under section 53 of the *Family Law Act*.

2. (1) Repeal of common law functions.— In so far as it is within the jurisdiction of the Legislature, the common law as it relates to the functions, powers and duties of coroners within Ontario is repealed.

(2) **Inquest not criminal court of record.—** The powers conferred on a coroner to conduct an inquest shall not be construed as creating a criminal court of record.

3. (1) Appointment of coroners.— The Lieutenant Governor in Council may appoint one or more legally qualified medical practitioners to be coroners for Ontario who, subject to subsections (2), (3) and (4), shall hold office during pleasure.

(2) **Tenure.—** A coroner ceases to hold office,

> (*a*) upon attaining the age of seventy years; or

> (*b*) upon ceasing to be a legally qualified medical practitioner. ...

(7) **Appointments continued.—** All persons holding appointments as coroners under *The Coroners Act*, being chapter 87 of the Revised Statutes of Ontario, 1970, shall be deemed to have been appointed in accordance with this Act.

4. (1) Chief Coroner and duties.— The Lieutenant Governor in Council may appoint a coroner to be Chief Coroner for Ontario who shall,

> (*a*) administer this Act and the regulations;

> (*b*) supervise, direct and control all coroners in Ontario in the performance of their duties;

> (*c*) conduct programs for the instruction of coroners in their duties;

> (*d*) bring the findings and recommendations of coroners' juries to the attention of appropriate persons, agencies and ministries of government;

> (*e*) prepare, publish and distribute a code of ethics for the guidance of coroners;

> (*f*) perform such other duties as are assigned to him or her by or under this or any other Act or by the regulations or by the Lieutenant Governor in Council.

(2) **Deputy Chief Coroner.**— The Lieutenant Governor in Council may appoint a coroner to be Deputy Chief Coroner for Ontario who shall act as and have all the powers and authority of the Chief Coroner during the absence of the Chief Coroner or his or her inability to act.

5. (1) **Regional coroners.**— The Lieutenant Governor in Council may appoint a coroner as a regional coroner for such region of Ontario as is described in the appointment.

(2) **Duties.**— A regional coroner shall assist the Chief Coroner in the performance of his or her duties in the region and shall perform such other duties as are assigned to him or her by the Chief Coroner. ...

8. Authority for judge to act as coroner.— Subject to subsection 15(1), a provincial judge may perform any of the duties and exercise any of the powers of a coroner in a territorial district in the absence of a coroner.

9. (1) **Police assistance.**— The police force having jurisdiction in a municipality shall make available to the coroner the assistance of such police officers as are necessary for the purpose of carrying out the coroner's duties.

(2) **Idem.**— The Chief Coroner in any case he or she considers appropriate may request that the criminal investigation branch of the Ontario Provincial Police provide assistance to a coroner in an investigation or inquest.

10. (1) **Duty to give information.**— Every person who has reason to believe that a deceased person died,

(a) as a result of,

(i) violence,

(ii) misadventure,

(iii) negligence,

(iv) misconduct, or

(v) malpractice;

(b) by unfair means;

(c) during pregnancy or following pregnancy in circumstances that might reasonably be attributable thereto;

(d) suddenly and unexpectedly;

(e) from disease or sickness for which he or she was not treated by a legally qualified medical practitioner;

(f) from any cause other than disease; or

(g) under such circumstances as may require investigation,

shall immediately notify a coroner or a police officer of the facts and circumstances relating to the death, and where a police officer is notified he or she shall in turn immediately notify the coroner of such facts and circumstances.

(2) **Deaths to be reported.**— Where a person dies while resident or an inpatient in,

(a) a charitable institution as defined in the *Charitable Institutions Act*;

(b) a children's residence under Part IX (Licensing) of the *Child and Family Services Act* or premises approved under subsection 9(1) of Part I (Flexible Services) of that Act; ...

(d) a home for retarded persons as defined in the *Homes for Retarded Persons Act*;

(e) a psychiatric facility designated under the *Mental Health Act*;

(f) an institution under the *Mental Hospitals Act*; ...

(*h*) a public or private hospital to which the person was transferred from a facility, institution or home referred to in clauses (a) to (g),

the person in charge of the hospital, facility, institution, residence or home shall immediately give notice of the death to a coroner, and the coroner shall investigate the circumstances of the death and, if as a result of the investigation he or she is of the opinion that an inquest ought to be held, the coroner shall issue his or her warrant and hold an inquest upon the body.

(2.1) **Deaths in nursing homes and homes for the aged.**— Where a person dies while resident in a home for the aged to which the *Homes for the Aged and Rest Homes Act* or the *Charitable Institutions Act* applies or a nursing home to which the *Nursing Homes Act* applies, the person in charge of the home shall immediately give notice of the death to a coroner and, if the coroner is of the opinion that the death ought to be investigated, he or she shall investigate the circumstances of the death and, if as a result of the investigation he or she is of the opinion that an inquest ought to be held, the coroner shall issue his or her warrant and hold an inquest upon the body. 1994, c. 27, s. 136(2).

(3) **Inmate off premises.**— Where a person dies while,

(*a*) a patient of a psychiatric facility;

(*b*) committed to a correctional institution; or

(*c*) committed to secure custody or open custody under the *Young Offenders Act* (Canada),

but while not on the premises or in actual custody of the facility, institution or place of custody, as the case may be, subsections (1) and (2) apply as if the person were a resident of an institution named therein. 1984, c. 55, s. 212(2) part, revised.

(4) **Persons in custody.**— Where a person dies while detained by or in the actual custody of a peace officer or while an inmate on the premises of a correctional institution, lock-up, or place or facility designated as a place of secure custody under section 24.1 of the *Young Offenders Act* (Canada), the peace officer or officer in charge of the institution, lock-up or place or facility, as the case may be, shall immediately give notice of the death to a coroner and the coroner shall issue a warrant to hold an inquest upon the body. 1984, c. 55, s. 212(2), part.

(5) **Notice of death resulting from accident at or in construction project, mining plant or mine.**— Where a worker dies as a result of an accident occurring in the course of the worker's employment at or in a construction project, mining plant or mine, including a pit or quarry, the person in charge of such project, mining plant or mine shall immediately give notice of the death to a coroner and the coroner shall issue a warrant to hold an inquest upon the body.

(6) **Certificate as evidence.**— A statement as to the notification or non-notification of a coroner under this section, purporting to be certified by the coroner is without proof of the appointment or signature of the coroner, receivable in evidence as proof, in the absence of evidence to the contrary of the facts stated therein for all purposes in any action, proceeding or prosecution.

11. Interference with body.— No person who has reason to believe that a person died in any of the circumstances mentioned in section 10 shall interfere with or alter the body or its condition in any way until the coroner so directs by a warrant.

12. (1) **Power of coroner to take charge of wreckage.**— Where a coroner has issued a warrant to take possession of the body of a person who has met death by violence in a wreck, the coroner may, with the approval of the Chief Coroner, take charge of the wreckage and place one or more police officers in charge of it so as to prevent persons from disturbing it until the jury at the inquest has viewed it, or the coroner has made such examination as he or she considers necessary.

(2) **View to be expedited.**— The jury or coroner, as the case may be, shall view the wreckage at the earliest moment possible. ...

15. (1) **Warrant for possession of body; investigation.**— Where a coroner is informed that there is in his or her jurisdiction the body of a person and that there is reason to believe that the person died in any of the circumstances mentioned in section 10, the coroner shall issue a warrant to take possession of the body and shall view the body and make such further investigation as is required to enable the coroner to determine whether or not an inquest is necessary.

(2) **Idem.**— Where the Chief Coroner has reason to believe that a person died in any of the circumstances mentioned in section 10 and no warrant has been issued to take possession of the body, he or she may issue the warrant or direct any coroner to do so.

(3) **Jurisdiction.**— After the issue of the warrant, no other coroner shall issue a warrant or interfere in the case, except the Chief Coroner or except under the instructions of the Minister. ...

(5) **No warrant.**— A coroner may proceed with an investigation without taking possession of the body where the body has been destroyed in whole or in part or is lying in a place from which it cannot be recovered or has been removed from Ontario.

16. (1) **Investigative powers.**— A coroner may,

(*a*) view or take possession of any dead body, or both; and

(*b*) enter and inspect any place where a dead body is and any place from which the coroner has reasonable grounds for believing the body was removed.

(2) **Idem.**— A coroner who believes on reasonable and probable grounds that to do so is necessary for the purposes of the investigation may,

(*a*) inspect any place in which the deceased person was, or in which the coroner has reasonable grounds to believe the deceased person was, prior to his or her death;

(*b*) inspect and extract information from any records or writings relating to the deceased or his or her circumstances and reproduce such copies therefrom as the coroner believes necessary;

(*c*) seize anything that the coroner has reasonable grounds to believe is material to the purposes of the investigation.

(3) **Delegation of powers.**— A coroner may authorize a legally qualified medical practitioner or a police officer to exercise all or any of the coroner's powers under subsection (1).

(4) **Idem.**— A coroner may, where in his or her opinion it is necessary for the purposes of the investigation, authorize a legally qualified medical practitioner or a police officer to exercise all or any of the coroner's powers under clauses (2)(a), (b) and (c) but, where such power is conditional on the belief of the coroner, the requisite belief shall be that of the coroner personally.

(5) **Return of things seized.**— Where a coroner seizes anything under clause (2)(c), he or she shall place it in the custody of a police officer for safekeeping and shall return it to the person from whom it was seized as soon as is practicable after the conclusion of the investigation or, where there is an inquest, of the inquest, unless the coroner is authorized or required by law to dispose of it otherwise.

(6) **Obstruction of coroner.**— No person shall knowingly,

    (*a*) hinder, obstruct or interfere with or attempt to hinder, obstruct or interfere with; or

    (*b*) furnish with false information or refuse or neglect to furnish information to,

a coroner in the performance of his or her duties or a person authorized by the coroner in connection with an investigation.

17. (1) **Transfer of investigation.**— A coroner may at any time transfer an investigation to another coroner where in his or her opinion the investigation may be continued or conducted more conveniently by that other coroner or for any other good and sufficient reason.

(2) **Investigation and inquest.**— The coroner to whom an investigation is transferred shall proceed with the investigation in the same manner as if he or she had issued the warrant to take possession of the body. ...

18. (1) **Statement where inquest unnecessary.**— Where the coroner determines that an inquest is unnecessary, the coroner shall forthwith transmit to the Chief Coroner, and a copy to the Crown Attorney, a signed statement setting forth briefly the result of the investigation, and shall also forthwith transmit to the division registrar a notice of the death in the form prescribed by the *Vital Statistics Act*.

(2) **Record of investigations.**— Every coroner shall keep a record of the cases reported in which an inquest has been determined to be unnecessary, showing for each case the identity of the deceased and the coroner's findings of the facts as to how, when, where and by what means the deceased came by his or her death, including the relevant findings of the post mortem examination and of any other examinations or analyses of the body carried out, and such information shall be available to the spouse, parents, children, brothers and sisters of the deceased and to his or her personal representative, upon request.

19. Warrant for inquest.— Where the coroner determines that an inquest is necessary, the coroner shall issue his or her warrant for an inquest, and shall forthwith transmit to the Chief Coroner, and a copy to the Crown Attorney, a signed statement setting forth briefly the result of the investigation and the grounds upon which the coroner determined that an inquest should be held.

20. What coroner shall consider and have regard to.— When making a determination whether an inquest is necessary or unnecessary, the coroner shall have regard to whether the holding of an inquest would serve the public interest and, without restricting the generality of the foregoing, shall consider,

    (*a*) whether the matters described in clauses 31(1)(a) to (e) are known;

    (*b*) the desirability of the public being fully informed of the circumstances of the death through an inquest; and

    (*c*) the likelihood that the jury on an inquest might make useful recommendations directed to the avoidance of death in similar circumstances.

21. Where body destroyed or removed from Ontario.— Where a coroner has reason to believe that a death has occurred in circumstances that warrant the holding of an inquest but, owing to the destruction of the body in whole or in part or to the fact that the body is lying in a place from which it cannot be recovered, or that the body has been removed from Ontario, an inquest cannot be held except by virtue of this section, he or she shall report the facts to the Chief Coroner who may direct an inquest to be held touching the death, in which case an inquest shall be held by the coroner making the report or by such other coroner as the Chief Coroner directs, and the law relating to coroners and coroners' inquests applies with such modifications as are necessary in consequence of the inquest being held otherwise than on or after a view of the body.

22. Minister may direct coroner to hold inquest.— Where the Minister has reason to believe that a death has occurred in Ontario in circumstances that warrant the holding of an inquest, the Minister may direct any coroner to hold an inquest and the coroner shall hold the inquest into the death in accordance with this Act, whether or not he or she or any other coroner has viewed the body, made an investigation, held an inquest, determined an inquest was unnecessary or done any other act in connection with the death. ...

24. Minister may direct that body be disinterred.— Despite anything in the *Cemeteries Act*, the Minister may, at any time where he or she considers it necessary for the purposes of an investigation or an inquest, direct that a body be disinterred under and subject to such conditions as the Minister considers proper.

25. (1) Direction by Chief Coroner.— The Chief Coroner may direct any coroner in respect of any death to issue a warrant to take possession of the body, conduct an investigation or hold an inquest, or may direct any other coroner to do so or may intervene to act as coroner personally for any one or more of such purposes.

(2) **Inquest into multiple deaths.**— Where two or more deaths appear to have occurred in the same event or from a common cause, the Chief Coroner may direct that one inquest be held into all of the deaths. ...

26. (1) Request by relative for inquest.— Where the coroner determines that an inquest is unnecessary, the spouse, parent, child, brother, sister or personal representative of the deceased person may request the coroner in writing to hold an inquest, and the coroner shall give the person requesting the inquest an opportunity to state his or her reasons, either personally, by the person's agent or in writing, and the coroner shall advise the person in writing within sixty days of the receipt of the request of the coroner's final decision and where the decision is to not hold an inquest shall deliver the reasons therefor in writing.

(2) **Review of refusal.**— Where the final decision of a coroner under subsection (1) is to not hold an inquest, the person making the request may, within twenty days after the receipt of the decision of the coroner, request the Chief Coroner to review the decision and the Chief Coroner shall review the decision of the coroner after giving the person requesting the inquest an opportunity to state his or her reasons either personally, by the person's agent or in writing. ...

27. (1) Where criminal offence charged.— Where a person is charged with an offence under the *Criminal Code* (Canada) arising out of a death, an inquest touching the death shall be held only upon the direction of the Minister and, when held, the person charged is not a compellable witness.

(2) **Idem.**— Where during an inquest a person is charged with an offence under the *Criminal Code* (Canada) arising out of the death, the coroner shall discharge the jury and close the inquest, and shall then proceed as if he or she had determined that an inquest was unnecessary, but the Minister may direct that the inquest be reopened.

(3) **Where charge or appeal finally disposed of.**— Despite subsections (1) and (2), where a person is charged with an offence under the *Criminal Code* (Canada) arising out of the death and the charge or any appeal from a conviction or an acquittal of the offence charged has been finally disposed of or the time for taking an appeal has expired, the coroner may issue a warrant for an inquest and the person charged is a compellable witness at the inquest.

28. (1) **Post mortem examinations and analyses.**— A coroner may at any time during an investigation or inquest issue a warrant for a post mortem examination of the body, an analysis of the blood, urine or contents of the stomach and intestines, or such other examination or analysis as the circumstances warrant.

(2) **Report.**— The person who performs the post mortem examination shall forthwith report his or her findings in writing only to the coroner who issued the warrant, the Crown Attorney, the regional coroner and the Chief Coroner and the person who performs any other examination or analysis shall forthwith report his or her findings in writing only to the coroner who issued the warrant, the person who performed the post mortem examination, the Crown Attorney, the regional coroner and the Chief Coroner. ...

30. (1) **Notice to Crown Attorney.**— Every coroner before holding an inquest shall notify the Crown Attorney of the time and place at which it is to be held and the Crown Attorney or a barrister and solicitor or any other person designated by him or her shall attend the inquest and shall act as counsel to the coroner at the inquest.

(2) **Counsel for Minister.**— The Minister may be represented at an inquest by counsel and shall be deemed to be a person with standing at the inquest for the purpose.

31. (1) **Purposes of inquest.**— Where an inquest is held, it shall inquire into the circumstances of the death and determine,

> (*a*) who the deceased was;
>
> (*b*) how the deceased came to his or her death;
>
> (*c*) when the deceased came to his or her death;
>
> (*d*) where the deceased came to his or her death; and
>
> (*e*) by what means the deceased came to his or her death.

(2) **Idem.**— The jury shall not make any finding of legal responsibility or express any conclusion of law on any matter referred to in subsection (1).

(3) **Authority of jury to make recommendations.**— Subject to subsection (2), the jury may make recommendations directed to the avoidance of death in similar circumstances or respecting any other matter arising out of the inquest.

(4) **Improper finding.**— A finding that contravenes subsection (2) is improper and shall not be received.

(5) **Failure to make proper finding.**— Where a jury fails to deliver a proper finding it shall be discharged.

32. Inquest public.— An inquest shall be open to the public except where the coroner is of the opinion that national security might be endangered or where a person is charged with an indictable offence under the *Criminal Code* (Canada) in which cases the coroner may hold the hearing concerning any such matters in the absence of the public.

33. (1) **Juries.**— Except as provided in subsection (4), every inquest shall be held with a jury composed of five persons.

(2) **Jurors.**— The coroner shall direct a constable to select from the list of names of persons provided under subsection 34(2) five persons who in his or her opinion are suitable to serve as jurors at an inquest and the constable shall summon them to attend the inquest at the time and place appointed.

(3) **Idem.**— Where fewer than five of the jurors so summoned attend at the inquest, the coroner may name and appoint so many persons then present or who can be found as will make up a jury of five.

(4) **Inquest without jury in territorial district.**— With the consent of the Chief Coroner, an inquest in a territorial district may be held without a jury.

34. (1) **List of jurors.**— A coroner may by his or her warrant require the sheriff for the area in which an inquest is to be held to provide a list of the names of such number of persons as the coroner specifies in the warrant taken from the jury roll prepared under the *Juries Act.*

(2) **Idem.**— Upon receipt of the warrant, the sheriff shall provide the list containing names of persons in the number specified by the coroner, taken from the jury roll prepared under the *Juries Act,* together with their ages, places of residence and occupations.

(3) **Eligibility.**— No person who is ineligible to serve as a juror under the *Juries Act* shall be summoned to serve or shall serve as a juror at an inquest.

(4) **Idem.**— An officer, employee or inmate of a hospital or an institution referred to in subsection 10(2) or (3) shall not serve as a juror at an inquest upon the death of a person who died therein.

(5) **Excusing from service.**— The coroner may excuse any person on the list from being summoned or from serving as a juror on the grounds of illness or hardship.

(6) **Exclusion of juror with interest.**— The coroner presiding at an inquest may exclude a person from being sworn as a juror where the coroner believes there is a likelihood that the person, because of interest or bias, would be unable to render a verdict in accordance with the evidence.

(7) **Excusing of juror for illness.**— Where in the course of an inquest the coroner is satisfied that a juror should not, because of illness or other reasonable cause, continue to act, the coroner may discharge the juror.

(8) **Continuation with reduced jury.**— Where in the course of an inquest a member of the jury dies or becomes incapacitated from any cause or is excluded or discharged by the coroner under subsection (6) or (7) or is found to be ineligible to serve, the jury shall, unless the coroner otherwise directs and if the number of jurors is not reduced below three, be deemed to remain properly constituted for all purposes of the inquest. ...

37. (1) **View of body may be directed.**— The jury shall view the body where the coroner directs them to do so.

(2) **Questions by jury.**— The jurors are entitled to ask relevant questions of each witness.

38. Majority.— A verdict or finding may be returned by a majority of the jurors sworn.

39. Service of summonses.— A summons to a juror or to a witness may be served by personal service or by sending it by registered mail addressed to the usual place of abode of the person summoned.

40. (1) **Summonses.**— A coroner may require any person by summons,

(*a*) to give evidence on oath or affirmation at an inquest; and

(*b*) to produce in evidence at an inquest documents and things specified by the coroner,

relevant to the subject-matter of the inquest and admissible.

(2) **Form and service of summonses.**— A summons issued under subsection (1) shall be in Form 1 and shall be signed by the coroner.

(3) **Bench warrants.**— Upon proof to the satisfaction of a judge of the Ontario Court (General Division) of the service of a summons under this section upon a person and that,

(*a*) such person has failed to attend or to remain in attendance at an inquest in accordance with the requirements of the summons; and

(*b*) the person's presence is material to the inquest,

the judge may, by a warrant in Form 2, directed to any sheriff or police officer, cause such witness to be apprehended anywhere within Ontario and forthwith to be brought to the inquest and to be detained in custody as the judge may order until the person's presence as a witness at the inquest is no longer required, or, in the discretion of the judge, to be released on a recognizance (with or without sureties) conditioned for appearance to give evidence.

(4) **Proof of service.**— Service of a summons may be proved by affidavit in an application under subsection (3). ...

41. (1) **Persons with standing at inquest.**— On the application of any person before or during an inquest, the coroner shall designate the person as a person with standing at the inquest if the coroner finds that the person is substantially and directly interested in the inquest.

(2) **Rights of persons with standing at inquest.**— A person designated as a person with standing at an inquest may,

(*a*) be represented by counsel or an agent;

(*b*) call and examine witnesses and present arguments and submissions;

(*c*) conduct cross-examinations of witnesses at the inquest relevant to the interest of the person with standing and admissible.

42. (1) **Protection for witnesses.**— A witness at an inquest shall be deemed to have objected to answer any question asked the witness upon the ground that his or her answer may tend to criminate the witness or may tend to establish his or her liability to civil proceedings at the instance of the Crown, or of any person, and no answer given by a witness at an inquest shall be used or be receivable in evidence against the witness in any trial or other proceedings against him or her thereafter taking place, other than a prosecution for perjury in giving such evidence.

(2) **Right to object under *Canada Evidence Act*.**— Where it appears at any stage of the inquest that the evidence that a witness is about to give would tend to criminate the witness, it is the duty of the coroner and of the Crown Attorney

to ensure that the witness is informed of his or her rights under section 5 of the *Canada Evidence Act.*

43. (1) Rights of witnesses to counsel.— A witness at an inquest is entitled to be advised by his or her counsel or agent as to his or her rights but such counsel or agent may take no other part in the inquest without leave of the coroner. ...

44. (1) What is admissible in evidence at inquest.— Subject to subsections (2) and (3), a coroner may admit as evidence at an inquest, whether or not admissible as evidence in a court,

(*a*) any oral testimony; and

(*b*) any document or other thing,

relevant to the purposes of the inquest and may act on such evidence, but the coroner may exclude anything unduly repetitious or anything that the coroner considers does not meet such standards of proof as are commonly relied on by reasonably prudent persons in the conduct of their own affairs and the coroner may comment on the weight that ought to be given to any particular evidence.

(2) **What is inadmissible in evidence at inquest.**— Nothing is admissible in evidence at an inquest,

(*a*) that would be inadmissible in a court by reason of any privilege under the law of evidence; or

(*b*) that is inadmissible by the statute under which the proceedings arise or any other statute.

(3) **Conflicts.**— Nothing in subsection (1) overrides the provisions of any Act expressly limiting the extent to or purposes for which any oral testimony, documents or things may be admitted or used in evidence.

(4) **Copies.**— Where the coroner is satisfied as to their authenticity, a copy of a document or other thing may be admitted as evidence at an inquest. ...

47. Maintenance of order at inquest.— A coroner may make such orders or give such directions at an inquest as he or she considers necessary for the maintenance of order at the inquest, and, if any person disobeys or fails to comply with any such order or direction, the coroner may call for the assistance of any peace officer to enforce the order or direction, and every peace officer so called upon shall take such action as is necessary to enforce the order or direction and may use such force as is reasonably required for that purpose. ...

48. (2) Constables at inquest.— A coroner may appoint such persons as constables as the coroner considers necessary for the purpose of assisting the coroner in an inquest and, on the request of the coroner, the police force having jurisdiction in the locality in which an inquest is held shall provide a police officer for the purpose and, before acting, every such constable shall take oath or affirm that he or she will faithfully perform his or her duties.

49. Administration of oaths.— The coroner conducting an inquest has power to administer oaths and affirmations for the purpose of the inquest.

50. (1) Abuse of processes.— A coroner may make such orders or give such directions at an inquest as the coroner considers proper to prevent abuse of its processes.

(2) **Limitation on cross-examination.**— A coroner may reasonably limit further cross-examination of a witness where the coroner is satisfied that the cross-examination of the witness has been sufficient to disclose fully and fairly the facts in relation to which the witness has given evidence.

(3) **Exclusion of agents.**— A coroner may exclude from a hearing anyone, other than a barrister and solicitor qualified to practise in Ontario, appearing as an agent advising a witness if the coroner finds that such person is not competent properly to advise the witness or does not understand and comply at the inquest with the duties and responsibilities of an adviser.

51. **Contempt proceedings.**— Where any person without lawful excuse,

(*a*) on being duly summoned as a witness or a juror at an inquest makes default in attending at the inquest; or

(*b*) being in attendance as a witness at an inquest, refuses to take an oath or to make an affirmation legally required by the coroner to be taken or made, or to produce any document or thing in his or her power or control legally required by the coroner to be produced by the person or to answer any question to which the coroner may legally require an answer; or

(*c*) does any other thing that would, if the inquest had been a court of law having power to commit for contempt, have been contempt of that court,

the coroner may state a case to the Divisional Court setting out the facts and that court may, on application on behalf of and in the name of the coroner, inquire into the matter and, after hearing any witnesses who may be produced against or on behalf of that person and after hearing any statement that may be offered in defence, punish or take steps for the punishment of that person in like manner as if he or she had been guilty of contempt of the court.

52. (1) **Return of verdict.**— The coroner shall forthwith after an inquest return the verdict or finding, with the evidence where the Minister, Crown Attorney or Chief Coroner has ordered it to be transcribed, to the Chief Coroner, and shall transmit a copy of the verdict and recommendations to the Crown Attorney.

(2) **Release of exhibits.**— After an inquest is concluded, the coroner shall, upon request, release documents and things put in evidence at the inquest to the lawful owner or person entitled to possession thereof.

53. **Protection from liability.**— No action or other proceeding for damages lies or shall be instituted against a coroner or any person acting under the coroner's authority for an act done by him or her in good faith in the performance or intended performance of any power or duty under this Act or the regulations, or for any neglect or default in the performance in good faith of any such power or duty. ...

55. **Penalty.**— Any person who contravenes section 10, 11, 13 or subsection 16 (6) is guilty of an offence and on conviction is liable to a fine of not more than $1,000 or to imprisonment for a term of not more than six months, or to both.

56. **Regulations.**— The Lieutenant Governor in Council may make regulations,

(*a*) prescribing powers and duties of the Chief Coroner; ...

(*d*) providing for the selecting, recording, summoning, attendance and service of persons as jurors at inquests;

(*e*) prescribing the contents of oaths and affirmations required or authorized by this Act;

(*f*) prescribing matters that may be grounds for disqualification because of interest or bias of jurors for the purposes of subsection 34(6); ...

(*h*) prescribing additional rules of procedure for inquests.

(2) **Same.**— The Minister may make regulations.

    (*a*) prescribing forms and providing for their use;

    (*b*) prescribing fees and allowances that shall be paid to persons rendering services in connection with coroners' investigations and inquests and providing for the adjustment of such fees and allowances in special circumstances. …

FORM 1

Coroners Act

(Section 40(2))

SUMMONS TO A WITNESS BEFORE AN INQUEST

RE: ...., deceased

TO:

You are hereby summoned and required to attend before an inquest to be held at .... in the .... of .... on .... day, the .... day of .... 19 ...., at the hour of .... o'clock in the .... noon (local time), and so from day to day until the inquest is concluded or the coroner otherwise orders, to give evidence on oath or affirmation touching the matters in question in the proceedings and to bring with you and produce at such time and place ....

....

Dated this .... day of ...., 19 ......

....
Coroner

NOTE:

If you fail to attend and give evidence at the inquest, or to produce the documents or things specified, at the time and place specified, without lawful excuse, you are liable to punishment by a judge of the Ontario Court (General Division) in the same manner as if for contempt of that court for disobedience to a summons.

FORM 2
Coroners Act
(Section 40(3))

BENCH WARRANT

PROVINCE OF ONTARIO

TO: A.B., Sheriff, etc.

WHEREAS proof has been made before me that C.D. was duly summoned to appear before an inquest into the death of .... deceased, at Toronto (or as the case may be) on the .... day of ...., 19 ..... ; that the presence of the said C.D. is material to the inquest, and that the said C.D. has failed to attend in accordance with the requirements of the summons.

THESE are therefore to command you to take the said C.D. to bring and have him (or her) before the said inquest at Toronto (or as the case may be) there to testify what he (or she) may know concerning the matters in question in the said inquest, and that you detain him (or her) in your custody until he (or she) has given his (or her) evidence or until the said inquest has ended or until other orders may be made concerning him (or her).

GIVEN UNDER MY HAND this .... day of ...., 19 ......, at ....

....

Judge of the Ontario Court
(General Division)

EXERCISES

■ TRUE OR FALSE

T 1. The police are mandated by the *Coroners Act* to provide whatever assistance is required by the coroner within their territorial jurisdiction.

F 2. During an inquest, jurors may ask relevant questions of witnesses.

F 3. A summons to a witness for an inquest must be served personally upon him or her.

T 4. Any person who has an interest in an inquest may be designated as a person with standing at an inquest.

F 5. The jury at an inquest determines who was at fault in causing a death.

T 6. A person who has been served with a summons to attend an inquest as a witness and refuses to, or who fails to attend and give testimony, may be convicted of contempt.

____ 7. A coroner may, by warrant, require the sheriff in the jurisdiction in which the inquest is to be held to provide a list of potential jurors from the voters' list.

____ 8. If, during the course of an inquest, a juror becomes ill or dies, the inquest will be postponed until another juror can be selected.

____ 9. Once a citizen is selected to be a member of a jury at an inquest, there are no reasons other than illness or death for being excused from a jury.

____ 10. The jury's recommendations must be acted upon within one year and one day of the conclusion of the inquest.

■ MULTIPLE CHOICE

Circle the correct response(s).

1. A jury for an inquest shall be composed of _____ jurors.

    a. 12

    b. 9

    c. 5

    d. 7

2. Which of the following is not a purpose of an inquest?

    a. to determine how the deceased died

    b. to determine who was responsible for the death

    c. to determine when the deceased died

    d. to determine where the deceased died

    e. to determine by what means the deceased came to his or her death

3. A person designated as a person with standing at an inquest may:

    a. be represented by counsel or agent

    b. call and examine witnesses

    c. conduct cross-examinations of witnesses

    d. all of the above

    e. a and b

4. A coroner must be notified of a death if the death occurred as a result of:

    a. violence

    b. negligence

    c. under such circumstances as may require investigation

    d. all of the above

    e. a and b

5. A coroner must hold an inquest if a death occurs at any one of the following facilities:

    a. a nursing home

    b. a mental hospital

    c. a home for retarded persons

    d. a police lockup

    e. all of the above

■ SHORT ANSWER

In the following situations, indicate whether an inquest should be considered and explain your rationale.

1. A person who is an involuntary patient of a psychiatric facility goes AWOL and while walking along a railway line is struck and killed by the train.

2. Two young people climb the fence at the local zoo. They enter the buffalo pen and start harassing the animals. Eight buffalo stampede and trample both youths to death.

3. An ambulance is called to a local residence to attend a young child who has stopped breathing. The paramedics are unable to revive the child. It is believed that the child died of sudden infant death syndrome (SIDS).

4. An inmate at the local jail uses his shorts to hang himself. The police do not discover the death for one hour.

5. A 40-year-old man passes out and dies of a heart attack while walking his dog along the city's waterfront. He had no history of heart problems.

6. Three elderly people die of a mysterious ailment. All three are residents of a home for the aged.

7. A man is arrested for being intoxicated in a public place. While being transported to the local jail in the back of the police paddy wagon, he dies. It is later learned that the man was diabetic.

■ CASE STUDY #1

You are a member of a small-town OPP detachment. OPP Officer Smith is dispatched to the site of an open pit mine just north of town, regarding an accident. On arrival, Smith finds that a large Euclid truck has run over and crushed a pickup truck. It appears that there was one occupant in the truck; he is crushed beyond recognition. The coroner arrives and pronounces the occupant of the truck dead at the scene. The incident is investigated and is ruled accidental. This is the third fatality at the mining site in the last 12 months.

The coroner issues a warrant to take possession of the body and an autopsy is conducted. The coroner appoints Smith as the investigating officer. You are appointed to act as the coroner's constable for the inquest.

1. What information will you need from Officer Smith to allow you to complete the documentation required for the inquest?

2. How will you select the jury? Are there any restrictions on the selection of jurors for the inquest?

3. How can you ensure that any potential juror whom you select does not have any conflict of interest? Who would be considered to have a conflict of interest in this particular scenario?

■ CASE STUDY #2

You are a police officer with your local police service. You are sent to investigate an apparent suicide at a home in the south end of your town. On arrival you find that a white male, approximately 50 years of age, is lying on the basement floor. You also notice that a rope is hanging from the rafters and that a noose is on the floor beside the man. The man has no pulse and is not breathing. The coroner is called to the scene and the man is pronounced dead. The coroner tells the family that he must take possession of the body and that an autopsy must be performed. The family pleads with the coroner not to desecrate the body and that, according to their faith, he must be buried within 24 hours. Several members of the family place themselves around the body and do not allow the body to be removed. Additional police are called and two family members are arrested.

1. Given the sensitive nature of this investigation, should the family members be charged with an offence under the *Coroners Act*? Explain.

2. Suggest alternative methods of dealing with this crisis situation.

CHAPTER 8
The Family Law Act

CHAPTER OBJECTIVES

After completing this chapter, you should be able to:

◆ Understand key terms defined in the *Family Law Act*.

◆ State the powers of arrest granted to police officers under the Act.

◆ Identify offences under the Act and list the facts in issue for those offences.

◆ Describe processes under the Act that allow for the possession of the matrimonial home, the disposition of property, the commencement of harassment proceedings, and proceedings against an absconding spouse.

◆ Describe the use of the criminal harassment sections of the *Criminal Code* in relation to occurrences under the Act.

◆ Identify common problems associated with the application of the statute.

◆ Be prepared to apply the provisions of the Act in a hypothetical fact situation.

INTRODUCTION

The *Family Law Act* is a statute that, for most people, becomes important only when a marriage or common law relationship breaks down. It applies to spouses in different kinds of relationships. It applies to married couples and to couples who cohabit in a conjugal or romantic relationship outside of marriage. If the couple has children, the Act determines the basic responsibilities that each ex-spouse has for the children.

In the event of a breakup, each spouse has an obligation to any children the couple may have. Each spouse must provide economic support for children who are unmarried minors; however, adult children and married children are expected to provide for themselves.

The obligation to support one's children is an important obligation that gives authority to the courts for the ordering of appropriate child support payments. If one parent fails to provide support, the Act provides for serious consequences. The courts also have the power to order child custody and access arrangements where the spouses cannot informally agree on living arrangements. In some cases, the courts may also place an obligation upon one spouse to pay support to the other spouse. Whether an amount is awarded will depend on many factors, such as the length of the relationship; whether the spouses are employed; and how much money each is earning.

When a couple's marriage has come to an end, the *Family Law Act* determines how the couple's property should be divided. Usually the couple's home, if owned, is the most valuable piece of property. The Act describes what happens to the matrimonial home in the event of a breakup. The term "matrimonial home" refers to the place in which the couple was living at the time of the breakup.

The *Family Law Act* gives the police the power to possess the matrimonial home and dispose of property in certain limited cases. It deals with separation agreements; harassment proceedings; proceedings against an absconding spouse; and restraining orders. It also gives the police and the courts the power to deal with situations where one spouse is harassing the other.

FAMILY LAW ACT

RSO 1990, Chapter F.3

Whereas it is desirable to encourage and strengthen the role of the family; and whereas for that purpose it is necessary to recognize the equal position of spouses as individuals within marriage and to recognize marriage as a form of partnership; and whereas in support of such recognition it is necessary to provide in law for the orderly and equitable settlement of the affairs of the spouses upon the breakdown of the partnership, and to provide for other mutual obligations in family relationships, including the equitable sharing by parent of responsibility for their children;

Therefore, Her Majesty, by and with the advice and consent of the Legislative Assembly of the Province of Ontario, enacts as follows:

1. (1) **Definitions.**— In this Act,
"child" includes a person whom a parent has demonstrated a settled intention to treat as a child of his or her family, except under an arrangement where the child is placed for valuable consideration in a foster home by a person having lawful custody; ...

[handwritten margin note: INTENT TO CARE FOR THAT PERSON.]

"cohabit" means to live together in a conjugal relationship, whether within or outside marriage; ...

"parent" includes a person who has demonstrated a settled intention to treat a child as a child of his or her family, except under an arrangement where the child is placed for valuable consideration in a foster home by a person having lawful custody; ...

[handwritten margin note: INTENT TO CARE FOR A CHILD]

"spouse" means either or a man and woman who,

> (a) are married to each other, or
>
> (b) have together entered into a marriage that is voidable or void, in good faith on the part of the person asserting a right under this Act.

(2) **Polygamous marriages.**— In the definition of "spouse", a reference to marriage includes a marriage that is actually or potentially polygamous, if it was celebrated in a jurisdiction whose system of law recognizes it as valid. ...

PART I

FAMILY PROPERTY

4. (1) **Definitions.**— In this Part, ...
"matrimonial home" means a matrimonial home under section 18 and includes property that is a matrimonial home under that section at the valuation date; ...

"property" means any interest, present or future, vested or contingent, in real or personal property and includes,

> (a) property over which a spouse has, alone or in conjunction with another person, a power of appointment exercisable in favour of himself or herself,
>
> (b) property disposed of by a spouse but over which the spouse has, alone or in conjunction with another person, a power to revoke the disposition or a power to consume or dispose of the property, and

(c) in the case of a spouse's rights under a pension plan that have vested, the spouse's interest in the plan including contributions made by other persons; ...

(2) **Excluded property.**— The value of the following property that a spouse owns on the valuation date does not form part of the spouse's net family property:

1. Property, other than a matrimonial home, that was acquired by gift or inheritance from a third person after the date of the marriage.

2. Income from property referred to in paragraph 1, if the donor or testator has expressly stated that it is to be excluded from the spouse's net family property.

3. Damages or a right to damages for personal injuries, nervous shock, mental distress or loss of guidance, care and companionship, or the part of a settlement that represents those damages.

4. Proceeds or a right to proceeds of a policy of life insurance, as defined in the *Insurance Act*, that are payable on the death of the life insured.

5. Property, other than a matrimonial home, into which property referred to in paragraphs 1 to 4 can be traced.

6. Property that the spouses have agreed by a domestic contract is not to be included in the spouse's net family property. ...

5. (1) **Equalization of net family properties.**— When a divorce is granted or a marriage is declared a nullity, or when the spouses are separated and there is no reasonable prospect that they will resume cohabitation, the spouse whose net family property is the lesser of the two net family properties is entitled to one-half the difference between them.

(2) **Idem.**— When a spouse dies, if the net family property of the deceased spouse exceeds the net family property of the surviving spouse, the surviving spouse is entitled to one-half the difference between them.

(3) **Improvident depletion of spouse's net family property.**— When spouses are cohabiting, if there is a serious danger that one spouse may improvidently deplete his or her net family property, the other spouse may on an application under section 7 have the difference between the net family properties divided as if the spouses were separated and there were no reasonable prospect that they would resume cohabitation. ...

PART II
MATRIMONIAL HOME

• • •

18. (1) **Matrimonial home.**— Every property in which a person has an interest and that is or, if the spouses have separated, was at the time of separation ordinarily occupied by the person and his or her spouse as their family residence is their matrimonial home. ...

19. (1) **Possession of matrimonial home.**— Both spouses have an equal right to possession of a matrimonial home.

(2) **Idem.**— When only one of the spouses has an interest in a matrimonial home, the other spouse's right of possession,

(*a*) is personal as against the first spouse; and

(*b*) ends when they cease to be spouses, unless a separation agreement or court order provides otherwise. ...

24. (1) **Order for possession of matrimonial home.**— Regardless of the ownership of a matrimonial home and its contents, and despite section 19 (spouse's right of possession), the court may on application, by order,

(*a*) provide for the delivering up, safekeeping and preservation of the matrimonial home and its contents;

(*b*) direct that one spouse be given exclusive possession of the matrimonial home or part of it for the period that the court directs and release other property that is a matrimonial home from the application of this Part;

(*c*) direct a spouse to whom exclusive possession of the matrimonial home is given to make periodic payments to the other spouse;

(*d*) direct that the contents of the matrimonial home, or any part of them,

(i) remain in the home for the use of the spouse given possession, or

(ii) be removed from the home for the use of a spouse or child;

(*e*) order a spouse to pay for all or part of the repair and maintenance of the matrimonial home and of other liabilities arising in respect of it, or to make periodic payments to the other spouse for those purposes;

(*f*) authorize the disposition or encumbrance of a spouse's interest in the matrimonial home, subject to the other spouse's right of exclusive possession as ordered; and

(*g*) where a false statement is made under subsection 21(3), direct,

(i) the person who made the false statement, or

(ii) a person who knew at the time he or she acquired an interest in the property that the statement was false and afterwards conveyed the interest,

to substitute other real property for the matrimonial home, or direct the person to set aside money or security to stand in place of it, subject to any conditions that the court considers appropriate.

(2) **Temporary or interim order.**— The court may, on motion, make a temporary or interim order under clause (1)(a), (b), (c), (d) or (e).

(3) **Order for exclusive possession: criteria.**— In determining whether to make an order for exclusive possession, the court shall consider,

(*a*) the best interests of the children affected;

(*b*) any existing orders under Part I (Family Property) and any existing support orders;

(*c*) the financial position of both spouses;

(*d*) any written agreement between the parties;

(*e*) the availability of other suitable and affordable accommodation; and

(*f*) any violence committed by a spouse against the other spouse or the children.

(4) **Best interests of child.**— In determining the best interests of a child, the court shall consider,

(*a*) the possible disruptive effects on the child of a move to other accommodation; and

(*b*) the child's views and preferences, if they can reasonably be ascertained.

(5) **Offence.**— A person who contravenes an order for exclusive possession is guilty of an offence and upon conviction is liable,

(*a*) in the case of a first offence, to a fine of not more than $5,000 or to imprisonment for a term of not more than three months, or to both; and

(*b*) in the case of a second or subsequent offence, to a fine of not more than $10,000 or to imprisonment for a term of not more than two years, or to both.

(6) **Arrest without warrant.**— A police officer may arrest without warrant a person the police officer believes on reasonable and probable grounds to have contravened an order for exclusive possession.

(7) **Existing orders.**— Subsections (5) and (6) also apply in respect of contraventions, committed on or after the 1st day of March, 1986, of orders for exclusive possession made under Part III of the *Family Law Reform Act*, being chapter 152 of the Revised Statutes of Ontario, 1980. ...

27. Registration of order.— Orders made under this Part or under Part III of the *Family Law Reform Act*, being chapter 152 of the Revised Statutes of Ontario, 1980 are registrable against land under the *Registry Act* and the *Land Titles Act*. ...

PART III
SUPPORT OBLIGATIONS

• • •

31. (1) **Obligation of parent to support child.**— Every parent has an obligation to provide support for his or her unmarried child who is a minor or is enrolled in a full time program of education, to the extent that the parent is capable of doing so.

(2) **Idem.**— The obligation under subsection (1) does not extend to a child who is sixteen years of age or older and has withdrawn from parental control. ...

33. (1) **Order for support.**— A court may, on application, order a person to provide support for his or her dependants and determine the amount of support. ...

(7) **Purposes of order for support of child.**— An order for the support of a child should,

(*a*) recognize that each parent has an obligation to provide support for the child;

(*b*) apportion the obligation according to the child support guidelines.

(8) **Purposes of order for support of spouse.**— An order for the support of a spouse should,

(*a*) recognize the spouse's contribution to the relationship and the economic consequences of the relationship for the spouse;

(*b*) share the economic burden of child support equitably;

(*c*) make fair provision to assist the spouse to become able to contribute to his or her own support; and

(*d*) relieve financial hardship, if this has not been done by orders under Parts I (Family Property) and II (Matrimonial Home). ...

43. (1) **Arrest of absconding debtor.**— If an application is made under section 33 or 37 and the court is satisfied that the respondent is about to leave Ontario and that there are reasonable grounds for believing that the respondent intends to evade his or her responsibilities under this Act, the court may issue a warrant for the respondent's arrest for the purpose of bringing him or her before the court. ...

46. (1) **Order restraining harassment.**— On application, a court may make an interim or final order restraining the applicant's spouse or former spouse from molesting, annoying or harassing the applicant or children in the applicant's lawful custody, or from communicating with the applicant or children, except as the order provides, and may require the applicant's spouse or former spouse to enter into the recognizance that the court considers appropriate.

(2) **Offence.**— A person who contravenes a restraining order is guilty of an offence and upon conviction is liable,

(a) in the case of a first offence, to a fine of not more than $5,000 or to imprisonment for a term of not more than three months, or to both; and

(b) in the case of a second or subsequent offence, to a fine of not more than $10,000 or to imprisonment for a term of not more than two years, or to both.

(3) **Arrest without warrant.**— A police officer may arrest without warrant a person the police officer believes on reasonable and probable grounds to have contravened a restraining order. ...

49. (1) **Contempt of orders of Ontario Court (Provincial Division).**— In addition to its powers in respect of contempt, the Ontario Court (Provincial Division) may punish by fine or imprisonment, or by both, any wilful contempt of or resistance to its process, rules or orders under this Act, but the fine shall not exceed $5,000 nor shall the imprisonment exceed ninety days.

(2) **Conditions of imprisonment.**— An order for imprisonment under subsection (1) may be conditional upon default in the performance of a condition set out in the order and may provide for the imprisonment to be served intermittently.

50. (1) **Limitation.**— No action or application for an order for the support of a spouse shall be brought under this Part after two years from the day the spouses separate. ...

PART IV
DOMESTIC CONTRACTS

• • •

54. Separation agreements.— A man and a woman who cohabited and are living separate and apart may enter into an agreement in which they agree on their respective rights and obligations, including,

(a) ownership in or division of property;

(b) support obligations;

(c) the right to direct the education and moral training of their children;

(d) the right to custody of and access to their children; and

(e) any other matter in the settlement of their affairs.

EXERCISES

■ SHORT ANSWER

Define the following terms:

1. child

IS ANY PERSON TO WHOM A PARENT HAS THE INTENTION TO CARE FOR.

2. parent

IS ANY PERSON THAT HAS DEMONSTRATED ~~TO~~ THE INTENTION TO CARE FOR A CHILD.

3. spouse IS THE PERSON OF THE OPOSITE SEX THAT IS LIVING IN A CONJUGAL

MARRIED. RELATION SHIP. (MARRIED).

4. matrimonial home IS THE PROPERTY THAT A COUPLE GOT WHILE THEY WERE MARRIED.

5. property: INCLUDE MONEY, INTEREST AND ANYTHING THAT THE COUPLE OBTAINED DURING THEIR MARRIAGE

■ TRUE OR FALSE

F 1. In a marriage breakup, the spouse who generally looks after the children has the right of possession of the matrimonial home.

F 2. When only one of the spouses has an interest in a matrimonial home, the other spouse's right of possession automatically ends when they cease to be spouses.

T 3. A separation agreement or court order can determine which of the spouses has the right to the matrimonial home.

T 4. In determining the best interests of the child, the court will base its decision on what the child prefers.

T 5. A police officer may arrest without warrant any person whom he or she finds in contravention of an order for exclusive possession of the matrimonial home.

F 6. Every parent has an obligation to provide support for his or her unmarried child who is a minor under the age of (18) years.   → 16.

F 7. A child who has withdrawn from parental control may demand that the parent with the child support obligation to continue with the support obligations.

T 8. Family court may make an order restraining the applicant's spouse or former spouse from molesting, annoying, or harassing the applicant or the children.

F 9. A person convicted of harassment under the *Family Law Act* will be subject to a fine of up to $10,000, but under no circumstances will this person be sentenced to serve jail time because jail will not permit the person to meet any support obligations.

F 10. The limitation period for commencement of spousal support proceedings is 12 months.

■ MULTIPLE CHOICE

Circle the correct response(s).

1. The definition of spouse under the *Family Law Act* includes:

    a a man and a woman who are married to each other

    b. a man and a woman who have lived in a common law relationship in excess of two months

    c. two men or two women who have been legally married in a jurisdiction that permits same-sex marriages

    d. all of the above

■ CASE STUDY #1

1. You are a police officer with your local police service. You are dispatched to 123 Northern Ave. regarding a domestic dispute. When you arrive you are met by a woman, Alice Graves, who claims that she and her husband, Peter Graves, are separated and that she has exclusive possession of the house. She states that he refuses to leave. She shows you a document, signed by her lawyer, for possession of the family home, and again states that she wants him removed. Given these circumstances, you would:

    a. arrest her husband for contravening an order for exclusive possession

    b. ask the husband to leave quietly and say that no charges will be processed

    c. determine whether the document is a valid court order and then take appropriate action

2. Two months later you are again dispatched to 123 Northern Ave. Alice Graves explains that she and her husband are legally separated and going through divorce proceedings. She shows you all of the legal documentation. While you are speaking with her, the phone rings. It is her husband; he pleads with her not to divorce him. She hangs up. She claims that he has been calling 20 times a day for the last week. She has all of the times recorded. Given these circumstances, you could:

    a. report the incident and seek an arrest warrant for Peter Graves for harassment under the *Family Law Act*

    b. suggest to the wife that she make application to the court for a restraining order against her husband

    c. report the incident and ask for a warrant for the arrest of her husband for harassment under the *Criminal Code*

    d. report the incident and request that a summons be issued charging the husband with harassment under the *Criminal Code*

    e. b or d

3. The next day, you stop a motor vehicle for a routine traffic violation. The driver gives his name as Peter Graves and his address as 123 Northern Ave. You recognize him as the husband who has been making harassing phone calls. Aside from processing the traffic violation, you would:

    a. arrest him for making harassing phone calls

    b. advise him that he may be charged under the *Criminal Code* for making harassing phone calls and warn him to discontinue

    c. arrest him under the authority of the *Family Law Act* on reasonable and probable grounds that he harassed his wife

4. Alice Graves has heard from several friends that her husband is about to leave the country and discontinue making support payments to her and her two children. You are again dispatched to 123 Northern Ave. She explains the situation to you and wants to know what can be done to stop him. You advise her that:

    a. he can be arrested on reasonable grounds—namely, that he is about to flee Ontario and avoid his responsibilities

    b. she could make application to the court for a warrant for his arrest

    c. this is not a police matter and she should contact her lawyer as soon as possible

■ CASE STUDY #2

You are a police officer with your local police service. You are dispatched to 452 Queen St., apartment 402, regarding a domestic dispute. Maria Oliver states that she has been living common law with Fred Braithwaite for almost two years; that they have a five-month-old baby boy; and that she is sick and tired of having Fred come home drunk every night and yell and scream at her. Fred has never struck her or the child. She is planning on leaving him. However, before she does anything, she needs answers to some questions. She has a list of questions for you and wants some advice.

1. Because Marie and Fred have been living together for two years and have a child, is their common law relationship treated the same as a lawful marriage?

   YES

2. Marie and Fred purchased furniture when they moved in together. Who gets the apartment and the furniture, and how is that determined?

   BOOTH AAVE RIGHT TO THEM BUT IT THE JUDGE WHO DESIDED

3. How will custody of the baby be determined?

   CUSTODY WILL BE DETTERMINED PROBLABLY TO THE MOTHER

4. Is there a way of ensuring that Fred won't bother Marie anymore?

    YES, ORDER OF RESTRAINING

5. Are there any community agencies that help women and children in distress, and do they have accommodations available until a separation is formalized?

    YES WOMEN'S COMMUNITY HOUSE

6. What else could you suggest to Maria to facilitate matters?

CHAPTER 9
The Mental Health Act

CHAPTER OBJECTIVES

After completing this chapter, you should be able to:

◆ Understand key terms defined in the *Mental Health Act*.

◆ Explain the purpose of the Act.

◆ List the criteria that a police officer must consider before apprehending and taking a person who is apparently suffering from a mental disorder to an appropriate place for assessment.

◆ Distinguish the authority given to a police officer by an order signed by a justice from the authority given by an application signed by a physician.

◆ State the authority given to a police officer in apprehending a person who is away without leave from a psychiatric facility.

◆ Know whose permission must be obtained before a person can be admitted to a psychiatric facility as a patient.

◆ Explain the time-frame requirements for a physician's application, justice of the peace order, and absence without leave.

◆ Explain the difference between a judge's order for examination and a judge's order for admission.

◆ Be prepared to apply the provisions of the Act in a hypothetical fact situation.

INTRODUCTION

It is challenging and often difficult for a police officer to deal with seriously mentally ill individuals. Sensitivity and care should be taken in this area.

It is sometimes necessary for a police officer to apprehend an individual under the *Mental Health Act* (pursuant to a form 1) if there is a possibility that the person is a danger to himself or herself and/or to others. In addition, a police officer may develop concerns in the course of an arrest as to the fitness of an individual. It is important to be aware of the provisions of the *Mental Health Act*. It is a complicated and extensive statute and can be difficult to both read and apply. Advice may be required in applying its provisions.

MENTAL HEALTH ACT

RSO 1990, Chapter M.7

1. (1) Definitions.— In this Act,

"attending physician" means the physician to whom responsibility for the observation, care and treatment of a patient has been assigned; ...

"Deputy Minister" means the Deputy Minister of Health;

"informal patient" means a person who is a patient in a psychiatric facility, having been admitted with the consent of another person under section 24 of the *Health Care Consent Act, 1996*.

"involuntary patient" means a person who is detained in a psychiatric facility under a certificate of involuntary admission or a certificate of renewal; ...

"mental disorder" means any disease or disability of the mind;

"mentally competent" means having the ability to understand the subject-matter in respect of which consent is requested and able to appreciate the consequences of giving or withholding consent;

"Minister" means the *Minister of Health*; ...

"officer in charge" means the officer who is responsible for the administration and management of a psychiatric facility;

"out-patient" means a person who is registered in a psychiatric facility for observation or treatment or both, but who is not admitted as a patient and is not the subject of an application for assessment;

"patient" means a person who is under observation, care and treatment in a psychiatric facility;

"physician" means a legally qualified medical practitioner;

"prescribed" means prescribed by the regulations;

"psychiatric facility" means a facility for the observation, care and treatment of persons suffering from mental disorder, and designated as such by the regulations;

"psychiatrist" means a physician who holds a specialist's certificate in psychiatry issued by The Royal College of Physicians and Surgeons of Canada or equivalent qualification acceptable to the Minister;

"regulations" means the regulations made under this Act; ...

"restrain" means place under control when necessary to prevent serious bodily harm to the patient or to another person by the minimal use of such force, mechanical means or chemicals as is reasonable having regard to the physical and mental condition of the patient; ...

6. Effect of Act on rights and privileges.— Nothing in this Act shall be deemed to affect the rights or privileges of any person except as specifically set out in this Act.

PART I
STANDARDS

7. Application of Act.— This Act applies to every psychiatric facility. ...

PART II
HOSPITALIZATION

11. Where admission may be refused.— Despite this or any other Act, admission to a psychiatric facility may be refused where the immediate needs in the case of the proposed patient are such that hospitalization is not urgent or necessary.

12. Admission of informal or voluntary patients.— Any person who is believed to be in need of the observation, care and treatment provided in a psychiatric facility may be admitted thereto as an informal or voluntary patient upon the recommendation of a physician. ...

14. Informal or voluntary patient.— Nothing in this Act authorizes a psychiatric facility to detain or to restrain an informal or voluntary patient.

15. (1) Application for psychiatric assessment.— Where a physician examines a person and has reasonable cause to believe that the person,

> (a) has threatened or attempted or is threatening or attempting to cause bodily harm to himself or herself;

> (b) has behaved or is behaving violently towards another person or has caused or is causing another person to fear bodily harm from him or her; or

> (c) has shown or is showing a lack of competence to care for himself or herself,

and if in addition the physician is of the opinion that the person is apparently suffering from mental disorder of a nature or quality that likely will result in,

> (d) serious bodily harm to the person;

> (e) serious bodily harm to another person; or

> (f) imminent and serious physical impairment of the person,

the physician may make application in the prescribed form for a psychiatric assessment of the person.

(2) **Contents of application.—** An application under subsection (1) shall set out clearly that the physician who signs the application personally examined the person who is the subject of the application and made careful inquiry into all of the facts necessary for him or her to form his or her opinion as to the nature and quality of the mental disorder of the person.

(3) **Idem.—** A physician who signs an application under subsection (1),

> (a) shall set out in the application the facts upon which he or she formed his or her opinion as to the nature and quality of the mental disorder;

> (b) shall distinguish in the application between the facts observed by him or her and the facts communicated to him or her by others; and

> (c) shall note in the application the date on which he or she examined the person who is the subject of the application.

(4) **Signing of application.—** An application under subsection (1) is not effective unless it is signed by the physician within seven days after he or she examined the person who is the subject of the examination.

(5) **Authority of application.**— An application under subsection (1) is sufficient authority for seven days from and including the day on which it is signed by the physician,

(*a*) to any person to take the person who is the subject of the application in custody to a psychiatric facility forthwith; and

(*b*) to detain the person who is the subject of the application in a psychiatric facility and to restrain, observe and examine him or her in the facility for not more than 72 hours.

16. (1) **Justice of the peace's order for psychiatric examination.**— Where information upon oath is brought before a justice of the peace that a person within the limits of the jurisdiction of the justice,

(*a*) has threatened or attempted or is threatening or attempting to cause bodily harm to himself or herself;

(*b*) has behaved or is behaving violently towards another person or has caused or is causing another person to fear bodily harm from him or her; or

(*c*) has shown or is showing a lack of competence to care for himself or herself,

and in addition based upon the information before him or her the justice of the peace has reasonable cause to believe that the person is apparently suffering from mental disorder of a nature or quality that likely will result in,

(*d*) serious bodily harm to the person;

(*e*) serious bodily harm to another person; or

(*f*) imminent and serious physical impairment of the person,

the justice of the peace may issue an order in the prescribed form for the examination of the person by a physician.

(2) **Idem.**— An order under this section may be directed to all or any police officers or other peace officers of the locality within which the justice has jurisdiction and shall name or otherwise describe the person with respect to whom the order has been made.

(3) **Authority of order.**— An order under this section shall direct, and, for a period not to exceed seven days from and including the day that it is made, is sufficient authority for any police officer or other peace officer to whom it is addressed to take the person named or described therein in custody forthwith to an appropriate place where he or she may be detained for examination by a physician.

17. Action by peace officer.— Where a constable or other peace officer observes a person who acts in a manner that in a normal person would be disorderly and has reasonable cause to believe that the person,

(*a*) has threatened or attempted or is threatening or attempting to cause bodily harm to himself or herself;

(*b*) has behaved or is behaving violently towards another person or has caused or is causing another person to fear bodily harm from him or her; or

(*c*) has shown or is showing a lack of competence to care for himself or herself,

and in addition the constable or other peace officer is of the opinion that the person is apparently suffering from mental disorder of a nature or quality that likely will result in,

(*d*) serious bodily harm to the person;

(*e*) serious bodily harm to another person; or

(*f*) imminent and serious physical impairment of the person,

and that it would be dangerous to proceed under section 16, the police officer or other peace officer may take the person in custody to an appropriate place for examination by a physician.

18. Place of psychiatric examination.— An examination under section 16 or 17 shall be conducted by a physician forthwith after receipt of the person at the place of examination and where practicable the place shall be a psychiatric facility or other health facility.

19. Change from informal or voluntary patient to involuntary patient.— Subject to subsection 20(5), the attending physician may change the status of an informal or voluntary patient to that of an involuntary patient by completing and filing with the officer in charge a certificate of involuntary admission.

20. (1) Duty of attending physician.— The attending physician, after observing and examining a person who is the subject of an application for assessment under section 15 or who is the subject of an order under section 32,

(*a*) shall release the person from the psychiatric facility if the attending physician is of the opinion that the person is not in need of the treatment provided in a psychiatric facility;

(*b*) shall admit the person as an informal or voluntary patient if the attending physician is of the opinion that the person is suffering from mental disorder of such a nature or quality that the person is in need of the treatment provided in a psychiatric facility and is suitable for admission as an informal or voluntary patient; or

(*c*) shall admit the person as an involuntary patient by completing and filing with the officer in charge a certificate of involuntary admission if the attending physician is of the opinion both that the person is suffering from mental disorder of a nature or quality that likely will result in,

(i) serious bodily harm to the person,

(ii) serious bodily harm to another person, or

(iii) imminent and serious physical impairment of the person,

unless the person remains in the custody of a psychiatric facility and that the person is not suitable for admission as an informal or voluntary patient.

(2) **Physician who completes certificate of involuntary admission.**— The physician who completes a certificate of involuntary admission pursuant to clause (1)(c) shall not be the same physician who completed the application for psychiatric assessment under section 15.

(3) **Release of person by officer in charge.**— The officer in charge shall release a person who is the subject of an application for assessment under section 15 or who is the subject of an order under section 32 upon the completion of 72 hours of detention in the psychiatric facility unless the attending physician has released the person, has admitted the person as an informal or voluntary patient or has admitted the person as an involuntary patient by completing and filing with the officer in charge a certificate of involuntary admission.

(4) **Authority of certificate.**— An involuntary patient may be detained, restrained, observed and examined in a psychiatric facility,

(*a*) for not more than two weeks under a certificate of involuntary admission; and (*b*) for not more than,

   (i) one additional month under a first certificate of renewal,

   (ii) two additional months under a second certificate of renewal, and

   (iii) three additional months under a third or subsequent certificate of renewal,

that is completed and filed with the officer in charge by the attending physician.

(5) **Conditions precedent to making of certificate of involuntary admission or certificate of renewal.** — The attending physician shall not complete a certificate of involuntary admission or a certificate of renewal unless, after he or she has examined the patient, he or she is of the opinion both,

   (*a*) that the patient is suffering from mental disorder of a nature or quality that likely will result in,

      (i) serious bodily harm to the patient,

      (ii) serious bodily harm to another person, or

      (iii) imminent and serious physical impairment of the patient,

   unless the patient remains in the custody of a psychiatric facility; and

   (*b*) that the patient is not suitable for admission or continuation as an informal or voluntary patient.

(6) **Change of status, where period of detention has expired.** — An involuntary patient whose authorized period of detention has expired shall be deemed to be an informal or voluntary patient.

(7) **Idem, where period of detention has not expired.** — An involuntary patient whose authorized period of detention has not expired may be continued as an informal or voluntary patient upon completion of the prescribed form by the attending physician. ...

21. (1) Judge's order for examination. — Where a judge has reason to believe that a person who appears before him or her charged with or convicted of an offence suffers from mental disorder, the judge may order the person to attend a psychiatric facility for examination.

(2) **Senior physician's report.** — Where an examination is made under this section, the senior physician shall report in writing to the judge as to the mental condition of the person.

22. (1) Judge's order for admission. — Where a judge has reason to believe that a person in custody who appears before him or her charged with an offence suffers from mental disorder, the judge may, by order, remand that person for admission as a patient to a psychiatric facility for a period of not more than two months.

(2) **Senior physician's report.** — Before the expiration of the time mentioned in such order, the senior physician shall report in writing to the judge as to the mental condition of the person.

23. Condition precedent to judge's order. — A judge shall not make an order under section 21 or 22 until he or she ascertains from the senior physician of a psychiatric facility that the services of the psychiatric facility are available to the person to be named in the order.

24. Contents of senior physician's report. — Despite this or any other Act or any regulation made under any other Act, the senior physician may report all or any part of the information compiled by the psychiatric facility to any person where, in the opinion of the senior physician, it is in the best interests of the person who is the subject of an order made under section 21 or 22.

25. Persons detained under *Criminal Code* (Canada).— Any person who, under the *Criminal Code* (Canada), is,

(*a*) remanded to custody for observation; or

(*b*) detained under the authority of a warrant of the Lieutenant Governor,

may be admitted to, detained in, and discharged from a psychiatric facility in accordance with the law.

26. (1) Communications to and from patients.— Except as provided in this section, no communication written by a patient or sent to a patient shall be opened, examined or withheld, and its delivery shall not in any way be obstructed or delayed. ...

28. (1) Unauthorized absence.— Where a person who is subject to detention is absent without leave from a psychiatric facility, a police officer or other peace officer or any one appointed by the officer in charge may return the person to the psychiatric facility or take the person to the psychiatric facility nearest to the place where the person is apprehended,

(*a*) within twenty-four hours after his or her absence becomes known to the officer in charge; or

(*b*) under the authority of an order in the prescribed form issued by the officer in charge, within one month after his or her absence becomes known to the officer in charge.

(2) **Detention during return.—** A patient who is being returned under subsection (1) may be detained in an appropriate place in the course of his or her return.

(3) **Period of detention upon return.—** For the purposes of this Act, a patient who is returned under subsection (1) may be detained for the remainder of the period of detention to which he or she was subject when his or her absence became known to the officer in charge.

(4) **Where not returned.—** Where a patient is not returned within one month after his or her absence became known to the officer in charge, he or she shall, unless subject to detention otherwise than under this Act, be deemed to be discharged from the psychiatric facility.

(5) **Prohibitions.—** No person shall do or omit to do any act for the purpose of aiding, assisting, abetting or counselling a patient in a psychiatric facility to be absent without authorization. ...

33. Duty of police officer, other peace officer or other person.— A police officer or other peace officer or any one who takes a person in custody to a psychiatric facility shall remain at the facility and retain custody of the person so taken until the facility accepts the custody of the person.

EXERCISES

■ SHORT ANSWER

1. Define the following terms:

   a. involuntary patient

   A PERSON WHO IS DETAINED AND TAKEN INTO A PSYCHIATRIC FACILITY TO BE OBSERVED.

   b. officer in charge

   IS THE OFFICER IN CHARGE OF THE ADMINISTRATION OF THE PSYCHIATRIC FACILITY

   c. psychiatric facility

   IT'S A FACILITY WHERE PATIENTS SUFFERING FROM MENTAL DISORDER ARE OBSERVED AND CARED.

   d. restrain IS TO TAKE CONTROL OF A PERSON USING THE MINIMUN AMOUNT OF FORCE, CHEMICAL OR MECHANICAL TO PREVENT BODILY HARM FROM THE PATIEN OR OTHER

   e. mentally competent
   MEANS THAT THE PERSON IS ABLE TO UNDERSTAND AND COMPREHEND MATTER AND CONSEQUENCES

2. What is the purpose of the *Mental Health Act*?

■ TRUE OR FALSE

T 1. A person who is brought to a psychiatric facility by a police officer must be admitted and examined by a duly qualified medical practitioner.

F 2. A person, once admitted to a psychiatric facility as a voluntary or involuntary patient, can be detained until the officer in charge of the facility discharges him or her.

F 3. The physician's application is authority for any person to take a person in custody who is the subject of an application to a psychiatric facility forthwith.

T 4. A justice of the peace's order for examination is directed to all police and peace officers in Canada.

T 5. A police officer who takes a person in custody to a psychiatric facility shall remain at the facility with the person until it is safe to leave.

■ MULTIPLE CHOICE

Circle the correct response(s).

1. An application to a physician for psychiatric assessment shall:

    ⓐ be signed by the physician that examined the person

    b. be signed by the officer in charge of a psychiatric facility

    c. signed by a justice of the peace

2. A physician's application for psychiatric assessment of a person must be signed within:

    a. 24 hours of the examination

    ⓑ 7 days of the examination

    c. 1 month of the examination

3. A person who has been taken into custody under the authority of a physician's application may be detained for observation and examination for not more than:

    a. 24 hours

    b. 48 hours

    ⓒ 72 hours

    d. 7 days

4. A JP's order for examination is valid for:

   a. 3 days, including the day that it was made

   b. 7 days, including the day that it was made

   c. 14 days, including the day that it was made

   d. one month

5. When a patient is not returned to a psychiatric facility within _____ after his or her absence became known to the officer in charge, the patient shall, unless he or she is subject to detention otherwise under the *Mental Health Act*, be deemed to be discharged from the psychiatric facility.

   a. 14 days

   b. 21 days

   c. 3 months

   d. 1 month

   e. 30 days

■ CASE STUDY #1

Andrew Appleby is a real estate salesman in a metropolitan area. Because of a depressed economy, few homes are being sold. In fact, Andrew has not sold a home in five months. He has fallen behind in his mortgage payments and his car has been repossessed. Over the past week, Andrew has locked himself in his room, sat on his bed, and rocked back and forth. He has said very little and, with the exception of going to the bathroom and eating potato chips, he has done nothing. His wife, Vera, has attempted, with the help of relatives, to get him to see a doctor, but he has refused to see anyone. Vera, in desperation, calls the police. You and your partner arrive and she pleads for help.

1. Given the situation, describe in detail the appropriate course of action that you and your partner would take. Explain your decision(s).

2. Suggest a referral agency to the spouse. Explain the role of the agency.

■ CASE STUDY #2

You are a police officer with your local police service. On Friday, June 4, at 11:25 p.m. you and your partner are dispatched to 862 Dundas St., apartment 1203. On arrival you are met by a woman in her mid forties. She is crying and starts pleading with you to help her husband. She tells you that he has just recently been fired from the steel mill and that he has locked himself in the bedroom and is sitting in the corner. He is holding a large knife in his hand and keeps repeating that he has had enough. He has been in this state for an hour. He has not threatened anyone with the knife.

1. Explain officer safety considerations in dealing with this situation. (This question requires background from the conflict management course.)

2. Given the situation, describe in detail the appropriate course of action that you and your partner would take. Explain your decision(s).

3. Suggest a referral agency to the spouse. Explain the role of the agency.

■ CASE STUDY #3

You are a police officer with your local police service. You receive an all-points bulletin that Alf Smith has walked away from the psychiatric ward at the General Hospital. You have been provided with a description of the subject. While proceeding to the area of the hospital, you observe Alf walking west on Queen Street.

1. Before you approach Smith, what information do you need to determine the appropriate course of action?

2. Smith refuses to be returned to the hospital. What course of action is available to you if Smith is a voluntary patient? State your authority.

3. Smith refuses to be returned to the hospital. What course of action is available to you if Smith is an involuntary patient? State your authority.

■ CASE STUDY #4

You and your partner are dispatched to University College residence regarding a disturbance. On arrival you find a large crowd gathered in the lobby of the building. They are staring at a student, Dave Johns, who is running and banging himself against the wall. He is screaming, "get that awful thing off my back." A student tells you that Johns just came back from a party. The student believes that someone spiked Johns's drink with LSD. Johns struck his head against the wall and is now bleeding profusely.

1. Given the situation, describe in detail the appropriate course of action that you and your partner would take. Explain your decision(s).

■ CASE STUDY #5

While on routine patrol, you and your partner stop a cyclist for a red-light violation. A check on the individual, who identifies himself as Fred Hodges, indicates that he has been absent without leave from the Penetanguishine Hospital for the criminally insane for 45 days. Hodges had been serving four years at Kingston Penitentiary for a wounding charge and was sent to the hospital when he developed a mental disorder.

1. Are there any time restrictions for returning residents of a psychiatric facility who have been convicted of a criminal offence?

2. Has Hodges committed any offence by being absent without leave from the facility?

3. Explain how this situation differs from cases that involve involuntary patients who are absent without leave from a psychiatric facility?

CHAPTER 10

The Child and Family Services Act

CHAPTER OBJECTIVES

After completing this chapter, you should be able to:

◆ Understand key terms defined in the *Child and Family Services Act*.

◆ Explain a police officer's authority in relation to the commencement of child protection proceedings.

◆ Describe a police officer's authority with respect to bringing a child in need of protection to a place of safety, dealing with a child under the age of 12 who has committed an offence, apprehending a child who is absent without leave from a place of open temporary detention, and apprehending a young person who is absent from custody.

◆ State the curfew for children as defined in part III of the Act.

◆ Locate and interpret offences dealing with child abuse and leaving children unattended.

◆ Describe the obligations placed on citizens and professionals to report child abuse.

◆ Describe the role of the Children's Aid Society in assisting the police with investigations under the Act.

◆ Be prepared to apply the provisions of the Act in a hypothetical fact situation.

INTRODUCTION

The *Child and Family Services Act* deals with important and wide-ranging issues concerning children. Its paramount objective is to promote the best interests, protection, and well-being of children. Sensitivity and care must be taken in dealing with the provisions of this Act.

The Act sets out the authority of the state to bring an abused child into a place of safety, and places obligations on citizens and professionals to report child abuse. It establishes a curfew for children under 14 years of age. It prevents parents from leaving young children alone for any period of time. It also deals with the functions of children's aid societies.

Part III of the Act deals specifically with child protection. This part applies only to minors and not to children who are actually or apparently 16 years of age or more. Part III sets out the circumstances in which a child is deemed to be in need of protection. It also establishes how a children's aid society may commence child protection proceedings, and gives important rights to child protection workers. For example, a child protection worker who brings a child in need of protection to a place of safety, and who believes that no less restrictive course of action is feasible, may detain that child in a place of safety—namely, a place of open temporary detention as defined in part IV of the Act. If the young person subsequently leaves that place of temporary detention, the young person may be apprehended.

CHILD AND FAMILY SERVICES ACT

RSO 1990, Chapter C.11

1. Declaration of principles.— The purposes of this Act are,

(*a*) as a paramount objective, to promote the best interests, protection and well-being of children;

(*b*) to recognize that while parents often need help in caring for their children, that help should give support to the autonomy and integrity of the family unit and, wherever possible, be provided on the basis of mutual consent;

(*c*) to recognize that the least restrictive or disruptive course of action that is available and is appropriate in a particular case to help a child or family should be followed;

(*d*) to recognize that children's services should be provided in a manner that,

(i) respects children's needs for continuity of care and for stable family relationships, and

(ii) takes into account physical and mental developmental differences among children;

(*e*) to recognize that, wherever possible, services to children and their families should be provided in a manner that respects cultural, religious and regional differences; and

(*f*) to recognize that Indian and native people should be entitled to provide, wherever possible, their own child and family services, and that all services to Indian and native children and families should be provided in a manner that recognizes their culture, heritage and traditions and the concept of the extended family.

2. (1) **French language services.**— Service providers shall, where appropriate, make services to children and their families available in the French language.

(2) **Duties of service providers.**— Service providers shall ensure,

(*a*) that children and their parents have an opportunity where appropriate to be heard and represented when decisions affecting their interests are made and to be heard when they have concerns about the services they are receiving; and

(*b*) that decisions affecting the interests and rights of children and their parents are made according to clear, consistent criteria and are subject to procedural safeguards.

INTERPRETATION

3. (1) **Definitions.**— In this Act,

"agency" means a corporation;

"approved agency" means an agency that is approved under subsection 8(1) of Part I (Flexible Services);

"approved service" means a service provided,

(a) under subsection 7(1) of Part I or with the support of a grant or contribution made under subsection 7(2) of that Part,

(b) by an approved agency, or

(c) under the authority of a licence;

"band" has the same meaning as in the *Indian Act* (Canada); ...

"child" means a person under the age of eighteen years;

"child development service" means a service for a child with a developmental or physical handicap, for the family of a child with a developmental or physical handicap, or for the child and the family;

"child treatment service" means a service for a child with a mental or psychiatric disorder, for the family of a child with a mental or psychiatric disorder, or for the child and the family;

"child welfare service" means,

(a) a residential or non-residential service, including a prevention service,

(b) a service provided under Part III (Child Protection),

(c) a service provided under Part VII (Adoption), or

(d) individual or family counselling; ...

"court" means the Ontario Court (Provincial Division) or the Unified Family Court; ...

"residential service" means boarding, lodging and associated supervisory, sheltered or group care provided for a child away from the home of the child's parent, and "residential care" and "residential placement" have corresponding meanings;

"service" means,

(a) a child development service,

(b) a child treatment service,

(c) a child welfare service,

(d) a community support service, or

(e) a young offenders service;

"service provider" means

(a) the Minister,

(b) an approved agency,

(c) a society,

(d) a licensee, or

(e) a person who provides an approved service or provides a service purchased by the Minister or an approved agency,

but does not include a foster parent;

"society" means an approved agency designated as a children's aid society under subsection 15(2) of Part I (Flexible Services);

"young offenders service" means a service provided under Part IV (Young Offenders) or under a program established under that Part.

(2) **Idem: "parent".**— In this act, a reference to a child's parent shall be deemed to be a reference to,

(*a*) both parents, where both have custody of the child;

(*b*) one parent, where that parent has lawful custody of the child or the other parent is unavailable or unable to act as the context requires; or

(*c*) another individual, where that individual has lawful custody of the child,

except where this Act provides otherwise. ...

CHILDREN'S AID SOCIETIES

• • •

(3) **Functions of society.**— The functions of a children's aid society are to,

(*a*) investigate allegations or evidence that children who are under the age of sixteen years or are in the society's care or under its supervision may be in need of protection;

(*b*) protect, where necessary, children who are under the age of sixteen years or are in the society's care or under its supervision;

(*c*) provide guidance, counselling and other services to families for protecting children or for the prevention of circumstances requiring the protection of children;

(*d*) provide care for children assigned or committed to its care under this Act;

(*e*) supervise children assigned to its supervision under this Act;

(*f*) place children for adoption under Part VII; and

(*g*) perform any other duties given to it by this or any other Act. ...

17. (2) **Director may designate places of safety.**— A Director may designate a place as a place of safety, and may designate a class of places as places of safety, for the purposes of Part III (Child Protection). ...

OFFENCES

25. Offence.— A person who knowingly,

(*a*) fails to furnish a report required by the Minister under subsection 5(5);

(*b*) contravenes subsection 6(2) or (3) (obstructing program supervisor, etc.); or

(*c*) furnishes false information in an application under this Part or in a report or return required under this Part or the regulations,

and a director, officer or employee of a corporation who authorizes, permits or concurs in such a contravention or furnishing by the corporation, is guilty of an offence and is liable upon conviction to a fine of not more than $2,000. ...

PART III

CHILD PROTECTION

37. (1) **Definitions.**— In this Part,

"child" does not include a child as defined in subsection 3(1) who is actually or apparently sixteen years of age or older, unless the child is the subject of an order under this Part;

"child protection worker" means a Director, a local director or a person authorized by a Director or local director for the purposes of section 40 (commencing child protection proceedings); ...

"parent", when used in reference to a child, means each of,

(a) the child's mother,

(b) an individual described in one of paragraphs 1 to 6 of subsection 8(1) of the *Children's Law Reform Act*, unless it is proved on a balance of probabilities that he is not the child's natural father,

(c) the individual having lawful custody of the child,

(d) an individual who, during the twelve months before intervention under this Part, has demonstrated a settled intention to treat the child as a child of his or her family, or has acknowledged parentage of the child and provided for the child's support,

(e) an individual who, under a written agreement or a court order, is required to provide for the child, has custody of the child or has a right of access to the child, and

(f) an individual who has acknowledged parentage of the child in writing under section 12 of the *Children's Law Reform Act*,

but does not include a foster parent;

"place of safety" means a foster home, a hospital, and a place or one of a class of places designated as such by a Director under subsection 17(2) of Part I (Flexible Services), but does not include,

(a) a place of secure custody as defined in Part IV (Young Offenders), or

(b) a place of secure temporary detention as defined in Part IV.

(2) **Child in need of protection.**— A child is in need of protection where,

(*a*) the child has suffered physical harm, inflicted by the person having charge of the child or caused by that person's failure to care and provide for or supervise and protect the child adequately;

(*b*) there is a substantial risk that the child will suffer physical harm inflicted or caused as described in clause (a);

(*c*) the child has been sexually molested or sexually exploited, by the person having charge of the child or by another person where the person having charge of the child knows or should know of the possibility of sexual molestation or sexual exploitation and fails to protect the child;

(*d*) there is a substantial risk that the child will be sexually molested or sexually exploited as described in clause (c);

(*e*) the child requires medical treatment to cure, prevent or alleviate physical harm or suffering and the child's parent or the person having charge of the child does not provide, or refuses or is unavailable or unable to consent to, the treatment;

(*f*) the child has suffered emotional harm, demonstrated by severe,

(i) anxiety,

(ii) depression,

(iii) withdrawal, or

(iv) self-destructive or aggressive behaviour,

and the child's parent or the person having charge of the child does not provide, or refuses or is unavailable or unable to consent to, services or treatment to remedy or alleviate the harm;

(*g*) there is a substantial risk that the child will suffer emotional harm of the kind described in clause (f), and the child's parent or the person having charge of the child does not provide, or refuses or is unavailable or unable to consent to, services or treatment to prevent the harm;

(*h*) the child suffers from a mental, emotional or developmental condition that, if not remedied, could seriously impair the child's development and the child's parent or the person having charge of the child does not provide, or refuses or is unavailable or unable to consent to, treatment to remedy or alleviate the condition;

(*i*) the child has been abandoned, the child's parent has died or is unavailable to exercise his or her custodial rights over the child and has not made adequate provision for the child's care and custody, or the child is in a residential placement and the parent refuses or is unable or unwilling to resume the child's care and custody;

(*j*) the child is less than twelve years old and has killed or seriously injured another person or caused serious damage to another person's property, services or treatment are necessary to prevent a recurrence and the child's parent or the person having charge of the child does not provide, or refuses or is unavailable or unable to consent to, those services or treatment;

(*k*) the child is less than twelve years old and has on more than one occasion injured another person or caused loss or damage to another person's property, with the encouragement of the person having charge of the child or because of that person's failure or inability to supervise the child adequately; or

(*l*) the child's parent is unable to care for the child and the child is brought before the court with the parent's consent and, where the child is twelve years of age or older, with the child's consent, to be dealt with under this Part.

(3) **Best interests of child.**— Where a person is directed in this Part to make an order or determination in the best interests of a child, the person shall take into consideration those of the following circumstances of the case that he or she considers relevant:

1. The child's physical, mental and emotional needs, and the appropriate care or treatment to meet those needs.

2. The child's physical, mental and emotional level of development.

3. The child's cultural background.

4. The religious faith, if any, in which the child is being raised.

5. The importance for the child's development of a positive relationship with a parent and a secure place as a member of a family.

6. The child's relationships by blood or through an adoption order.

7. The importance of continuity in the child's care and the possible effect on the child of disruption of that continuity.

8. The merits of a plan for the child's care proposed by a society including a proposal that the child be placed for adoption or adopted, compared with the merits of the child remaining with or returning to a parent.

9. The child's views and wishes, if they can be reasonably ascertained.

10. The effects on the child of delay in the disposition of the case.

11. The risk that the child may suffer harm through being removed from, kept away from, returned to or allowed to remain in the care of a parent.

12. The degree of risk, if any, that justified the finding that the child is in need of protection.

13. Any other relevant circumstance.

(4) **Where child an Indian or native person.**— Where a person is directed in this Part to make an order or determination in the best interests of a child and the child is an Indian or native person, the person shall take into consideration the importance, in recognition of the uniqueness of Indian and native culture, heritage and traditions, of preserving the child's cultural identity.

LEGAL REPRESENTATION

38. (1) **Legal representation of child.**— A child may have legal representation at any stage in a proceeding under this Part.

(2) **Court to consider issue.**— Where a child does not have legal representation in a proceeding under this Part, the court,

(*a*) shall, as soon as practicable after the commencement of the proceeding; and

(*b*) may, at any later stage in the proceeding,

determine whether legal representation is desirable to protect the child's interests.

(3) **Direction for legal representation.**— Where the court determines that legal representation is desirable to protect a child's interests, the court shall direct that legal representation be provided for the child.

(4) **Criteria.**— Where,

(*a*) the court is of the opinion that there is a difference of views between the child and a parent or a society, and the society proposes that the child be removed from a person's care or be made a society or Crown ward under paragraph 2 or 3 of subsection 57(1);

(*b*) the child is in the society's care and,

(i) no parent appears before the court, or

(ii) it is alleged that the child is in need of protection within the meaning of clause 37(2)(a), (c), (f) or (h); or

(*c*) the child is not permitted to be present at the hearing,

legal representation shall be deemed to be desirable to protect the child's interests, unless the court is satisfied, taking into account the child's views and wishes if they can be reasonably ascertained, that the child's interests are otherwise adequately protected. ...

PARTIES AND NOTICE

39. (1) **Parties.—** The following are parties to a proceeding under this Part:

1. The applicant.

2. The society having jurisdiction in the matter.

3. The child's parent.

4. Where the child is an Indian or a native person, a representative chosen by the child's band or native community. ...

COMMENCING CHILD PROTECTION PROCEEDINGS

40. (1) **Application.—** A society may apply to the court to determine whether a child is in need of protection.

(2) **Warrant to apprehend child.—** A justice of the peace may issue a warrant authorizing a child protection worker to bring a child to a place of safety if the justice of the peace is satisfied on the basis of a child protection worker's sworn information that there are reasonable and probable grounds that,

(a) the child is in need of protection; and

(b) a less restrictive course of action is not available or will not protect the child adequately.

(3) **Idem.—** A justice of the peace shall not refuse to issue a warrant under subsection (2) by reason only that the child protection worker may bring the child to a place of safety under subsection (7).

(4) **Order to produce or apprehend child.—** Where the court is satisfied, on a person's application upon notice to a society, that there are reasonable and probable grounds to believe that,

(a) a child is in need of protection, the matter has been reported to the society, the society has not made an application under subsection (1), and no child protection worker has sought a warrant under subsection (2) or apprehended the child under subsection (7); and

(b) the child cannot be protected adequately otherwise than by being brought before the court,

the court may order,

(c) that the person having charge of the child produce him or her before the court at the time and place named in the order for a hearing under subsection 47(1) to determine whether he or she is in need of protection; or

(d) where the court is satisfied that an order under clause (c) would not protect the child adequately, that a child protection worker employed by the society bring the child to a place of safety. ...

(6) **Authority to enter, etc.—** A child protection worker authorized to bring a child to a place of safety by a warrant issued under subsection (2) or an order made under clause (4)(d) may at any time enter any premises specified in the warrant or order, by force if necessary, and may search for and remove the child.

(7) **Apprehension without warrant.**— A child protection worker who believes on reasonable and probable grounds that,

    (*a*) a child is in need of protection; and

    (*b*) there would be a substantial risk to the child's health or safety during the time necessary to bring the matter on for a hearing under subsection 47(1) or obtain a warrant under subsection (2),

may without a warrant bring the child to a place of safety.

(8) **Police assistance.**— A child protection worker acting under this section may call for the assistance of a peace officer.

(9) **Consent to examine child.**— A child protection worker acting under subsection (7) or under a warrant issued under subsection (2) or an order made under clause (4)(d) may authorize the child's medical examination where a parent's consent would otherwise be required.

(10) **Place of open temporary detention.**— Where a child protection worker who brings a child to a place of safety under this section believes on reasonable and probable grounds that no less restrictive course of action is feasible, the child may be detained in a place of safety that is a place of open temporary detention as defined in Part IV (Young Offenders).

(11) **Right of entry, etc.**— A child protection worker who believes on reasonable and probable grounds that a child referred to in subsection (7) is on any premises may without a warrant enter the premises, by force, if necessary, and search for and remove the child.

(12) **Regulations re power of entry.**— A child protection worker authorized to enter premises under subsection (6) or (11) shall exercise the power of entry in accordance with the regulations.

(13) **Peace officer has powers of child protection worker.**— Subsections (2), (6), (7), (10), (11) and (12) apply to a peace officer as if the peace officer were a child protection worker.

(14) **Protection from personal liability.**— No action shall be instituted against a peace officer or child protection worker for any act done in good faith in the execution or intended execution of that person's duty under this section or for an alleged neglect or default in the execution in good faith of that duty.

SPECIAL CASES OF APPREHENSION OF CHILDREN

41. (1) **Warrant to apprend child in care.**— A justice of the peace may issue a warrant authorizing a peace officer or child protection worker to bring a child to a place of safety if the justice of the peace is satisfied on the basis of a peace officer's or child protection worker's sworn information that,

    (*a*) the child is actually or apparently under the age of sixteen years and has left or been removed from a society's lawful care and custody without its consent; and

    (*b*) there are reasonable and probable grounds to believe that there is no course of action available other than bringing the child to a place of safety that would adequately protect the child.

(2) **Idem.**— A justice of the peace shall not refuse to issue a warrant to a person under subsection (1) by reason only that the person may bring the child to a place of safety under subsection (4).

(3) **No need to specify premises.—** It is not necessary in a warrant under subsection (1) to specify the premises where the child is located.

(4) **Apprehension of child in care without warrant.—** A peace officer or child protection worker who believes on reasonable and probable grounds that,

(*a*) a child is actually or apparently under the age of sixteen years and has left or been removed from a society's lawful care and custody without its consent; and

(*b*) there would be a substantial risk to the child's health or safety during the time necessary to obtain a warrant under subsection (1),

may without a warrant bring the child to a place of safety.

(5) **Apprehension of child absent from place of open temporary detention.—** Where a child is detained under this Part in a place of safety that has been designated as a place of open temporary detention as defined in Part IV (Young Offenders) and leaves the place without the consent of,

(*a*) the society having care, custody and control of the child; and

(*b*) the person in charge of the place of safety,

a peace officer, the person in charge of the place of safety or that person's delegate may apprehend the child without a warrant.

(6) **Idem.—** A person who apprehends a child under subsection (5) shall,

(*a*) take the child to a place of safety to be detained until the child can be returned to the place of safety the child left; or

(*b*) return the child or arrange for the child to be returned to the place of safety the child left.

42. (1) **Apprehension of child under twelve.—** A peace officer who believes on reasonable and probable grounds that a child actually or apparently under twelve years of age has committed an act in respect of which a person twelve years of age or older could be found guilty of an offence may apprehend the child without a warrant and on doing so,

(*a*) shall return the child to the child's parent or other person having charge of the child as soon as practicable; or

(*b*) where it is not possible to return the child to the parent or other person within a reasonable time, shall take the child to a place of safety to be detained there until the child can be returned to the parent or other person.

(2) **Notice to parent, etc.—** The person in charge of a place of safety in which a child is detained under subsection (1) shall make reasonable efforts to notify the child's parent or other person having charge of the child of the child's detention so that the child may be returned to the parent or other person.

(3) **Where child not returned to parent, etc., within twelve hours.—** Where a child detained in a place of safety under subsection (1) cannot be returned to the child's parent or other person having charge of the child within twelve hours of being taken to the place of safety, the child shall be dealt with as if the child had been taken to a place of safety under subsection 40(7) and not apprehended under subsection (1).

43. (1) **Application.—** In this section, "parent" includes,

(*a*) an approved agency that has custody of the child;

(*b*) a person who has care and control of the child.

(2) **Warrant to apprehend runaway child.—** A justice of the peace may issue a warrant authorizing a peace officer or child protection worker to apprehend a

child if the justice of the peace is satisfied on the basis of the sworn information of a parent of the child that,

    (a) the child is under the age of sixteen years;

    (b) the child has withdrawn from the parent's care and control without the parent's consent; and

    (c) the parent believes on reasonable and probable grounds that the child's health or safety may be at risk if the child is not apprehended.

(3) **Idem.**— A person who apprehends a child under subsection (2) shall return the child to the child's parent as soon as practicable and where it is not possible to return the child to the parent within a reasonable time, take the child to a place of safety.

(4) **Notice to parent, etc.**— The person in charge of a place of safety to which a child is taken under subsection (3) shall make reasonable efforts to notify the child's parent that the child is in the place of safety so that the child may be returned to the parent.

(5) **Where child not returned to parent within twelve hours.**— Where a child taken to a place of safety under subsection (3) cannot be returned to the child's parent within twelve hours of being taken to the place of safety, the child shall be dealt with as if the child had been taken to a place of safety under subsection 40(2) and not apprehended under subsection (2).

(6) **Where custody enforcement proceedings more appropriate.**— A justice of the peace shall not issue a warrant under subsection (2) where a child has withdrawn from the care and control of one parent with the consent of another parent under circumstances where a proceeding under section 36 of the *Children's Law Reform Act* would be more appropriate.

(7) **No need to specify premises.**— It is not necessary in a warrant under subsection (2) to specify the premises where the child is located.

(8) **Child protection proceedings.**— Where a peace officer or child protection worker believes on reasonable and probable grounds that a child apprehended under this section is in need of protection and there may be a substantial risk to the health or safety of the child if the child were returned to the parent,

    (a) the peace officer or child protection worker may take the child to a place of safety under subsection 40(7); or

    (b) where the child has been taken to a place of safety under subsection (5), the child shall be dealt with as if the child had been taken there under subsection 40(7).

POWER OF ENTRY AND OTHER PROVISIONS FOR SPECIAL CASES OF APPREHENSION

44. (1) Authority to enter, etc.— A person authorized to bring a child to a place of safety by a warrant issued under subsection 41(1) or 43(2) may at any time enter any premises specified in the warrant, by force, if necessary, and may search for and remove the child.

(2) **Right of entry, etc.**— A person authorized under subsection 41(4) or (5) or 42(1) who believes on reasonable and probable grounds that a child referred to in the relevant subsection is on any premises may without a warrant enter the premises, by force, if necessary, and search for and remove the child.

(3) **Regulations re power of entry.**— A person authorized to enter premises under this section shall exercise the power of entry in accordance with the regulations.

(4) **Police assistance.**— A child protection worker acting under section 41 or 43 may call for the assistance of a peace officer. ...

(6) **Place of open temporary detention.**— Where a person who brings a child to a place of safety under section 41 or 42 believes on reasonable and probable grounds that no less restrictive course of action is feasible, the child may be detained in a place of safety that is a place of open temporary detention as defined in Part IV (Young Offenders).

(7) **Protection from personal liability.**— No action shall be instituted against a peace officer or child protection worker for any act done in good faith in the execution or intended execution of that person's duty under this section or section 41, 42 or 43 or for an alleged neglect or default in the execution in good faith of that duty.

HEARINGS AND ORDERS

• • •

45. (8) **Prohibition: identifying child.**— No person shall publish or make public information that has the effect of identifying a child who is a witness at or a participant in a hearing or the subject of a proceeding, or the child's parent or foster parent or a member of the child's family.

(9) **Idem: order re adult.**— The court may make an order prohibiting the publication of information that has the effect of identifying a person charged with an offence under this Part. ...

46. (1) **Time of detention limited.**— As soon as practicable, but in any event within five days after a child is brought to a place of safety under section 40 or subsection 79(6) or a homemaker remains or is placed on premises under subsection 78(2),

(*a*) the matter shall be brought before a court for a hearing under subsection 47(1) (child protection hearing);

(*b*) the child shall be returned to the person who last had charge of the child or, where there is an order for the child's custody that is enforceable in Ontario, to the person entitled to custody under the order; or

(*c*) a temporary care agreement shall be made under subsection 29(1) of Part II (Voluntary Access to Services).

(2) **Idem: place of open temporary detention.**— Within twenty-four hours after a child is brought to a place of safety that is a place of open temporary detention, or as soon thereafter as is practicable, the matter shall be brought before a court for a hearing and the court shall,

(*a*) where it is satisfied that no less restrictive course of action is feasible, order that the child remain in the place of open temporary detention for a period or periods not exceeding an aggregate of thirty days and then be returned to the care and custody of the society;

(*b*) order that the child be discharged from the place of open temporary detention and returned to the care and custody of the society; or

(*c*) make an order under subsection 51(2) (temporary care and custody).

47. (1) **Child protection hearing.**— Where an application is made under sub-section 40(1) or a matter is brought before the court to determine whether the child is in need of protection, the court shall hold a hearing to determine the issue and make an order under section 57.

(2) **Child's name, age, etc.**— As soon as practicable, and in any event before determining whether a child is in need of protection, the court shall determine,

(*a*) the child's name and age;

(*b*) the religious faith, if any, in which the child is being raised;

(*c*) whether the child is an Indian or a native person and, if so, the child's band or native community; and

(*d*) where the child was brought to a place of safety before the hearing, the location of the place from which the child was removed.

(3) **Where sixteenth birthday intervenes.**— Despite anything else in this Part, where the child was under the age of sixteen years when the proceeding was commenced or when the child was apprehended, the court may hear and determine the matter and make an order under this Part as if the child were still under the age of sixteen years. ...

ASSESSMENTS

• • •

57. (1) **Order where child in need of protection.**— Where the court finds that a child is in need of protection and is satisfied that intervention through a court order is necessary to protect the child in the future, the court shall make one of the following orders, in the child's best interests:

1. Supervision order   That the child be placed with or returned to a parent or another person, subject to the supervision of the society, for a specified period of at least three and not more than twelve months.

2. Society wardship   That the child be made a ward of the society and be placed in its care and custody for a specified period not exceeding twelve months.

3. Crown wardship   That the child be made a ward of the Crown, until the wardship is terminated under section 65 or expires under subsection 71(1), and be placed in the care of the society.

4. Consecutive orders of society of wardship and supervision   That the child be made a ward of the society under paragraph 2 for a specified period and then be returned to a parent or another person under paragraph 1, for a period or periods not exceeding an aggregate of twelve months. ...

(9) **Where no court order necessary.**— Where the court finds that a child is in need of protection but is not satisfied that a court order is necessary to protect the child in the future, the court shall order that the child remain with or be returned to the person who had charge of the child immediately before intervention under this Part. ...

DUTY TO REPORT

72. (1) **Definition.**— In this section and in sections 73, 74 and 75, "to suffer abuse", when used in reference to a child, means to be in need of protection within the meaning of clause 37(2)(a), (c), (e), (f) or (h).

(2) **Duty to report that child in need of protection.**— A person who believes on reasonable grounds that a child is or may be in need of protection shall forthwith report the belief and the information upon which it is based to a society.

(3) **Idem: professional or official duties, suspicion of abuse.**— Despite the provisions of any other Act, a person referred to in subsection (4) who, in the course of his or her professional or official duties, has reasonable grounds to suspect that a child is or may be suffering or may have suffered abuse shall forthwith report the suspicion and the information on which it is based to a society.

(4) **Application of subs. (3).**— Subsection (3) applies to every person who performs professional or official duties with respect to a child, including,

(*a*) a health care professional, including a physician, nurse, dentist, pharmacist and psychologist;

(*b*) a teacher, school principal, social worker, family counsellor, priest, rabbi, member of the clergy, operator or employee of a day nursery and youth and recreation worker;

(*c*) a peace officer and a coroner;

(*d*) a solicitor; and

(*e*) a service provider and an employee of a service provider. ...

(6) **Duty of society.**— A society that obtains information that a child in its care and custody is or may be suffering or may have suffered abuse shall forthwith report the information to a Director.

(7) **Section overrides privilege.**— This section applies although the information reported may be confidential or privileged, and no action for making the report shall be instituted against a person who acts in accordance with subsection (2) or (3) unless the person acts maliciously or without reasonable grounds for the belief or suspicion, as the case may be.

(8) **Exception: solicitor client privilege.**— Nothing in this section abrogates any privilege that may exist between a solicitor and his or her client. ...

OFFENCES, RESTRAINING ORDERS, RECOVERY ON CHILD'S BEHALF

79. (1) **Definition.**— In this section, "abuse" means a state or condition of being physically harmed, sexually molested or sexually exploited.

(2) **Child abuse.**— No person having charge of a child shall,

(*a*) inflict abuse on the child; or

(*b*) by failing to care and provide for or supervise and protect the child adequately,

(i) permit the child to suffer abuse, or

(ii) permit the child to suffer from a mental, emotional or developmental condition that, if not remedied, could seriously impair the child's development.

(3) **Leaving child unattended.**— No person having charge of a child less than sixteen years of age shall leave the child without making provision for his or her supervision and care that is reasonable in the circumstances.

(4) **Reverse onus.**— Where a person is charged with contravening subsection (3) and the child is less than ten years of age, the onus of establishing that the person made provision for the child's supervision and care that was reasonable in the circumstances rests with the person.

(5) **Allowing child to loiter, etc.**— No parent of a child less than sixteen years of age shall permit the child to,

> (*a*) loiter in a public place between the hours of midnight and 6 a.m.; or

> (*b*) be in a place of public entertainment between the hours of midnight and 6 a.m., unless the parent accompanies the child or authorizes a specified individual eighteen years of age or older to accompany the child.

(6) **Police may take child home or to place of safety.**— Where a child who is actually or apparently less than sixteen years of age is in a place to which the public has access between the hours of midnight and 6 a.m. and is not accompanied by a person described in clause (5)(b), a peace officer may apprehend the child without a warrant and proceed as if the child had been apprehended under subsection 42(1).

(7) **Child protection hearing.**— The court may, in connection with a case arising under subsection (2), (3) or (5), proceed under this Part as if an application had been made under subsection 40(1) (child protection proceeding) in respect of the child.

80. (1) **Restraining order.**— Where the court finds that a child is in need of protection, the court may, instead of or in addition to making an order under subsection 57(1), make an order in the child's best interests restraining or prohibiting a person's access to or contact with the child, and may include in the order such directions as the court considers appropriate for implementing the order and protecting the child.

(2) **Idem: notice.**— An order shall not be made under subsection (1) unless notice of the proceeding has been served personally on the person to be named in the order.

(3) **Six month maximum.**— An order made under subsection (1) shall be in force for a specified period not exceeding six months. ...

81. (1) **Definition.**— In this section, "to suffer abuse", when used in reference to a child, means to be in need of protection within the meaning of clause 37(2)(a), (c), (e), (f) or (h). ...

82. Prohibition.— No person shall place a child in the care and custody of a society, and no society shall take a child into its care and custody, except,

> (*a*) in accordance with this Part; or

> (*b*) under an agreement made under subsection 29(1) or 30(1) (temporary care or special needs agreement) of Part II (Voluntary Access to Services).

83. Offence.— Where a child is the subject of an order for society supervision, society wardship or Crown wardship under subsection 57(1), no person shall,

> (*a*) induce or attempt to induce the child to leave the care of the person with whom the child is placed by the court or by the society, as the case may be;

> (*b*) detain or harbour the child after the person or society referred to in clause (a) requires that the child be returned;

> (*c*) interfere with the child or remove or attempt to remove the child from any place; or

(*d*) for the purpose of interfering with the child, visit or communicate with the person referred to in clause (a).

84. Offence.— No person shall,

(*a*) knowingly give false information in an application under this Part; or

(*b*) obstruct, interfere with or attempt to obstruct or interfere with a child protection worker or a peace officer who is acting under section 40, 41, 42, 43 or 44.

85. (1) **Offences.—** A person who contravenes,

(*a*) an order for access made under subsection 58(1);

(*b*) subsection 72(3) (reporting child abuse);

(*c*) subsection 74(5) (disclosure of information obtained by court order);

(*d*) subsection 75(6) or (10) (confidentiality of child abuse register);

(*e*) an order made under subsection 76(8) (amendment of society's records);

(*f*) subsection 79(3) or (5) (leaving child unattended, etc.);

(*g*) a restraining order made under subsection 80(1);

(*h*) section 82 (unauthorized placement);

(*i*) any provision of section 83 (interference with child, etc.); or

(*j*) clause 84(a) or (b).

and a director, officer or employee of a corporation who authorizes, permits or concurs in such a contravention by the corporation is guilty of an offence and on conviction is liable to a fine of not more than $1,000 or, except in the case of a contravention of subsection 72(3), to imprisonment for a term of not more than one year, or to both.

(2) **Idem.—** A person who contravenes subsection 79(2) (child abuse), and a director, officer or employee of a corporation who authorizes, permits or concurs in such a contravention by the corporation is guilty of an offence and on conviction is liable to a fine of not more than $2,000 or to imprisonment for a term of not more than two years, or to both.

(3) **Idem.—** A person who contravenes subsection 45(8) or 76(11) (publication of identifying information) or an order prohibiting publication made under clause 45(7)(c) or subsection 45(9), and a director, officer or employee of a corporation who authorizes, permits or concurs in such a contravention by the corporation, is guilty of an offence and on conviction is liable to a fine of not more than $10,000 or to imprisonment for a term of not more than three years, or to both. ...

APPREHENSION OF YOUNG PERSONS WHO ARE ABSENT FROM CUSTODY WITHOUT PERMISSION

98. (1) **Apprehension of young person absent from place of temporary detention.—** A peace officer, the person in charge of a place of temporary detention or that person's delegate, who believes on reasonable and probable grounds that a young person detained under the federal Act or the *Provincial Offences Act* in a place of temporary detention has left the place without the consent of the person in charge and fails or refuses to return there may apprehend the young person with or without a warrant and take the young person or arrange for the young person to be taken to a place of temporary detention.

(2) **Idem: place of open custody.**— A peace officer, the person in charge of a place of open custody or that person's delegate, who believes on reasonable and probable grounds that a young person held in a place of open custody as described in section 95,

    (*a*) has left the place without the consent of the person in charge and fails or refuses to return there; or

    (*b*) fails or refuses to return to the place of open custody upon completion of a period of temporary release under clause 95(b).

may apprend the young person with or without a warrant and take the young person or arrange for the young person to be taken to a place of open custody or a place of temporary detention.

(3) **Young person to be returned within forty-eight hours.**— A young person who is apprehended under this section shall be returned to the place from which he or she is absent within forty-eight hours after being apprehended unless the provincial director detains the young person in secure temporary detention under paragraph 2 of subsection 93(2).

(4) **Warrant to apprehend young person.**— A justice of the peace who is satisfied on the basis of a sworn information that there are reasonable and probable grounds to believe that a young person held in a place of temporary detention or open custody,

    (*a*) has left the place without the consent of the person in charge and fails or refuses to return there; or

    (*b*) fails or refuses to return to a place of open custody upon completion of a period of temporary release under clause 95(b),

may issue a warrant authorizing a peace officer, the person in charge of the place of temporary detention or open custody or that person's delegate to apprehend the young person.

(5) **Authority to enter, etc.**— Where a person authorized to apprehend a young person under subsection (1) or (2) believes on reasonable and probable grounds that a young person referred to in the relevant subsection is on any premises, the person may with or without a warrant enter the premises, by force, if necessary, and search for and remove the young person.

(6) **Regulations re exercise of power of entry.**— A person authorized to enter premises under subsection (5) shall exercise the power of entry in accordance with the regulations.

PART V
RIGHTS OF CHILDREN

• • •

LOCKING UP

100. (1) **Locking up restricted.**— No service provider shall detain a child or permit a child to be detained in locked premises in the course of the provision of a service to the child, except as Part IV (Young Offenders) and Part VI (Extraordinary Measures) authorize.

EXERCISES

■ DEFINITIONS

Define the following terms:

1. child ⟶ A PERSON   UNDE THE AGE   OF   18 YR .

2. child (for the purposes of part III, Child Protection)

   A   PERSO UNDE   THE   AGE OF   16 .

3. child in need of protection :   A CHILD   UNDER 16
   - SUFFERED   PHYSICAL HARM
   - RISK OF SUFFER ↗
   - SUFFER OR IN RISK OF BEEING SEXUALY ABUSE
   -

4. abuse :   A CHILD IN NEED OF PROTECTION
   ↳ A STATE OF   BEING   PHYSICALLY HARMED
   SEXUALY MOLESTED   OR   EXPLOITED .

5. to suffer abuse (for the purposes of duty to report)

   IS A CHILD IN NEED OF PROTECTION

6. place of safety   HOSPITAL
   FOSTER HOME

7. parent   A PERSON WHO HAS CUSTODY OF
   A CHILD.   1PAREN / 2 PAREN
   ANYONE .

■ TRUE OR FALSE

T **1.** A police officer is considered a child protection worker with respect to the commencement of proceedings.

T **2.** A child protection worker may at any time enter a place and search for and remove a child that he or she thinks is in need of protection.

F **3.** A runaway child apprehended by a police officer must be returned to a place of open temporary detention until a hearing is held.

T **4.** Every person who suspects that a child is in need of protection has a legal duty to report the information to the police or a children's aid society.

F **5.** A parent who allows a child under 14 years of age to loiter in a public place between the hours of midnight and 6:00 a.m. is guilty of an offence under the *Child and Family Services Act*.

T **6.** First Nations people are entitled to provide their own child and family services.

T **7.** Under the *Child and Family Services Act*, a parent includes a person who has the lawful custody of the child.

T **8.** A function of the Children's Aid Society is to investigate allegations that children under its care are in need of protection.

■ **MULTIPLE CHOICE**

Circle the correct response(s).

1. Which of the following is not a place of safety as defined in part III (Child Protection) under the *Child and Family Services Act*:

   a. a foster home

   b. a place of secure temporary detention

   c. a hospital

   d. none of the above

2. Which of the following is not included in the definition of parent under part III of the *Child and Family Services Act*:

   a. an individual who has lawful custody of the child

   b. an individual who has acknowledged parentage of the child in writing under s. 12 of the *Children's Law Reform Act*

   c. a foster parent

   d. the child's mother

   e. none of the above

3. The police are called to investigate a complaint that two children, ages 8 and 5, have been left unattended in the west end of town. After knocking on the door several times, and getting no response, they hear the sound of a crying child. They continue to knock and get no reply. Given these circumstances, the police should:

   a. call the Children's Aid Society and wait for their arrival before they can take any action

   b. attempt to locate the parents to be let into the house

   c. force open the door and take the children

   d. send other officers to obtain a search warrant that will allow them to enter

4. Once the investigation into the incident from question #3 is complete, the police will turn the children over to:

   a. their parents

   b. the Children's Aid Society

   c. their closest relatives

5. The children in question #3 were found to be unharmed. After returning home and not finding her children, the single mother attended at the local police station. She explained that she had been at the casino for a couple of hours, and that she had left her children alone on other occasions because she believed that her 8-year-old daughter was mature enough to babysit. Given these circumstances, the police would:

   a. charge the mother under the *Child and Family Services Act* for failing to care for and supervise the children adequately

   b. charge the mother under the *Criminal Code* for failing to provide the necessaries of life

   c. charge the mother under the *Child and Family Services Act* for leaving her children unattended

   d. determine whether the 8-year-old is mature enough to babysit

   e. do nothing because this has happened before and the children have always been found safe

6. Under the *Child and Family Services Act*, a child under 10 years of age shall not be left without making provision for his or her supervision and care that is reasonable in the circumstances.

   a. 14 years

   b. 10 years

   c. 16 years

   d. 12 years

7. The responsibility for establishing that a person has made adequate provision for a child's supervision and care rests with:

   a. the Children's Aid Society

   b. the police and the courts

   c. the person

8. Several 17-year-old female high school students have complained to the school principal that their 53-year-old science teacher slaps them on their rear ends and is always trying to look up their skirts. The teacher has been at this school for 25 years and there has never been a complaint about his behaviour. Given these circumstances, the principal should:

   a. talk to the teacher and advise him of the complaint

   b. notify the Children's Aid Society

   c. notify the police because a criminal offence has been committed

   d. do nothing because the science teacher has an excellent reputation and these are unsubstantiated allegations

9. The police are called to the A & P store. The manager brings them to the office, where a clerk is holding a 10-year-old child. The child was caught shoplifting several chocolate bars. This is the third time in a week that he has been caught. In the past, when the child's mother picked up the child, she seemed indifferent about the situation. Given these circumstances, the police would:

    a. charge the child with theft under the *Young Offenders Act*

    b. take the child home and release him into his mother's care

    c. take the child to a place of safety

    d. let the child go because all kids do stuff like this

10. The police receive information that 13-year-old, Allison Brown is absent without leave from a place of temporary detention and is staying with 22-year-old Jason Smith at 123 Northern Ave. A warrant is obtained and the police arrive at the address. They find Smith in the shower with Brown. Given these circumstances, the police could:

    a. apprehend Brown with or without the warrant and return her to the place of temporary detention from which she escaped

    b. apprehend Brown with the warrant and return her to any place of temporary detention

    c. arrest Brown for escaping custody and bring her to the local jail

    d. any of the above

    e. a or b

11. In the circumstances described in question #10, Jason Smith would be:

    a. arrested and charged with contributing to juvenile delinquency

    b. arrested and charged with sexual exploitation under s. 153 of the *Criminal Code*

    c. warned and told that if he knew that Brown was absent without leave, he could be charged with being an accessory to the escape

■ SHORT ANSWER

1. The police have come across a 14-year-old boy who is absent without permission from a place of open temporary detention. Describe the options available to the police for dealing with this child. Provide the authority for your response.

   APPREHEND CHILD AND BRING HIM WITHIN THE NEXT 48 HOURS

2. The police receive information that Allison Brown has again gone absent without permission from a place of temporary detention (see multiple-choice question #10). They receive reliable information that she is currently at 123 Northern Ave. and that she has purchased a bus ticket for Toronto. Given this information, what are the police authorized to do? Provide the authority for your response.

   ARREST HER AND BRING HER   W/O WARRANT

3. List the offences and the section numbers with which police officers who are charged with the responsibility of enforcing the *Child and Family Services Act* must be familiar.

■ **CASE STUDY**

You are a safety officer for your police service and one of your responsibilities is to attend at the elementary schools in your district and to teach young children about the dangers of associating with strangers. After one of these sessions, a 9-year-old girl approaches you and informs you that sometimes parents do the same things as strangers. She tells you that sometimes her stepfather touches her in places that she doesn't like and that sometimes she gets locked in the closet for misbehaving or not doing what her stepfather tells her. You speak to the child's teacher and she informs you that sometimes the child has bruises on her, but that they appear to be the type of bruises that all kids get. She also informs you that sometimes the child is very withdrawn. Given this information, you commence an investigation into the child's allegations.

1. Specify exactly what actions could be taken. Itemize the actions. Provide the authority(ies) for your response.

   NOTIFY THE SOCIET CHILDREN AIDS SOCIETY
   THIS IS A CHILD IN RISK AND IN NEED
   OF PROTECTION

2. Describe how the Children's Aid Society could be used to assist you in your investigation.

   INTERROGATE HER STEP FATHER
   ISSUING A RESTRAIN ORDER

3. Assume that the investigation revealed some mispropriety on behalf of the stepfather. On the basis of the girl's description of events, what charges, under both the *Child and Family Services Act* and the *Criminal Code*, could be processed?

   CHILD ABUSE .
   SEXUAL EXPLOITAITION , MOLESTING.

CHAPTER 11
The Police Services Act

CHAPTER OBJECTIVES

After completing this chapter, you should be able to:

◆ Understand key terms defined in the *Police Services Act*.

◆ State the six principles set out in the Act.

◆ State the five core services as set out in the Act.

◆ List the duties and powers of police officers as set out in the Act.

◆ Identify situations where use-of-force reports are required.

◆ State who is responsible for both discipline and the initial investigation of allegations of police misconduct.

◆ State the geographical areas in which a police officer has authority to act.

◆ List the offences contained in the code of conduct and explain whether off-duty misconduct is subject to discipline.

◆ Explain "standard operating procedure" with respect to the SIU.

INTRODUCTION

The *Police Services Act* is a lengthy and important statute that you must become familiar with and refer to when needed. You are expected to act in accordance with this Act at all times.

The *Police Services Act* sets out the five core services provided by the police: crime prevention, law enforcement, assistance to victims of crime, maintenance of public order, and emergency response.

The Act also describes the appropriate principles of policing and establishes the duties and powers of police officers. It makes the solicitor general responsible for monitoring police forces to ensure that the necessary services are provided for at both the municipal and provincial levels. It gives the solicitor general the power to monitor boards and police forces.

The Act also deals with police misconduct, including off-duty police misconduct, and contains procedures for dealing with police complaints. It establishes the Special Investigations Unit (SIU) and sets out procedures that the SIU must follow.

The Act also sets out when use-of-force reports must be filled out by police officers. Use-of-force reports are reports that explain and justify the circumstances in which police officers used force. Use-of-force reports are required not only when shootings and deaths occur, but also in less serious circumstances.

It is crucial for you as a police officer to be aware of the provisions of the *Police Services Act* and to follow them at all times.

POLICE SERVICES ACT

RSO 1990, Chapter P.15

1. Declaration of principles.— Police services shall be provided throughout Ontario in accordance with the following principles:

1. The need to ensure the safety and security of all persons and property in Ontario.

2. The importance of safeguarding the fundamental rights guaranteed by the *Canadian Charter of Rights and Freedoms* and the *Human Rights Code*.

3. The need for co-operation between the providers of police services and the communities they serve.

4. The importance of respect for victims of crime and understanding of their needs.

5. The need for sensitivity to the pluralistic, multiracial and multi-cultural character of Ontario society.

6. The need to ensure that police forces are representative of the communities they serve.

2. Definitions.— In this Act,

"association" means an association whose members belong to one police force and whose objects include the improvement of their working conditions and remuneration;

"board" means a municipal police services board;

"chief of police" means a municipal chief of police or the Commissioner of the Ontario Provincial Police and includes an acting chief of police;

"Commission" means the Ontario Civilian Commission on Police Services;

"Commissioner" means the Commissioner of the Ontario Provincial Police;

"member of a police force" means a police officer, and in the case of a municipal police force includes an employee who is not a police officer;

"municipality" includes district, metropolitan and regional municipalities and the County of Oxford;

"police force" means the Ontario Provincial Police or a municipal police force;

"police officer" means a chief of police or any other police officer, but does not include a special constable, a First Nations Constable, a municipal law enforcement officer or an auxiliary member of a police force;

"prescribed" means prescribed by the regulations;

"regulations" means the regulations made under this Act;

"Solicitor General" means the Solicitor General and Minister of Correctional Services or such other member of the Executive Council as may be designated by the Lieutenant Governor in Council.

PART I
RESPONSIBILITY FOR POLICE SERVICES

SOLICITOR GENERAL

3. (1) **Administration of Act.**— This Act shall be administered by the Solicitor General.

(2) **Duties and powers of Solicitor General.**— The Solicitor General shall,

(*a*) monitor police forces to ensure that adequate and effective police services are provided at the municipal and provincial levels;

(*b*) monitor boards and police forces to ensure that they comply with prescribed standards of service; ...

(*d*) develop and promote programs to enhance professional police practices, standards and training;

(*e*) conduct a system of inspection and review of police forces across Ontario;

(*f*) assist in the co-ordination of police services;

(*g*) consult with and advise boards, community policing advisory committees, municipal chiefs of police, employers of special constables and associations on matters relating to police and police services;

(*h*) develop, maintain and manage programs and statistical records and conduct research studies in respect of police services and related matters;

(*i*) provide to boards, community policing advisory committees and municipal chiefs of police information and advice respecting the management and operation of police forces, techniques in handling special problems and other information calculated to assist;

(*j*) issue directives and guidelines respecting policy matters;

(*k*) develop and promote programs for community-oriented police services;

(*l*) operate the Ontario Police College.

(3) **Ontario Police College continued.**— The police college known as the Ontario Police College for the training of members of police forces is continued.

MUNICIPALITIES

4. (1) **Police services in municipalities.**— Every municipality to which this subsection applies shall provide adequate and effective police services in accordance with its needs.

(2) **Core police services.**— Adequate and effective police services must include, at a minimum, all of the following police services:

1. Crime prevention.

2. Law enforcement.

3. Assistance to victims of crime.

4. Public order maintenance.

5. Emergency response.

(3) **Infrastructure for police services.**— In providing adequate and effective police services, a municipality shall be responsible for providing all the infrastructure and administration necessary for providing such services, including vehicles, boats, equipment, communication devices, buildings and supplies.

(4) **Application of subsection (1).**— Subsection (1) applies to,

(a) cities, towns, villages and townships (other than area municipalities within district, regional or metropolitan municipalities); and

(b) district municipalities, regional municipalities and metropolitan municipalities.

(5) **Exception, Oxford County.**— Subsection (1) does not apply to the County of Oxford but does apply to its area municipalities.

(6) **Same.**— Despite subsection (5) and sections 72, 73 and 74 of the *County of Oxford Act*, the councils of the County of Oxford and of all the area municipalities within the County of Oxford may agree to have subsection (1) apply to the County of Oxford and not to the area municipalities but, having made such agreement, the councils cannot thereafter revoke it. ...

5. Methods of providing municipal police services.— A municipality's responsibility to provide police services shall be discharged in one of the following ways:

1. The council may establish a police force, the members of which shall be appointed by the board under clause 31(1)(a).

2. The council may enter into an agreement under section 33 with one or more other councils to constitute a joint board and the joint board may appoint the members of a police force under clause 31(1)(a).

3. The council may enter into an agreement under section 6 with one or more other councils to amalgamate their police forces.

4. The council may enter into an agreement under section 6.1 with the council of another municipality to have its police services provided by the board of the other municipality, on the conditions set out in the agreement, if the municipality that is to receive the police services is contiguous to the municipality that is to provide the police services or is contiguous to any other municipality that receives police services from the same municipality.

5. The council may enter into an agreement under section 10, alone or jointly with one or more other councils, to have police services provided by the Ontario Provincial Police.

6. With the Commission's approval, the council may adopt a different method of providing police services.

5.1 (1) If municipality fails to provide police services.— If a municipality does not provide police services by one of the ways set out in section 5, the Ontario Provincial Police shall provide police services to the municipality.

(2) **Municipality to pay for O.P.P. services.**— A municipality that is provided police services by the Ontario Provincial Police under subsection (1) shall pay the Minister of Finance for the services, in the amount and the manner provided by the regulations.

(3) **Same.**— The amount owed by a municipality for the police services provided by the Ontario Provincial Police, if not collected by other means, may be deducted from any grant payable to the municipality out of provincial funds or may be recovered by a court action, with costs, as a debt due to Her Majesty.

(4) **Community policing advisory committee.**— One or more municipalities served by the same Ontario Provincial Police detachment that provides police services under this section may establish a community policing advisory committee.

(5) **Composition.**— If a community policing advisory committee is established, it shall be composed of one delegate for each municipality that is served by the same Ontario Provincial Police detachment and that chooses to send a delegate.

(6) **Functions.**— A community policing advisory committee shall advise the detachment commander of the Ontario Provincial Police detachment assigned to the municipality or municipalities, or his or her designate, with respect to objectives and priorities for police services in the municipality or municipalities.

(7) **Term of office.**— The term of office for a delegate to a community policing advisory committee shall be as set out by the council in his or her appointment, but shall not exceed the term of office of the council that appointed the delegate.

(8) **Same, and reappointment.**— A delegate to a community policing advisory committee may continue to sit after the expiry of the term of office of the council that appointed him or her until the appointment of his or her successor, and is eligible for reappointment.

(9) **Protection from liability.**— No action or other proceeding for damages shall be instituted against a community policing advisory committee or a delegate to a community policing advisory committee for any act done in good faith in the execution or intended execution of a duty or for any alleged neglect or default in the execution in good faith of a duty.

6. (1) Amalgamation of police forces.— Despite any other Act, the councils of two or more municipalities that have police forces may enter into an agreement to amalgamate them.

(2) **Contents of amalgamation agreement.**— The agreement shall deal with,

(*a*) the establishment and, subject to section 33, the composition of a joint board for the amalgamated police force.

(*b*) the amalgamation of the police forces and the appointment or transfer of their members;

(*c*) the joint board's use of the assets and its responsibility for the liabilities associated with the police forces;

(*d*) the budgeting of the cost for the operation of the amalgamated police force;

(*e*) any other matter that is necessary or advisable to effect the amalgamation.

(3) **Commission's approval.**— The agreement does not take effect until the Commission has approved the organization of the amalgamated police force.

(4) **Exception, board appointments.**— Appointments to a joint board for an amalgamated police force may be made before the agreement takes effect.

6.1 (1) Municipal agreements for providing police services.— The councils of two municipalities may enter into an agreement for the provision of police services for one municipality by the board of the other municipality, on the conditions set out in the agreement, if the municipality that is to receive the police services is contiguous to the municipality that is to provide the police services or is contiguous to any other municipality that receives police services from the same municipality.

(2) **Advisors to board.**— The council of a municipality that receives police services pursuant to an agreement made under subsection (1) may select a person to advise the other municipality's board with respect to objectives and priorities for police services in the municipality that receives the police services.

(3) **Term of office.**— The term of office for a person selected to advise another municipality's board shall be as set by the council when the person is selected, but shall not exceed the term of office of the council that selected him or her.

(4) **Same and reappointment.**— A person selected to advise another municipality's board may continue to sit after the expiry of the term of office of the council that selected him or her until the selection of his or her successor, and is eligible for reappointment.

(5) **Protection from liability.**— No action or other proceeding for damages shall be instituted against a person selected to advise another municipality's board for any act done in good faith in the execution or intended execution of a duty or for any alleged neglect or default in the execution in good faith of a duty.

7. (1) **Municipal agreements for sharing police services.**— Two or more boards may agree that one board will provide some police services to the other or others, on the conditions set out in the agreement.

(2) **Limitation.**— Two or more boards may not agree under subsection (1) that the police force of one board will provide the other board or boards with all the police services that a municipality is required to provide under section 4.

(3) **Municipal agreements with O.P.P.**— The board of a municipality may agree with the Commissioner or with the local detachment commander of the Ontario Provincial Police that the Ontario Provincial Police will provide some police services to the municipality, on the conditions set out in the agreement, and subsections 10(7) and (8) apply to the agreement.

8. (1) **Additional municipal police forces.**— A municipality to which subsection 4(1) (obligation to provide police services) does not apply may, with the Commission's approval, establish and maintain a police force.

(2) **Transition.**— An approval given or deemed to have been given under section 19 of the *Police Act*, being chapter 381 of the Revised Statutes of Ontario, 1980, in respect of a police force that was being maintained on the 30th day of December, 1990, shall be deemed to have been given under this section.

(3) **Revocation.**— The Commission may revoke an approval given or deemed to have been given under this section.

9. (1) **Failure to provide police services.**— If the Commission finds that a municipality to which subsection 4(1) applies is not providing police services, it may request that the Commissioner have the Ontario Provincial Police give assistance.

(2) **Inadequate police services.**— If the Commission finds that a municipal police force is not providing adequate and effective police services or is not complying with this Act or the regulations, it may communicate that finding to the board of the municipality and direct the board to take the measures that the Commission considers necessary.

(3) **Idem.**— If the board does not comply with the direction, the Commission may request that the Commissioner have the Ontario Provincial Police give assistance.

(4) **Crown Attorney's request.**— In any area for which a municipality is required to provide police services, the Crown Attorney may request that the Commissioner have the Ontario Provincial Police give assistance.

(5) **Board's request.**— A board may, by resolution, request that the Commissioner have the Ontario Provincial Police give assistance.

(6) **Request of chief of police in emergency.**— A municipal chief of police who is of the opinion that an emergency exists in the municipality may request that the Commissioner have the Ontario Provincial Police give assistance.

(7) **Chief of police to advise board.**— A chief of police who makes a request under subsection (6) shall advise the chair of the board of the fact as soon as possible.

(8) **Assistance of O.P.P.**— When a request is made under this section, the Commissioner shall have the Ontario Provincial Police give such temporary or emergency assistance as he or she considers necessary and shall have the Ontario Provincial Police stop giving temporary or emergency assistance when he or she considers it appropriate to do so.

(9) **Cost of services.**— The Commissioner shall certify the cost of the services provided under this section by the Ontario Provincial Police and, unless the Solicitor General directs otherwise, the municipality shall pay that amount to the Minister of Finance.

(10) **Same.**— The amount owed by a municipality for the police services provided by the Ontario Provincial Police, if not collected by other means, may be deducted from any grant payable to the municipality out of provincial funds or may be recovered by a court action, with costs, as a debt due to Her Majesty.

10. (1) **Municipal agreements for provision of police services by O.P.P.**— The Solicitor General may enter into an agreement with the council of a municipality or jointly with the councils of two or more municipalities for the provision of police services for the municipality or municipalities by the Ontario Provincial Police.

(2) **Board required.**— In order for a municipality to enter into art agreement under this section, the municipality must have a board.

(3) **Same.**— In order for two or more municipalities to enter into an agreement under this section, the municipalities must have a joint board.

(4) **Transition.**— If an agreement under this section was entered into, before section 10 of the Police Services Amendment Act, 1997 comes into force, by a municipality that did not have a board at the time, the agreement remains valid and enforceable despite subsection (2), but the agreement may not be renewed unless the municipality has a board.

(5) **Collective bargaining.**— No agreement shall be entered into under this section if, in the Solicitor General's opinion, a council seeks the agreement for the purpose of defeating the collective bargaining provisions of this Act.

(6) **Duties of O.P.P.**— When the agreement comes into effect, the Ontario Provincial Police detachment assigned to the municipality or municipalities shall provide police services for the municipality or municipalities, and shall

perform any other duties, including by-law enforcement, that are specified in the agreement.

(7) **Payment into Consolidated Revenue Fund.**— The amounts received from municipalities under agreements entered into under this section shall be paid into the Consolidated Revenue Fund.

(8) **Collection of amounts owed.**— The amount owed by a municipality under the agreement, if not collected by other means, may be deducted from any grant payable to the municipality out of provincial funds or may be recovered by a court action, with costs, as a debt due to Her Majesty.

(9) **Role of board.**— If one or more municipalities enters into an agreement under this section, the board or joint board shall advise the Ontario Provincial Police detachment commander assigned to the municipality or municipalities, or his or her designate, with respect to police services in the municipality or municipalities and shall,

(*a*) participate in the selection of the detachment commander of the detachment assigned to the municipality or municipalities;

(*b*) generally determine objectives and priorities for police services, after consultation with the detachment commander or his or her designate;

(*c*) establish, after consultation with the detachment commander or his or her designate, any local policies with respect to police services (but the board or joint board shall not establish provincial policies of the Ontario Provincial Police with respect to police services);

(*d*) monitor the performance of the detachment commander;

(*e*) receive regular reports from the detachment commander or his or her designate on disclosures and decisions made under section 49 (secondary activities);

(*f*) review the detachment commander's administration of the complaints system under Part V and receive regular reports from the detachment commander or his or her designate on his or her administration of the complaints system.

(10) **Non-application of certain sections.**— If one or more municipalities enters into an agreement under this section, section 31 (responsibilities of board), section 38 (municipal police force) and section 39 (estimates) do not apply to the municipality or municipalities.

11. (1) **Fines.**— This section applies if a municipality is entitled to receive fines paid as a result of prosecutions instituted by police officers of the municipal police force.

(2) **Idem.**— If the municipality does not have its own police force because of an agreement under section 7 or 10, the police officers who are assigned to the municipality under the agreement shall, for the purposes of determining entitlement to fines, be deemed to be police officers of the municipal police force. ...

13. (1) **Special areas.**— If, because of the establishment of a business or for any other reason, special circumstances or abnormal conditions in an area make it inequitable, in the Solicitor General's opinion, to impose the responsibility for police services on a municipality or on the Province, the Lieutenant Governor in Council may designate the area as a special area.

(2) **Agreement for provision of police services by O.P.P.**— The person who operates the business or owns the special area shall enter into an agreement

with the Solicitor General for the provision of police services by the Ontario Provincial Police for the special area.

(3) **Duties of O.P.P., payment.**— Subsections 10(6) and (7) apply to the agreement with necessary modifications.

(4) **Failure to enter into agreement.**— If the person who operates the business or owns the special area does not enter into an agreement as subsection (2) requires, the Ontario Provincial Police shall provide police services for the area.

(5) **Cost of services.**— The costs of the services may be recovered from the person by a court action, with costs, as a debt due to Her Majesty.

14. Police services outside municipality.— A municipality that has an interest in land outside the territory of the municipality may agree to pay all or part of the cost of providing police services for the land.

15. (1) **Municipal by-law enforcement officers.**— A municipal council may appoint persons to enforce the by-laws of the municipality.

(2) **Peace officers.**— Municipal law enforcement officers are peace officers for the purpose of enforcing municipal by-laws.

16. Aid to survivors.— A municipal council may grant financial or other assistance for the benefit of the surviving spouses and children of members of the municipal police force who die from injuries received or illnesses contracted in the discharge of their duties.

ONTARIO PROVINCIAL POLICE

17. (1) **Commissioner.**— There shall be a Commissioner of the Ontario Provincial Police who shall be appointed by the Lieutenant Governor in Council.

(2) **Functions.**— Subject to the Solicitor General's direction, the Commissioner has the general control and administration of the Ontario Provincial Police and the employees connected with it. ...

(4) **Annual report.**— After the end of each calendar year, the Commissioner shall file with the Solicitor General an annual report on the affairs of the Ontario Provincial Police.

18. (1) **Composition of O.P.P.**— The Ontario Provincial Police shall consist of the Commissioner and other police officers appointed under the *Public Service Act*.

(2) **Ranks.**— The Commissioner shall establish the ranks within the Ontario Provincial Police and shall determine the rank of each police officer.

(3) **Commissioned officers.**— The Lieutenant Governor in Council may name police officers of the Ontario Provincial Police to the rank of commissioned officers and may authorize the issue of commissions to them under the Great Seal.

(4) **Employees.**— The Commissioner may appoint such other employees as are required in connection with the Ontario Provincial Police.

19. (1) **Responsibilities of O.P.P.**— The Ontario Provincial Police have the following responsibilities:

> 1. Providing police services in respect of the parts of Ontario that do not have municipal police forces other than municipal law enforcement officers.

2. Providing police services in respect of all navigable bodies and courses of water in Ontario, except those that lie within municipalities designated by the Solicitor General.

3. Maintaining a traffic patrol on the King's Highway, except the parts designated by the Solicitor General.

4. Maintaining a traffic patrol on the connecting links within the meaning of section 21 of the *Public Transportation and Highway Improvement Act* that are designated by the Solicitor General.

5. Maintaining investigative services to assist municipal police forces on the Solicitor General's direction or at the Crown Attorney's request.

(2) **Municipal by-laws.**— The Ontario Provincial Police have no responsibilities in connection with municipal by-laws, except under agreements made in accordance with section 10.

(3) **O.P.P. may charge for services.**— The Ontario Provincial Police may, with the approval of the Solicitor General, charge a municipality, a law enforcement agency or any prescribed corporation or organization for any service it provides to them under this Act.

(4) **Payment into Consolidated Revenue Fund.**— The amounts received pursuant to a charge imposed under subsection (3) shall be paid into the Consolidated Revenue Fund.

(5) **Collection of amounts owed.**— The amount owed pursuant to a charge imposed under subsection (3), if not collected by other means, may be recovered by a court action, with costs, as a debt due to Her Majesty and, if the amount is owed by a municipality, may be deducted from any grant payable to the municipality out of provincial funds.

20. Aid to survivors.— The Lieutenant Governor in Council may, out of money appropriated for that purpose by the Legislature, grant financial or other assistance for the benefit of the surviving spouses and children of members of the Ontario Provincial Police who die from injuries received or illnesses contracted in the discharge of their duties.

PART II

ONTARIO CIVILIAN COMMISSION ON POLICE SERVICES

21. (1) **Commission continued.**— The commission known in English as the Ontario Civilian Commission on Police Services and in French as Commission civile des services policiers de l'Ontario is continued.

(2) **Composition.**— The Commission shall consist of such members as are appointed by the Lieutenant Governor in Council.

(3) **Chair, vice-chairs.**— The Lieutenant Governor in Council may designate one of the members of the Commission to be the chair and one or more members of the Commission to be vice-chairs.

(4) **Employees.**— Such employees as the Commission considers necessary to carry out its duties may be appointed under the *Public Service Act*.

(5) **Delegation.**— The chair may authorize a member or employee of the Commission to exercise the Commission's powers and perform its duties with

respect to a particular matter, but the authority conferred on the Commission by sections 23 and 24 may not be delegated.

(6) **Quorum.**— The chair shall determine the number of members of the Commission that constitutes a quorum for any purpose, and may determine that one member constitutes a quorum.

(7) **Annual report.**— After the end of each calendar year, the Commission shall file with the Solicitor General an annual report on its affairs.

(8) **Expenses.**— The money required for the Commission's purposes shall be paid out of the amounts appropriated by the Legislature for that purpose.

(9) **Protection from personal liability.**— No action or other proceeding for damages shall be instituted against a member of the Commission for any act done in good faith in the execution or intended execution of his or her duty or for any alleged neglect or default in the execution in good faith of that duty.

(10) **Transition.**— The members of the Commission who are in office immediately before section 15 of the Police Services Amendment Act, 1997 comes into force may continue to be members until the expiry of their terms.

22. (1) **Powers and duties of Commission.**— The Commission's powers and duties include,

(*a*) if the Solicitor General advises the Commission that a board or municipal police force is not complying with prescribed standards of police services,

(i) directing the board or police force to comply, and

(ii) if the Commission considers it appropriate, taking measures in accordance with subsection 23(1); ...

(*c*) conducting investigations with respect to municipal police matters under section 25;

(*d*) conducting inquiries into matters relating to crime and law enforcement under section 26;

(*e*) conducting inquiries, on its own motion, in respect of a complaint or complaints made about the policies of or services provided by a police force or about the conduct of a police officer and the disposition of such complaint or complaints by a chief of police or board;

(*e.1*) conducting reviews under section 72, at the request of a complainant, into the decision that a complaint is about the policies of or services provided by a police force or is about the conduct of a police officer, that a complaint is frivolous or vexatious, made in bad faith or unsubstantiated, that the complaint will not be dealt with because it was made more than six months after the facts on which it is based occurred, that the complainant was not directly affected by the policy, service or conduct that is the subject of the complaint or that the misconduct or unsatisfactory work performance was not of a serious nature;

(*e.2*) making recommendations with respect to the policies of or services provided by a police force by sending the recommendations, with any supporting documents, to the Solicitor General, the chief of police, the association, if any, and, in the case of a municipal police force, the board.

(*f*) hearing and disposing of appeals by members of police forces and complainants in accordance with Part V.

(2) **Powers of Commission in investigations and inquiries.**— When the Commission conducts an investigation or inquiry, it has all the powers of a commission under Part II of the *Public Inquiries Act*, which Part applies to the investigation or inquiry as if it were an inquiry under that Act.

(3) *Statutory Powers Procedure Act* **applicable to hearings.**— The *Statutory Powers Procedure Act* does not apply to the Commission, except to a hearing conducted by the Commission under subsection 23(1), 25(4), (4.1) or (5), 39(5), 47(5), 65(9), 70(2), (3) or (4) or 116(1).

23. (1) **Sanctions for failure to comply with prescribed standards of police services.**— If the Commission is of the opinion, after holding a hearing, that a board or municipal police force has flagrantly or repeatedly failed to comply with prescribed standards of police services, the Commission may take any of the following measures or any combination of them:

1. Suspending the chief of police, one or more members of the board, or the whole board, for a specified period.

2. Removing the chief of police, one or more members of the board, or the whole board from office.

3. Disbanding the police force and requiring the Ontario Provincial Police to provide police services for the municipality.

4. Appointing an administrator to perform specified functions with respect to police matters in the municipality for a specified period. ...

(3) **Suspension with or without pay.**— If the Commission suspends the chief of police or members of the board who are entitled to remuneration under subsection 27(12), it shall specify whether the suspension is with or without pay. ...

(5) **Powers of administrator.**— An administrator appointed under paragraph 4 of subsection (1) has all the powers necessary for the performance of his or her functions.

(6) **Replacement of chief of police.**— If the Commission suspends or removes the chief of police, it may appoint a person to replace him or her.

(7) **Parties.**— The parties to the hearing are the chief of police, the board, any member of the board that the Commission designates and, if the Commission so directs, the association or associations representing members of the police force.

(8) **Idem.**— The Commission may add parties at any stage of the hearing on the conditions it considers proper.

(9) **Replacement of suspended or removed member.**— If the Commission suspends a member of a board or removes him or her from office, the municipal council or the Lieutenant Governor in Council, as the case may be, shall appoint a person to replace the member.

(10) **Consequences of removal and suspension.**— A member who has been removed shall not subsequently be a member of any board, and a member who has been suspended shall not be reappointed during the period of suspension.

(11) **Appeal to Divisional Court.**— A party may appeal to the Divisional Court within thirty days of receiving notice of the Commission's decision.

(12) **Grounds for appeal.**— An appeal may be made on a question that is not a question of fact alone, or from a penalty, or both. ...

24. (1) **Emergency, interim order.**— The Commission may make an interim order under subsection 23(1), without notice and without holding a hearing, if it is of the opinion that an emergency exists and that the interim order is necessary in the public interest.

(2) **Restriction.**— The Commission shall not remove a person from office or disband a police force by means of an interim order.

25. (1) **Investigations into police matters.**— The Commission may, at the Solicitor General's request, at a board's request, at a municipal council's request or of its own motion, investigate, inquire into and report on,

(a) the conduct or the performance of duties of a police officer, a municipal chief of police, an auxiliary member of a police force, a special constable, municipal law enforcement officer or a member of a board.

(b) the administration of a municipal police force;

(c) the manner in which police services are provided for a municipality;

(d) the police needs of a municipality.

(2) **Cost of investigation.**— The cost of an investigation conducted at a council's request shall be paid by the municipality, unless the Solicitor General directs otherwise.

(3) **Report.**— The Commission shall communicate its report of an investigation under subsection (1) to the Solicitor General at his or her request and to the board or council at its request, and may communicate the report to any other person as the Commission considers advisable.

(4) **Actions taken, police officer, municipal chief of police.**— If the Commission concludes, after a hearing, that the conduct of a police officer or municipal chief of police is proved on clear and convincing evidence to be misconduct or unsatisfactory work performance, it may direct that any action described in section 68, as specified by the Commission, be taken with respect to the police officer or municipal chief of police or it may direct that the police officer or municipal chief of police be retired if he or she is entitled to retire.

(4.1) **Actions taken, auxiliary member, special constable, municipal law enforcement officer.**— If the Commission concludes, after a hearing, that an auxiliary member of a police force, a special constable or a municipal law enforcement officer is not performing or is incapable of performing the duties of his or her position in a satisfactory manner, it may direct that,

(a) the person be demoted as the Commission specifies, permanently or for a specified period;

(b) the person be dismissed;

(c) the person be retired, if the person is entitled to retire; or

(d) the person's appointment be suspended or revoked.

(5) **Penalties, member of board.**— If the Commission concludes, after a hearing, that a member of a board is guilty of misconduct or is not performing or is incapable of performing the duties of his or her position in a satisfactory manner, it may remove or suspend the member.

(6) **Appeal to Divisional Court.**— A member of a police force or of a board on whom a penalty is imposed under subsection (4) or (5) may appeal to the Divisional Court within thirty days of receiving notice of the Commission's decision.

(7) **Grounds for appeal.**— An appeal may be made on a question that is not a question of fact alone, or from a penalty, or both.

(8) **Replacement of suspended or removed member.**— If the Commission suspends a member of a board or removes him or her from office, the municipal council or the Lieutenant Governor in Council, as the case may be, shall appoint a person to replace the member.

(9) **Consequences of removal and suspension.**— A member who has been removed shall not subsequently be a member of any board, and a member who has been suspended shall not be reappointed during the period of suspension.

26. (1) **Inquiries respecting crime and law enforcement.**— The Lieutenant Governor in Council may direct the Commission to inquire into and report to the Lieutenant Governor in Council on any matter relating to crime or law enforcement, and shall define the scope of the inquiry in the direction.

(2) *Public Inquiries Act* **applies.**— Section 6 (stated case) of the *Public Inquiries Act* applies to inquiries conducted under this section.

(3) **Rights of witnesses.**— Witnesses at inquiries conducted under this section have the right to retain and instruct counsel and all the other rights of witnesses in civil courts.

(4) **Offence.**— Any person who knowingly discloses, without the Commission's consent, evidence taken in private at an inquiry conducted under this section or information likely to identify the witness is guilty of an offence and on conviction is liable to a fine of not more than $5,000.

PART III
MUNICIPAL POLICE SERVICES BOARDS

27. (1) **Police services boards.**— There shall be a police services board for every municipality that maintains a police force.

(2) **Boards of commissioners of police continued as police services boards.**— Every board of commissioners of police constituted or continued under the *Police Act*, being chapter 381 of the Revised Statutes of Ontario, 1980, or any other Act and in existence on the 31st day of December, 1990, is continued as a police services board.

(3) **Name.**— A board shall be known as (insert name of municipality) Police Services Board and may also be known as Commission des services policiers de (insert name of municipality).

(4) **Three member boards in smaller municipalities.**— The board of a municipality whose population according to the last enumeration taken under section 15 of the *Assessment Act* does not exceed 25,000 shall consist of,

  (*a*) the head of the municipal council or, if the head chooses not to be a member of the board, another member of the council appointed by resolution of the council;

  (*b*) one person appointed by resolution of the council, who is neither a member of the council nor an employee of the municipality; and

  (*c*) one person appointed by the Lieutenant Governor in Council.

(5) **Five-member boards in larger municipalities.**— The board of a municipality, other than a district, regional or metropolitan municipality, whose population according to the last enumeration taken under section 15 of the *Assessment Act* exceeds 25,000 shall consist of,

(*a*) the head of the municipal council or, if the head chooses not to be a member of the board, another member of the council appointed by resolution of the council;

(*b*) one member of the council appointed by resolution of the council;

(*c*) one person appointed by resolution of the council, who is neither a member of the council nor an employee of the municipality; and

(*d*) two persons appointed by the Lieutenant Governor in Council.

(6) **Smaller municipalities, option to expand board.**— The council of a municipality to which subsection (4) would otherwise apply may determine, by resolution, that the composition of its board shall be as described in subsection (5).

(7) **Transition.**— A resolution passed under clause 8(2a)(b) of the *Police Act*, being chapter 381 of the Revised Statutes of Ontario, 1980, before the 31st day of December, 1990, shall be deemed to have been passed under subsection (6).

(8) **District, regional and metropolitan municipalities.**— The board of a district, regional or metropolitan municipality shall consist of,

(*a*) the head of the municipal council or, if the head chooses not to be a member of the board, another member of the council appointed by resolution of the council;

(*b*) one member of the council appointed by resolution of the municipal council;

(*c*) one person appointed by resolution of the council, who is neither a member of the council nor an employee of the district, regional or metropolitan municipality; and

(*d*) two persons appointed by the Lieutenant Governor in Council.

(9) **Seven-member boards in certain circumstances.**— The council of a municipality whose population according to the last enumeration taken under section 15 of the *Assessment Act* exceeds 300,000 may apply to the Lieutenant Governor in Council for an increase in the size of its board; if the Lieutenant Governor in Council approves the application, the board shall consist of,

(*a*) the head of the municipal council or, if the head chooses not to be a member of the board, another member of the council appointed by resolution of the council;

(*b*) two members of the council appointed by resolution of the council;

(*c*) one person appointed by resolution of the council, who is neither a member of the council nor an employee of the municipality; and

(*d*) three persons appointed by the Lieutenant Governor in Council,

(10) **Vacancies.**— If the position of a member appointed by the Lieutenant Governor in Council becomes vacant, the Solicitor General may appoint a replacement to act until the Lieutenant Governor in Council makes a new appointment.

(10.1) **Term of office.**— The term of office for a member appointed by resolution of a council shall be as set out by the council in his or her appointment, but shall not exceed the term of office of the council that appointed the member.

(10.2) **Same, and reappointment.**— A member appointed by resolution of a council may continue to sit after the expiry of his or her term of office until the appointment of his or her successor, and is eligible for reappointment.

(11) **Idem.**— If the position of a member who is appointed by a municipal council or holds office by virtue of being the head of a municipal council be-

comes vacant, the board shall notify the council, which shall forthwith appoint a replacement.

(12) **Remuneration.**— The council shall pay the members of the board who are appointed by the Lieutenant Governor in Council or Solicitor General remuneration that is at least equal to the prescribed amount.

(13) **Persons who are ineligible to be members of a board.**— A judge, a justice of the peace, a police officer and a person who practises criminal law as a defence counsel may not be a member of a board.

(14) **Transition.**— The members of a board, including persons described in subsection (13), who are in office immediately before subsection 19(3) of the Police Services Amendment Act, 1997 comes into force may continue to be members until the expiry of their terms. ...

28. (1) **Election of chair.**— The members of a board shall elect a chair at the board's first meeting in each year.

(2) **Vice-chair.**— The members of a board may also elect a vice-chair at the first meeting in each year, and the vice-chair shall act as the chair if the chair is absent or if the chair's position is vacant.

29. (1) **Protection from personal liability.**— No action or other proceeding for damages shall be instituted against a member of a board for any act done in good faith in the execution or intended execution of his or her duty or for any alleged neglect or default in the execution in good faith of that duty.

(2) **Board's liability.**— Subsection (1) does not relieve a board of liability for a member's acts or omissions, and the board is liable as if that subsection had not been enacted and as if the member were the board's employee.

30. (1) **Board may contract, sue and be sued.**— A board may contract, sue and be sued in its own name.

(2) **Members not liable for board's contracts.**— The members of a board are not personally liable for the board's contracts.

31. (1) **Responsibilities of boards.**— A board is responsible for the provision of adequate and effective police services in the municipality and shall,

(a) appoint the members of the municipal police force;

(b) generally determine, after consultation with the chief of police, objectives and priorities with respect to police services in the municipality;

(c) establish policies for the effective management of the police force;

(d) recruit and appoint the chief of police and any deputy chief of police, and annually determine their remuneration and working conditions, taking their submissions into account;

(e) direct the chief of police and monitor his or her performance;

(f) establish policies respecting the disclosure by chiefs of police of personal information about individuals;

(g) receive regular reports from the chief of police on disclosures and decisions made under section 49 (secondary activities);

(h) establish guidelines with respect to the indemnification of members of the police force for legal costs under section 50;

(i) establish guidelines for dealing with complaints made under Part V;

(j) review the chief of police's administration of the complaints system under Part V and receive regular reports from the chief of police on his or her administration of the complaints system.

(2) **Members of police force under board's jurisdiction.**— The members of the police force, whether they were appointed by the board or not, are under the board's jurisdiction.

(3) **Restriction.**— The board may give orders and directions to the chief of police, but not to other members of the police force, and no individual member of the board shall give orders or directions to any member of the police force.

(4) **Idem.**— The board shall not direct the chief of police with respect to specific operational decisions or with respect to the day-to-day operation of the police force.

(5) **Training of board members.**— The board shall ensure that its members undergo any training that the Solicitor General may provide or require.

(6) **Rules re management of police force.**— The board may, by by-law, make rules for the effective management of the police force.

(7) **Guidelines re secondary activities.**— The board may establish guidelines consistent with section 49 for disclosing secondary activities and for deciding whether to permit such activities.

32. Oath of office.— Before entering on the duties of office, a member of a board shall take an oath or affirmation of office in the prescribed form.

33. (1) **Agreement to constitute joint board.**— Despite any special Act, the councils of two or more municipalities may enter into an agreement to constitute a joint board.

(2) **Consent of Solicitor General required.**— The agreement must be authorized by by-laws of the councils of the participating municipalities and requires the consent of the Solicitor General.

(3) **Application of Act to joint boards.**— The provisions of this Act that apply to boards also apply with necessary modifications to joint boards.

(4) **Three-member joint boards.**— The joint board of municipalities whose combined population according to the last enumeration taken under section 15 of the *Assessment Act* does not exceed 25,000 shall consist of,

    (*a*) one person who is a member of the council of a participating municipality, appointed by agreement of the councils of the participating municipalities;

    (*b*) one person appointed by agreement of the councils of the participating municipalities, who is neither a member of a council of a participating municipality nor an employee of a participating municipality; and

    (*c*) one person appointed by the Lieutenant Governor in Council.

(5) **Five-member joint boards.**— The joint board of municipalities whose combined population according to the last enumeration taken under section 15 of the *Assessment Act* exceeds 25,000 shall consist of,

    (*a*) two persons who are members of the councils of any participating municipalities, appointed by agreement of the councils of the participating municipalities;

    (*b*) one person appointed by agreement of the councils of the participating municipalities, who is neither a member of a council of a participating municipality nor an employee of a participating municipality; and

    (*c*) two persons appointed by the Lieutenant Governor in Council.

(6) **Option to expand joint board.**— The councils of participating municipalities to which subsection (4) would otherwise apply may determine, by reso-

lution of each of them, that the composition of their joint board shall be as described in subsection (5).

(7) **Seven-member joint boards.**— Where the combined population of the participating municipalities according to the last enumeration taken under section 15 of the *Assessment Act* exceeds 300,000, the councils of the participating municipalities may apply to the Lieutenant Governor in Council for an increase in the size of their joint board; if the Lieutenant Governor in Council approves the application, the joint board shall consist of,

(*a*) three persons who are members of the councils of any participating municipalities, appointed by agreement of the councils of the participating municipalities;

(*b*) one person appointed by agreement of the councils of the participating municipalities, who is neither a member of a council of a participating municipality nor an employee of a participating municipality; and

(*c*) three persons appointed by the Lieutenant Governor in Council.

34. Delegation.— A board may delegate to two or more of its members any authority conferred on it by this Act, except, ...

(*b*) the authority to bargain under Part VIII, which the board may delegate to one or more members.

35. (1) **Meetings.**— The board shall hold at least four meetings each year.

(2) **Quorum.**— A majority of the members of the board constitutes a quorum.

(3) **Proceedings open to the public.**— Meetings and hearings conducted by the board shall be open to the public, subject to subsection (4), and notice of them shall be published in the manner that the board determines.

(4) **Exception.**— The board may exclude the public from all or part of a meeting or hearing if it is of the opinion that,

(*a*) matters involving public security may be disclosed and, having regard to the circumstances, the desirability of avoiding their disclosure in the public interest outweighs the desirability of adhering to the principle that proceedings be open to the public; or

(*b*) intimate financial or personal matters or other matters may be disclosed of such a nature, having regard to the circumstances, that the desirability of avoiding their disclosure in the interest of any person affected or in the public interest outweighs the desirability of adhering to the principle that proceedings be open to the public.

36. Admissibility of documents.— A document purporting to be a by-law of the board signed by a member or purporting to be a copy of such a by-law certified correct by a member is admissible in evidence without proof of the signature or authority of the person signing.

37. Rules and procedures.— A board shall establish its own rules and procedures in performing its duties under this Act and, except when conducting a hearing under subsection 65(9), the *Statutory Powers Procedure Act* does not apply to a board.

38. Municipal police force.— A municipal police force shall consist of a chief of police and such other police officers and other employees as are adequate, and shall be provided with adequate equipment and facilities.

39. (1) **Estimates.**— The board shall submit operating and capital estimates to the municipal council that will show, separately, the amounts that will be required, (*a*) to maintain the police force and provide it with equipment and facilities; and

(*b*) to pay the expenses of the board's operation other than the remuneration of board members.

(2) **Same.**— The format of the estimates, the period that they cover and the timetable for their submission shall be as determined by the council.

(3) **Budget.**— Upon reviewing the estimates, the council shall establish an overall budget for the board for the purposes described in clauses (1)(a) and (b) and, in doing so, the council is not bound to adopt the estimates submitted by the board.

(4) **Same.**— In establishing an overall budget for the board, the council does not have the authority to approve or disapprove specific items in the estimates.

(5) **Commission hearing in case of dispute.**— If the board is not satisfied that the budget established for it by the council is sufficient to maintain an adequate number of police officers or other employees of the police force or to provide the police force with adequate equipment or facilities, the board may request that the Commission determine the question and the Commission, shall, after a hearing, do so.

40. (1) **Reduction or abolition of police force.**— A board may terminate the employment of a member of the police force for the purpose of abolishing the police force or reducing its size if the Commission consents and if the abolition or reduction does not contravene this Act.

(2) **Criteria for Commission's consent.**— The Commission shall consent to the termination of the employment of a member of the police force under subsection (1) only if,

(*a*) the member and the board have made an agreement dealing with severance pay or agreed to submit the matter to arbitration; or

(*b*) the Commission has made an order under subsection (3).

(3) **Order imposing arbitration.**— If the member and the board do not make an agreement dealing with severance pay and do not agree to submit the matter to arbitration, the Commission, if it is of the opinion that it would be appropriate to permit the abolition of the police force or the reduction of its size, may order the member and the board to submit the matter to arbitration and may give any necessary directions in that connection.

(4) **Arbitration.**— Section 124 applies to an arbitration referred to in this section with necessary modifications.

PART IV
POLICE OFFICERS AND OTHER POLICE STAFF

CHIEF OF POLICE

41. (1) **Duties of chief of police.**— The duties of a chief of police include,

(*a*) in the case of a municipal police force, administering the police force and overseeing its operation in accordance with the objectives, priorities and policies established by the board under subsection 31(1);

(*b*) ensuring that members of the police force carry out their duties in accordance with this Act and the regulations and in a manner that reflects the needs of the community, and that discipline is maintained in the police force;

(c) ensuring that the police force provides community-oriented police services;

(d) administering the complaints system in accordance with Part V. ...

(1.1) **Power to disclose personal information.**— Despite any other Act, a chief of police, or a person designated by him or her for the purpose of this subsection, may disclose personal information about an individual in accordance with the regulations.

(1.2) **Purpose of disclosure.**— Any disclosure made under subsection (1.1) shall be for one or more of the following purposes:

1. Protection of the public.

2. Protection of victims of crime.

3. Keeping victims of crime informed of the law enforcement, judicial or correctional processes relevant to the crime that affected them.

4. Law enforcement.

5. Correctional purposes.

6. Administration of justice.

7. Enforcement of and compliance with any federal or provincial Act, regulation or government program.

8. Keeping the public informed of the law enforcement, judicial or correctional processes respecting any individual.

(1.3) **Same.**— Any disclosure made under subsection (1.1) shall be deemed to be in compliance with clauses 42(e) of the *Freedom of Information and Protection of Privacy Act* and 32(e) of the Municipal *Freedom of Information and Protection of Privacy Act*.

(1.4) **Same.**— If personal information is disclosed under subsection (1.1) to a ministry, agency or institution, the ministry, agency or institution shall collect such information and subsections 39(2) of the *Freedom of Information and Protection of Privacy Act* and 29(2) of the Municipal *Freedom of Information and Protection of Privacy Act* do not apply to that collection of personal information.

(2) **Chief of police reports to board.**— The chief of police reports to the board and shall obey its lawful orders and directions.

POLICE OFFICERS

42. (1) **Duties of police officer.**— The duties of a police officer include,

(a) preserving the peace;

(b) preventing crimes and other offences and providing assistance and encouragement to other persons in their prevention;

(c) assisting victims of crime;

(d) apprehending criminals and other offenders and others who may lawfully be taken into custody;

(e) laying charges and participating in prosecutions;

(*f*) executing warrants that are to be executed by police officers and performing related duties;

(*g*) performing the lawful duties that the chief of police assigns;

(*h*) in the case of a municipal police force and in the case of an agreement under section 10 (agreement for provision of police services by O.P.P.), enforcing municipal by-laws;

(*i*) completing the prescribed training.

(2) **Power to act throughout Ontario.**— A police officer has authority to act as such throughout Ontario.

(3) **Powers and duties of common law constable.**— A police officer has the powers and duties ascribed to a constable at common law.

43. (1) **Criteria for hiring.**— No person shall be appointed as a police officer unless he or she,

(*a*) is a Canadian citizen or a permanent resident of Canada;

(*b*) is at least eighteen years of age;

(*c*) is physically and mentally able to perform the duties of the position, having regard to his or her own safety and the safety of members of the public;

(*d*) is of good moral character and habits; and

(*e*) has successfully completed at least four years of secondary school education or its equivalent.

(2) **Idem.**— A candidate for appointment as a police officer shall provide any relevant information or material that is lawfully requested in connection with his or her application.

44. (1) **Probationary period.**— A municipal police officer's probationary period begins on the day he or she is appointed and ends on the later of,

(*a*) the first anniversary of the day of appointment;

(*b*) the first anniversary of the day the police officer completes an initial period of training at the Ontario Police College.

(2) **Time for completing initial training.**— The police officer shall complete the initial period of training within six months of the day of appointment.

(3) **Termination of employment during probationary period.**— A board may terminate a police officer's employment at any time during his or her probationary period but, before doing so, shall give the police officer reasonable information with respect to the reasons for the termination and an opportunity to reply, orally or in writing, as the board may determine.

(3.1) **Part V does not apply.**— Part V does not apply in the case of the termination of a police officer's employment under subsection (3).

(4) **Only one probationary period.**— Subsections (1), (2) and (3) do not apply to a police officer who has completed a probationary period with another municipal police force, the Ontario Provincial Police, the Royal Canadian Mounted Police or a prescribed police force outside Ontario.

45. Oaths of office and secrecy.— A person appointed to be a police officer shall, before entering on the duties of his or her office, take oaths or affirmations of office and secrecy in the prescribed form.

46. Political activity.— No municipal police officer shall engage in political activity, except as the regulations permit.

MEMBERS OF POLICE FORCES

47. (1) **Accommodation of needs of disabled member of municipal police force.**— Subject to subsection (2), if a member of a municipal police force becomes mentally or physically disabled and as a result is incapable of performing the essential duties of the position, the board shall accommodate his or her needs in accordance with the *Human Rights Code*.

(2) **Undue hardship.**— The board may discharge the member, or retire him or her if entitled to retire, if, after holding a hearing at which the evidence of two legally qualified medical practitioners is received, the board,

(*a*) determines, on the basis of that evidence, that the member is mentally or physically disabled and as a result incapable of performing the essential duties of the position, and what duties the member is capable of performing; and

(*b*) concludes that the member's needs cannot be accommodated without undue hardship on the board.

(3) **Idem, O.P.P.**— Subject to subsection (4), if a member of the Ontario Provincial Police becomes mentally or physically disabled and as a result is incapable of performing the essential duties of the position, the Commissioner shall accommodate the member's needs in accordance with the *Human Rights Code*.

(4) **Idem.**— The member may be discharged, or retired if entitled to retire, if, after holding a hearing at which the evidence of two legally qualified medical practitioners is received, the Commissioner or a person whom he or she designates,

(*a*) determines, on the basis of that evidence, that the member is mentally or physically disabled and as a result incapable of performing the essential duties of the position, and what duties the member is capable of performing; and

(*b*) concludes that the member's needs cannot be accommodated without undue hardship on the Crown in right of Ontario.

(5) **Appeal.**— A member of a police force who is discharged or retired under subsection (2) or (4) may appeal to the Commission by serving a written notice on the Commission and on the board or the Commissioner, as the case may be, within thirty days of receiving notice of the decision.

(6) **Powers of Commission.**— The Commission may confirm, alter or revoke the decision or may require the board or Commissioner, as the case may be, to rehear the matter.

(7) **Decision.**— The Commission shall promptly give written notice of its decision, with reasons, to the appellant and to the board or Commissioner, as the case may be.

(8) **Participation of members of Commission.**— No member of the Commission shall participate in the decision unless he or she was present throughout the hearing of the appeal and, except with the consent of the appellant, no decision of the Commission shall be given unless all members who were present throughout the hearing participate in the decision. ...

49. (1) **Restrictions on secondary activities.**— A member of a police force shall not engage in any activity,

(*a*) that interferes with or influences adversely the performance of his or her duties as a member of a police force, or is likely to do so;

(*b*) that places him or her in a position of conflict of interest, or is likely to do so;

(*c*) that would otherwise constitute full-time employment for another person; or

(*d*) in which he or she has an advantage derived from employment as a member of a police force.

(2) **Exception, paid duty.**— Clause (1)(d) does not prohibit a member of a police force from performing, in a private capacity, services that have been arranged through the police force.

(3) **Disclosure to chief of police.**— A member of a police force who proposes to undertake an activity that may contravene subsection (1) or who becomes aware that an activity that he or she has already undertaken may do so shall disclose full particulars of the situation to the chief of police, or, in the case of a chief of police, to the board.

(4) **Decision of chief of police.**— The chief of police or the board, as the case may be, shall decide whether the member is permitted to engage in the activity and the member shall comply with that decision.

50. (1) **Liability for torts.**— The board or the Crown in right of Ontario, as the case may be, is liable in respect of torts committed by members of the police force in the course of their employment.

(2) **Indemnification of member of municipal police force.**— The board may, in accordance with the guidelines established under clause 31(1)(h), indemnify a member of the police force for reasonable legal costs incurred,

(*a*) in the defence of a civil action, if the member is not found to be liable;

(*b*) in the defence of a criminal prosecution, if the member is found not guilty;

(*c*) in respect of any other proceeding in which the member's manner of execution of the duties of his or her employment was an issue, if the member is found to have acted in good faith.

(3) **Agreement.**— A majority of the members of a police force and the board may, in an agreement made under Part VIII, provide for indemnification for the legal costs of members of the police force, except the legal costs of a member who is found guilty of a criminal offence; if such an agreement exists, the board shall indemnify members in accordance with the agreement and subsection (2) does not apply.

(4) **Council responsible for board's liabilities.**— The council is responsible for the liabilities incurred by the board under subsections (1), (2) and (3).

(5) **Indemnification of member of O.P.P.**— The Minister of Finance may indemnify, out of the Consolidated Revenue Fund, a member of the Ontario Provincial Police for reasonable legal costs incurred,

(*a*) in the defence of a civil action, if the member is not found to be liable;

(*b*) in the defence of a criminal prosecution, if the member is found not guilty;

(*c*) in respect of any other proceeding in which the member's manner of execution of the duties of his or her employment was an issue, if the member is found to have acted in good faith.

(6) **Agreement.**— The Ontario Provincial Police Association and the Crown in right of Ontario may, in an agreement made under the *Public Service Act*, pro-

vide for indemnification for the legal costs of members of the police force, except the legal costs of a member who is found guilty of a criminal offence; if such an agreement exists, the Minister of Finance shall indemnify members in accordance with the agreement and subsection (5) does not apply.

51. (1) **Police cadets.—** With the board's approval, a municipal chief of police may appoint persons as police cadets to undergo training.

(2) **Idem.—** A police cadet is a member of the municipal police force.

52. (1) **Auxiliary members of municipal police force.—** With the Solicitor General's approval, a board may appoint auxiliary members of the police force.

(2) **Notice of suspension or termination.—** If the board suspends or terminates the appointment of an auxiliary member of the police force, it shall promptly give the Solicitor General written notice of the suspension or termination.

(3) **Auxiliary members of O.P.P.—** The Commissioner may appoint auxiliary members of the Ontario Provincial Police.

(3.1) **Same.—** The Commissioner also has the power to suspend or terminate the appointment of an auxiliary member of the police force.

(3.2) **Information and opportunity to reply.—** Before the auxiliary members appointment is terminated under subsection (2), or (3.1), he or she shall be given reasonable information with respect to the reasons for the termination and an opportunity to reply orally, or in writing, as the board or Commissioner, as the case may be, may determine.

(4) **Authority of auxiliary members of police force.—** An auxiliary member of a police force has the authority of a police officer if he or she is accompanied or supervised by a police officer and is authorized to perform police duties by the chief of police.

(5) **Restriction.—** The chief of police may authorize an auxiliary member of the police force to perform police duties only in special circumstances, including an emergency, that the police officers of the police force are not sufficiently numerous to deal with.

(6) **Oaths of office and secrecy.—** A person appointed to be an auxiliary member of a police force shall, before entering on the duties of his or her office, take oaths or affirmations of office and secrecy in the prescribed form.

SPECIAL CONSTABLES

53. (1) **Special constables appointed by board.—** With the Solicitor General's approval, a board may appoint a special constable to act for the period, area and purpose that the board considers expedient.

(2) **Special constables appointed by Commissioner.—** With the Solicitor General's approval, the Commissioner may appoint a special constable to act for the period, area and purpose that the Commissioner considers expedient.

(3) **Powers of police officer.—** The appointment of a special constable may confer on him or her the powers of a police officer, to the extent and for the specific purpose set out in the appointment.

(4) **Restriction.—** A special constable shall not be employed by a police force to perform on a permanent basis, whether part-time or full-time, all the usual duties of a police officer.

(5) **Idem.**— Subsection (4) does not prohibit police forces from authorizing special constables to escort and convey persons in custody and to perform duties related to the responsibilities of boards under Part X.

(6) **Suspension or termination of appointment.**— The power to appoint a special constable includes the power to suspend or terminate the appointment, but if a board or the Commissioner suspends or terminates an appointment, written notice shall promptly be given to the Solicitor General.

(7) **Same.**— The Solicitor General also has power to suspend or terminate the appointment of a special constable.

(8) **Information and opportunity to reply.**— Before a special constable's appointment is terminated, he or she shall be given reasonable information with respect to the reasons for the termination and an opportunity to reply, orally or in writing as the board, Commissioner or Solicitor General, as the case may be may determine.

(9) **Oaths of office and secrecy.**— A person appointed to be a special constable shall, before entering on the duties of his or her office, take oaths or affirmations of office and secrecy in the prescribed form.

FIRST NATIONS CONSTABLES

54. (1) **First Nations Constables.**— With the Commission's approval, the Commissioner may appoint a First Nations Constable to perform specified duties.

(2) **Further approval.**— If the specified duties of a First Nations Constable relate to a reserve as defined in the *Indian Act* (Canada), the appointment also requires the approval of the reserve's police governing authority or band council.

(3) **Powers of police officer.**— The appointment of a First Nations Constable confers on him or her the powers of a police officer for the purpose of carrying out his or her specified duties.

(4) **Duty to consult.**— The Commissioner shall not suspend or terminate the appointment of a First Nations Constable whose specified duties relate to a reserve without first consulting with the police governing authority or band council that approved the appointment.

(5) **Suspension or termination of appointment.**— The power to appoint a First Nations Constable includes the power to suspend or terminate the appointment, but if the Commissioner suspends or terminates an appointment, written notice shall promptly be given to the Commission.

(6) **Commission.**— The Commission also has power to suspend or terminate the appointment of a First Nations Constable.

(7) **Information and opportunity to reply.**— Before a First Nations Constable's appointment is terminated, he or she shall be given reasonable information with respect to the reasons for the termination and an opportunity to reply, orally or in writing as the Commissioner or Commission, as the case may be, may determine.

(8) **Oaths of office and secrecy.**— A person appointed to be a First Nations Constable shall, before entering on the duties of his or her office, take oaths or affirmations of office and secrecy in the prescribed form.

EMERGENCIES

55. (1) **Emergencies.**— In an emergency, the Solicitor General may make an agreement with the Crown in right of Canada or of another province or with any of its agencies for the provision of police services.

(2) **Authority to act as police officers.**— The agreement authorizes all peace officers to whom it relates to act as police officers in the area to which the agreement relates.

(3) **Application.**— For the purposes of the insurance plan established under the *Workplace Safety and Insurance Act, 1997*, the relationship between a member of a police force and the body that employs him or her continues as if an agreement had not been made under this section.

(4) **Expense of calling out Canadian Forces.**— If the services of the Canadian Forces are provided under this section, the municipality in whose territory the services are required shall pay all the related expenses.

(5) **Resignation during emergency prohibited.**— Subject to sections 33 and 34 of the *National Defence Act* (Canada), while an agreement made under this section is in force, no member of a police force that has jurisdiction in the area to which the agreement relates shall resign without the consent of the chief of police.

PART V
COMPLAINTS

56. (1) **Making a complaint.**— Any member of the public may make a complaint under this Part about the policies of or services provided by a police force or about the conduct of a police officer.

(2) **Same.**— The chief of police may also make a complaint under this Part about the conduct of a police officer.

(3) **Withdrawal of complaint.**— A complainant may withdraw his or her complaint at any time, but if the chief of police or board has begun to hold a hearing in respect of a complaint, the complaint shall not be withdrawn without the consent of the chief of police or board, as the case may be.

(4) **Notice of withdrawal.**— If a complaint is withdrawn, the chief of police or board shall notify the police officer who is the subject of the complaint, if any, of the fact within 30 days after the withdrawal.

(5) **Same.**— The chief of police or board may continue to deal with a complaint after the complaint is withdrawn, if the chief of police or board, as the case may be, considers it appropriate to do so.

(6) **Notice.**— If the chief of police or board continues to deal with a complaint after the complainant has asked that it be withdrawn, the chief of police or board shall notify the police officer who is the subject of the complaint, if any, within 30 days of deciding to continue.

(7) **Notice to police officer.**— Where a complaint is about the conduct of a police officer, the chief of police shall forthwith give the police officer notice of the substance of the complaint unless, in the chief of police's opinion, to do so might prejudice the investigation.

(8) **Interpretation—portion of a complaint.**— This part applies to a portion of a complaint as if it were a complaint.

57. (1) **Public complaints, restriction.**— A complaint may be made by a member of the public only if the complainant was directly affected by the policy, service or conduct that is the subject of the complaint.

(2) **Same, procedure for making.**— A complaint made by a member of the public must be in writing, signed by the complainant and delivered to any station or detachment of the police force to which the complaint relates or to the Commission, personally by the complainant or his or her agent, by mail or by telephone transmission of a facsimile.

(3) **Form may be used.**— If a complainant wants to make his or her complaint on a standard form, he or she may use a form approved for the purpose by the Commission; the approved form shall be available in every police station and detachment and in the Commission's offices.

(4) **Same, withdrawal.**— A withdrawal of a complaint by the member of the public who made the complaint must be in writing, signed by the complainant and delivered to any station or detachment of the police force to which the complaint relates or to the Commission, personally by the complainant or his or her agent, by mail or by telephone transmission of a facsimile.

(5) **Commission to send complaint to police force.**— If a complaint is made or withdrawn by delivering it to the Commission, the Commission shall forthwith send the complaint or withdrawal, or a copy of it, to the chief of police of the police force to which the complaint relates.

(6) **When complaint is made.**— For the purposes of this Part, a complaint is made,

(*a*) on the day on which it is delivered in person to a station or detachment of the police force to which the complaint relates;

(*b*) on the day that is five days after it is mailed to the station or detachment;

(*c*) on the day after it is sent by telephone transmission of a facsimile to the station or detachment;

(*d*) on the day that is five days after it is delivered in person, or sent by mail or by telephone transmission of a facsimile to the Commission.

(7) **Definition, member of the public.**— For the purposes of this Part, a member of the public does not include,

(*a*) the Solicitor General;

(*b*) a member or employee of the Commission;

(*c*) a member of a police force if that police force or another member of that police force is the subject of the complaint;

(*d*) a member or employee of a board if the board is responsible for the police force that is, or a member of which is, the subject of the complaint;

(*e*) a person selected by the council of a municipality to advise another municipality's board under subsection 6.1(2), if the board is responsible for the police force that is, or a member of which is, the subject of the complaint; or

(*f*) a delegate to a community policing advisory committee if the community policing advisory committee advises the detachment commander of the Ontario Provincial Police detachment that is, or a member of which is, the subject of the complaint.

58. (1) **Informal complaint resolution.**— If, at any time before or during an investigation into a complaint about the conduct of a police officer, the conduct appears to be obviously conduct that is not of a serious nature, the chief of police may resolve the matter informally, if the police officer and the complainant consent to the proposed resolution.

(2) **Same.**— If, at any time before or during an investigation into a complaint about the conduct of a chief of police or deputy chief of police, the conduct appears to be obviously conduct that is not of a serious nature, the board may resolve the matter informally, if the chief of police or deputy chief of police and the complainant consent to the proposed resolution.

(3) **Inadmissibility of statements.**— No statement made during an attempt at informal resolution of a complaint under this section is admissible in a civil proceeding, including a proceeding under subsection 64(15) or 65(17) or a hearing held under this Part, except with the consent of the person who made the statement.

(4) **Non-application of this Part.**— No other provisions of this Part apply in respect of an informal resolution under subsection (1) or (2).

59. (1) **Chief determines nature of complaints.**— The chief of police shall determine whether a complaint is about the policies of or services provided by the police force or the conduct of a police officer and shall ensure that every complaint is appropriately dealt with as provided by section 60.

(2) **Notice re nature of complaint.**— The chief of police shall notify the complainant in writing of his or her determination that the complaint is about the policies of or services provided by the police force or is about the conduct of a police officer and of the complainant's right to ask the Commission to review the determination within 30 days of receiving the notice.

(3) **Frivolous, vexatious, bad faith complaints.**— The chief of police may decide not to deal with any complaint about the police force or about a police officer, other than the chief of police or deputy chief of police, that he or she considers to be frivolous or vexatious or made in bad faith.

(4) **Complaint more than six months old.**— The chief of police may decide not to deal with any complaint made by a member of the public if the complaint is made more than six months after the facts on which it is based occurred.

(5) **Complainant not directly affected.**— The chief of police shall not deal with any complaint made by a member of the public if he or she decides that the complainant was not directly affected by the policy, service, or conduct that is the subject of the complaint.

(6) **Notice.**— If the chief of police decides not to deal with a complaint under subsection (3), (4) or (5), he or she shall notify the complainant and the police officer who is the subject of the complaint, if any, in writing, of the decision and of the complainant's right to ask the Commission to review the decision within 30 days of receiving the notice.

(7) **Time limit.**— The chief of police shall notify the complainant under subsection (2) or (6) within 30 days after the complaint was made unless the chief of police notifies the complainant in writing before the expiry of the 30-day period that he or she is extending the 30-day period.

(8) **Same.**— Subject to subsections (3), (4) and (5), the chief of police shall ensure that a review under section 61 is begun into every complaint made about the policies of or services provided by the police force, and that an investigation

under section 64 is begun into every complaint made about the conduct of a police officer, immediately upon the later of,

    (*a*) 30 days after the complainant was notified under subsection (2); and

    (*b*) notification of the Commission's decision after a review under section 72 with respect to a notice under subsection (2).

(9) **Same.**— Despite subsection (8), if the complainant notifies the chief of police in writing that he or she will not ask the Commission to conduct a review under section 72, the chief of police shall ensure that the review or investigation, as the case may be, is begun immediately after receiving such notification from the complainant.

60. (1) **Complaints about municipal force referred to chief.**— All complaints about the policies of or services provided by a municipal police force shall be referred to the chief of police and dealt with under section 61.

(2) **Complaints about local O.P.P. policies referred to detachment commander.**— All complaints about the local policies, established under clause 10(9)(c), of an Ontario Provincial Police detachment shall be referred to the detachment commander and dealt with under section 62.

(3) **Complaints about provincial O.P.P. policies referred to Commissioner.**— All complaints about the provincial policies of the Ontario Provincial Police shall be referred to the Commissioner and dealt with under section 63.

(4) **Complaints about officer referred to chief.**— All complaints about the conduct of a police officer, other than a chief of police or deputy chief of police, shall be referred to the chief of police and dealt with under section 64.

(5) **Complaints about chief deputy chief referred to board.**— All complaints about the conduct of a municipal chief of police or a municipal deputy chief of police shall be referred to the board and dealt with under section 65.

(6) **Complaints about Commissioner, deputy Commissioner referred to Solicitor General.**— All complaints about the conduct of the Commissioner or a deputy Commissioner shall be referred to the Solicitor General and dealt with under section 66. ...

61. (1) **Complaints about municipal force, chief to review.**— Subject to subsections 59(3), (4) and (5), the chief of police shall review every complaint that is made about the policies of or services provided by a municipal police force and shall take any action, or no action, in response to the complaint as he or she considers appropriate.

(2) **Report to board on disposition.**— The chief of police shall submit a written report to the board, as may be requested by the board, respecting every complaint about the policies of or services provided by the police force, including a complaint disposed of under subsection 59(3), (4) or (5), and his or her disposition of the complaint.

(3) **Notice to complainant.**— The chief of police shall notify the complainant, in writing, of his or her disposition of the complaint and of the complainant's right to request that the board review the complaint if the complainant is not satisfied with the disposition, and the chief of police shall do so within 60 days after the later of,

    (*a*) the expiry of the 30-day period in which the complainant may ask the Commission to review a decision, as set out in a notice under subsection 59(2) or (6); and

(b) notification of the Commission's decision after conducting the requested review.

(4) **If no action taken.**— If the chief of police decides to take no action with respect to the complaint, he or she shall provide the complainant with reasons for the decision.

(5) **Extension of time.**— The chief of police may extend the 60-day period set out in subsection (3) by notifying the complainant in writing of the extension before the expiry of the period being extended.

(6) **Deemed disposition.**— If the chief of police has not notified the complainant of his or her disposition of the complaint within the 60-day period required by subsection (3) or within the extended period established under subsection (5), the chief of police shall be deemed to have taken no action in response to the complaint and shall be deemed to have so notified the complainant.

(7) **Request for review by board.**— A complainant may, within 30 days after receiving the notice under subsection (3) or the deemed notice under subsection (6), request that the board review the complaint by serving a written request to that effect on the board.

(8) **Board to review and dispose of complaint.**— Upon receiving a written request for a review of a complaint previously dealt with by the chief of police, the board shall,

   (a) advise the chief of police of the request;

   (b) subject to subsection (9), review the complaint and take any action, or no action, in response to the complaint, as it considers appropriate; and

   (c) notify the complainant and the chief of police in writing of its disposition of the complaint.

(9) **Committee of board may review and report to board.**— A board that is composed of more than three members may appoint a committee of not fewer than three members of the board (two of whom constitute a quorum for the purpose of this subsection) to review a complaint and to make recommendations to the board after the review and the board shall consider the recommendations and shall take any action, or no action, in response to the complaint as the board considers appropriate.

(10) **Public meeting.**— In conducting a review under this section, the board or the committee of the board may hold a public meeting into the complaint.

62. (1) **Complaints re local O.P.P. policies, detachment commander to review.**— The detachment commander shall review every complaint that is made about the local policies, established under clause 10(9)(c), of the Ontario Provincial Police detachment that is providing police services pursuant to an agreement entered into under section 10 and shall take any action, or no action, in response to the complaint as he or she considers appropriate.

(2) **Frivolous, vexatious, bad faith complaints.**— The detachment commander may decide not to deal with any complaint described in subsection (1) that he or she considers to be frivolous or vexatious or made in bad faith.

(3) **Complaint more than six months old.**— The detachment commander may decide not to deal with any complaint described in subsection (1) if the complaint is made more than six months after the facts on which it is based occurred.

(4) **Complainant not directly affected.**— The detachment commander shall not deal with any complaint described in subsection (1) if he or she decides that the complainant was not directly affected by the policy that is the subject of the complaint.

(5) **Notice to complainant re decision not to deal with complaint.**— If the detachment commander decides not to deal with a complaint under subsection (2), (3) or (4), he or she shall notify the complainant, in writing, of the decision and of the complainant's right to ask the Commission to review the decision within 30 days of receiving in the notice.

(6) **Report to board on disposition.**— The detachment commander shall submit a written report to the board, as may be requested by the board, respecting every complaint about the local policies of the detachment, including a complaint disposed of under subsection (2), (3) or (4), and his or her disposition of the complaint.

(7) **Notice to complainant.**— The detachment commander shall notify the complainant, in writing, of his or her disposition of the complaint and of the complainant's right to request that the board review the complaint if the complainant is not satisfied with the disposition, and the detachment commander shall do so within 60 days after the later of,

(a) the expiry of the 30-day period in which the complainant may ask the Commission to review a decision, as set out in a notice under subsection 59(2) or subsection (5) of this section; and

(b) notification of the Commission's decision after conducting the requested review.

(8) **If no action taken.**— If the detachment commander decides to take no action with respect to the complaint, he or she shall provide the complainant with reasons for the decision.

(9) **Extension of time.**— The detachment commander may extend the 60-day period set out in subsection (7) by notifying the complainant in writing of the extension before the expiry of the period being extended.

(10) **Deemed disposition.**— If the detachment commander has not notified the complainant of his or her disposition of the complaint within the 60-day period required by subsection (7) or within the extended period established under subsection (9), the detachment commander shall be deemed to have taken no action in response to the complaint and shall be deemed to have so notified the complainant.

(11) **Request for review by board.**— A complainant may, within 30 days after receiving the notice under subsection (7) or the deemed notice under subsection (10), request that the board review the complaint by serving a written request to that effect on the board.

(12) **Board to review and dispose of complaint.**— Upon receiving a written request for a review of a complaint previously dealt with by a detachment commander, the board shall,

(a) advise the detachment commander of the request;

(b) subject to subsection (13), review the complaint and take any action, or no action, in response to the complaint, as it considers appropriate; and

(c) notify the complainant and the detachment commander in writing of its disposition of the complaint.

(13) **Committee of board may review and report to board.**— A board that is composed of more than three members may appoint a committee of not fewer than three members of the board (two of whom constitute a quorum for the purpose of this subsection) to review a complaint and to make recommendations to the board after the review and the board shall consider the recommendations and shall take any action, or no action, in response to the complaint as the board considers appropriate.

(14) **Public meeting.**— In conducting a review under this section, the board or the committee of the board may hold a public meeting into the complaint.

(15) **Delegation.**— A detachment commander may delegate any of his or her duties, functions or powers under this section to any police officer who is a member of the detachment.

63. (1) **Complaints re provincial O.P.P. policies, Commissioner to review.**— Subject to subsections 59(3), (4) and (5), the Commissioner shall review every complaint that is made about the provincial policies of the Ontario Provincial Police or about the services provided by the Ontario Provincial Police, other than services provided pursuant to an agreement under section 10, and shall take any action, or no action, in response to the complaint as he or she considers appropriate.

(2) **Notice to complainant.**— The Commissioner shall notify the complainant in writing of his or her disposition of the complaint.

(3) **If no action taken.**— If the Commissioner decides to take no action with respect to the complaint, he or she shall provide the complainant with reasons for the decision. ...

64. (1) **Complaints about police officer's conduct.**— Subject to subsections 59(3), (4) and (5), the chief of police shall cause every complaint made about the conduct of a police officer, other than the chief of police or deputy chief of police, to be investigated and the investigation to be reported on in a written report.

(2) **Investigation assigned to another police force.**— A municipal chief of police may, with the approval of the board and on written notice to the Commission, ask the chief of police of another police force to cause the complaint to be investigated and to report, in writing, back to him or her at the expense of the police force in respect of which the complaint is made.

(3) **Same, re O.P.P. officer.**— In the case of a complaint about the conduct of a police officer who is a member of the Ontario Provincial Police, the Commissioner may, on written notice to the Commission, ask the chief of police of another police force to cause the complaint to be investigated and to report, in writing, back to him or her at the expense of the Ontario Provincial Police.

(4) **Same, more than one force involved.**— If the complaint is about an incident that involved the conduct of two or more police officers who are members of different police forces, the chiefs of police whose police officers are the subjects of the complaint shall agree on which police force (which may be one of the police forces whose police officer is a subject of the complaint or another police force) is to investigate the complaint and report, in writing, back to the other chief or chiefs of police and how the cost of the investigation is to be shared.

(5) **Same.**— If the chiefs of police cannot agree under subsection (4), the Commission shall decide how the cost of the investigation is to be shared and,

(*a*) shall decide which of the chiefs of police whose police officer is a subject of the complaint shall cause the complaint to be investigated and report in writing back to the other chief or chiefs of police; or

(*b*) shall ask another chief of police to cause the complaint to be investigated and to report back in writing to the chiefs of police.

(6) **Unsubstantiated complaint.**— If, at the conclusion of the investigation and on review of the written report submitted to him or her, the chief of police is of the opinion that the complaint is unsubstantiated, the chief of police shall take no action in response to the complaint and shall notify the complainant and the police officer who is the subject of the complaint, in writing, together with a copy of the written report, of the decision and of the complainant's right to ask the Commission to review the decision within 30 days of receiving the notice.

(7) **Hearing to be held.**— Subject to subsection (11), if, at the conclusion of the investigation and on review of the written report submitted to him or her, the chief of police is of the opinion that the police officer's conduct may constitute misconduct, as defined in section 74, or unsatisfactory work performance, he or she shall hold a hearing into the matter.

(8) **Prosecutor at hearing.**— The chief of police shall designate to be the prosecutor at the hearing,

(*a*) a police officer from any police force of a rank equal to or higher than that of the police officer who is the subject of the hearing; or

(*b*) a legal counsel or agent.

(9) **Same.**— A police officer from another police force may be the prosecutor at the hearing only with the approval of his or her chief of police.

(10) **Findings and disposition after hearing.**— At the conclusion of the hearing, if misconduct or unsatisfactory work performance is proved on clear and convincing evidence, the chief of police shall take any action described in section 68.

(11) **Informal resolution if conduct not serious.**— If, at the conclusion of the investigation and on review of the written report submitted to him or her, the chief of police is of the opinion that there was misconduct or unsatisfactory work performance but that it was not of a serious nature, the chief of police may resolve the matter informally without holding a hearing, if the police officer and the complainant consent to the proposed resolution.

(12) **Notice to complainant.**— Before resolving the matter informally, the chief of police shall notify the complainant and the police officer, in writing, of his or her opinion that there was misconduct or unsatisfactory work performance that was not of a serious nature, and that the complainant may ask the Commission to review this decision within 30 days of receiving such notification.

(13) **No informal resolution until after Commission's review.**— The chief of police shall take no action to resolve the matter informally until,

(*a*) the 30-day period in which the complainant may ask for a review has expired without a review being requested; or

(*b*) if the complainant asked for a review within the 30-day period, the Commission has completed its review and them only if the Commission's decision is such that there may be an informal resolution of the complaint.

(14) **Same.**— Despite subsection (13), if the complainant notifies the chief of police in writing that he or she will not ask the Commission to conduct a review under section 72, the chief of police shall take action to resolve the matter informally immediately after receiving such notification from the complainant.

(15) **Disposition without a hearing if informal resolution fails.**— If an informal resolution of the matter is attempted but not achieved under subsection (11), the following rules apply:

 1. The chief of police shall provide the police officer with reasonable information concerning the matter and shall give him or her an opportunity to reply, orally or in writing.

 2. Subject to paragraph 3, the chief of police may impose on the police officer the penalty described in clause 68(1)(e) and may take any other action described in subsection 68(5) and may cause an entry concerning the matter, the penalty imposed or action taken and the police officer's reply to be made in his or her employment record.

 3. If the police officer refuses to accept the penalty imposed or action taken, the chief of police shall not impose a penalty or take any other action or cause any entry to be made in the police officer's employment record, but shall hold a hearing under subsection (7).

(16) **Employment record expunged.**— An entry made in the police officer's employment record under paragraph 2 of subsection (15) shall be expunged from the record two years after being made if during that time no other entries concerning misconduct or unsatisfactory work performance have been made in the record under this Part.

(17) **Agreement.**— Nothing in this section affects agreements between boards and police officers or associations that permit penalties or actions other than those permitted by this section, if the police officer in question consents, without hearing under subsection (7).

65. (1) **Complaints about chief's, deputy chief's conduct.**— The board shall review every complaint made about the conduct of the municipal chief of police or a municipal deputy chief of police and shall ensure that it begins the review immediately upon the later of,

　　(*a*) 30 days after the complainant was notified under subsection 59(2); and

　　(*b*) notification of the Commission's decision after reviewing a decision with respect to a notice under subsection 59(2).

(2) **Same.**— Despite subsection (1), if the complainant notifies the board in writing that he or she will not ask the Commission to conduct a review under section 72 with respect to a notice under subsection 59(2), the board shall ensure that it begins the review immediately alter receiving such notification from the complainant.

(3) **Frivolous, vexatious, bad faith complaints.**— The board may decide not to deal with any complaint that it considers to be frivolous or vexatious or made in bad faith and shall notify the complainant and the police officer who is the subject of the complaint in writing of the decision and of the complainant's right to ask the Commission to review the decision within 30 days of receiving the notice.

(4) **Complaint more than six months old.**— The board may decide not to deal with any complaint that was made more than six months after the facts on which it is based occurred and shall notify the complainant and the police officer who is the subject of the complaint in writing of the decision and of the complainant's right to ask the Commission to review the decision within 30 days of receiving the notice.

(5) **Complainant not directly affected.**— The board shall not deal with any complaint made by a member of the public if the board decides that the complainant was not directly affected by the conduct that is the subject of the complaint and shall notify the complainant and the police officer who is the subject of the complaint in writing of the decision and of the complainant's right to ask the Commission to review the decision within 30 days of receiving the notice.

(6) **Investigation assigned to another police force.**— If, at the conclusion of the review, the board is of the opinion that the chief of police's or deputy chief of police's conduct may constitute an offence under a law of Canada or of a province or territory, or misconduct, as defined in section 74, or unsatisfactory work performance, the board shall ask the Commission to assign the chief of police of another police force to cause the complaint to be investigated immediately and the investigation to be reported on in a written report.

(7) **Matter referred to board.**— If, at the conclusion of the investigation carried out by another police force, the chief of police of the other police force is of the opinion that the conduct of the chief of police or deputy chief of police under investigation may constitute misconduct, as defined in section 74, or unsatisfactory work performance, he or she shall refer the matter, together with the written report, to the board.

(8) **Unsubstantiated complaint.**— If, at the conclusion of the investigation carried out by another police force, the chief of police of the other police force is of the opinion that the complaint is unsubstantiated, the chief of police shall report that in writing to the board and the board shall take no action in response to the complaint and shall notify the complainant and the police officer who is the subject of the complaint, in writing, together with a copy of the written report, of the decision, and of the complainant's right to ask the Commission to review the decision within 30 days of receiving the notice.

(9) **Board or Commission to hold hearing.**— Subject to subsection (13), the board shall hold a hearing into a matter referred to it under subsection (7) or may refer the matter to the Commission to hold the hearing.

(10) **Prosecutor at hearing.**— The board or Commission, as the case may be, shall designate a legal counsel or agent to be the prosecutor at the hearing.

(11) **Board pays for prosecutor.**— The board shall pay the prosecutor's remuneration, whether the prosecutor has been designated by the board or by the Commission.

(12) **Findings and disposition after hearing.**— At the conclusion of a hearing by the board, if misconduct or unsatisfactory work performance is proved on clear and convincing evidence, the board shall take any action described in section 68; at the conclusion of a hearing by the Commission, if misconduct or unsatisfactory work performance is proved on clear and convincing evidence, the Commission shall direct the board to take any action, as specified by the Commission, under section 68 and the board shall take such action.

(13) **Informal resolution if conduct not serious.**— If the board is of the opinion, on a review of the written report, that there was misconduct or unsatisfactory work performance but that it was not of a serious nature, the board may resolve the matter informally without holding a hearing if the chief of police or deputy chief of police and the complainant consent to the proposed resolution.

(14) **Notice to complainant.**— Before resolving the matter informally, the board shall notify the complainant, in writing, of its opinion that there was misconduct or unsatisfactory work performance that was not of a serious nature, and that the complainant may ask the Commission to review this decision within 30 days of receiving such notification.

(15) **No informal resolution until after Commission's review.**— The board shall take no action to resolve the matter informally until,

(*a*) the 30-day period in which the complainant may ask for a review has expired, without a review being requested; or

(*b*) if the complainant asked for a review within the 30-day period, the Commission has completed its review and then, only if the Commission's decision is such that there may be informal resolution of the complaint.

(16) **Same.**— Despite subsection (15), if the complainant notifies the board in writing that he or she will not ask the Commission to conduct a review under section 72, the board shall take action to resolve the matter informally immediately after receiving such notification from the complainant.

(17) **Disposition without a hearing if informal resolution fails.**— If an informal resolution of the matter is attempted but not achieved under subsection (13), the following rules apply:

1. The board shall provide the chief of police or deputy chief of police with reasonable information concerning the matter and shall give him or her an opportunity to reply, orally or in writing.

2. Subject to paragraph 3, the board may impose on the chief of police or deputy chief of police the penalty described in clause 68(2)(e) and may take any other action described in subsection 68(5) and may cause an entry concerning the matter, the penalty imposed or action taken and the chief of police's or deputy chief of police's reply to be made in his or her employment record.

3. If the chief of police or deputy chief of police refuses to accept the penalty imposed or action taken, the board shall not impose a penalty or take any other action or cause any entry to be made in the employment record, but shall hold a hearing, or refer the matter to the Commission to hold a hearing, under subsection (9).

(18) **Employment record expunged.**— An entry made in the chief of police's or deputy chief of police's employment record under paragraph 2 of subsection (17) shall be expunged from the record two years after being made if during that time no other entries concerning misconduct or unsatisfactory work performance have been made in the record under this Part.

(19) **Agreement.**— Nothing in this section affects agreements between boards and chiefs of police or deputy chiefs of police that permit penalties or actions

other than those permitted by this section, if the chief of police or deputy chief of police in question consents, without a hearing under subsection (9).

66. Complaints about Commissioner's, deputy Commissioner's conduct.— The Solicitor General shall deal with all complaints about the conduct of the Commissioner or a deputy Commissioner as he or she sees fit and there is no appeal from a decision or action taken by the Solicitor General under this section.

67. (1) Suspension.— If a police officer, other than a chief of police or deputy chief of police, is suspected of or charged with an offence under a law of Canada or of a province or territory or is suspected of misconduct as defined in section 74, the chief of police may suspend him or her from duty with pay.

(2) **Same.—** If a chief of police or deputy chief of police is suspected of or charged with an offence under a law of Canada or of a province or territory or is suspected of misconduct as defined in section 74, the board may suspend him or her from duty with pay.

(3) **Revocation and reimposition of suspension.—** The chief of police or board may revoke the suspension and later reimpose it, repeatedly if necessary, as the chief of police or board, as the case may be, considers appropriate.

(4) **Duration of suspension.—** Unless the chief of police or board revokes the suspension, it shall continue until the final disposition of the proceeding in which the chief of police's, deputy chief of police's or other police officer's conduct is at issue.

(5) **Conditions of suspension.—** While suspended, the chief of police, deputy chief of police or other police officer shall not exercise any of the powers vested in him or her as a chief of police, deputy chief of police or police officer, or wear or use clothing or equipment that was issued to him or her in that capacity.

(6) **Suspension without pay.—** If a chief of police, deputy chief of police or other police officer is convicted of an offence and sentenced to a term of imprisonment, the chief of police or board, as the case may be, may suspend him or her without pay, even if the conviction or sentence is under appeal.

(7) **Earnings from other employment.—** If a chief of police, deputy chief of police or other police officer is suspended with pay, the pay for the period of suspension shall be reduced by the amount that he or she earns from other employment during that period.

(8) **Exception.—** Subsection (7) does not apply to earnings from other employment that was commenced before the period of suspension.

68. (1) Powers of chief of police.— The chief of police may, under subsection 64(10),

(a) dismiss the police officer from the police force;

(b) direct that the police officer be dismissed in seven days unless he or she resigns before that time;

(c) demote the police officer, specifying the manner and period of the demotion;

(d) suspend the police officer without pay for a period not exceeding 30 days or 240 hours, as the case may be;

(e) direct that the police officer forfeit not more than three days or 24 hours pay, as the case may be; or

(f) direct that the police officer forfeit not more than 20 days or 160 hours off, as the case may be.

(2) **Powers of board.**— The board may, under subsection 65(12),

(*a*) dismiss the chief of police or deputy chief of police from the police force;

(*b*) direct that the chief of police or deputy chief of police be dismissed in seven days unless he or she resigns before that time;

(*c*) demote the chief of police or deputy chief of police, specifying the manner and period of the demotion;

(*d*) suspend the chief of police or deputy chief of police without pay for a period not exceeding 30 days or 240 hours, as the case may be;

(*e*) direct that the chief of police or deputy chief of police forfeit not more than three days or 24 hours pay, as the case may be; or

(*f*) direct that the chief of police or deputy chief of police forfeit not more than 20 days or 160 hours off, as the case may be.

(3) **Calculation of penalties.**— Penalties imposed under clauses (1)(d), (e) and (f) and (2)(d), (e) and (f) shall be calculated in terms of days if the chief of police, deputy chief of police or other police officer normally works eight hours a day or less and in terms of hours if he or she normally works more than eight hours a day.

(4) **Same.**— If a penalty is imposed under clause (1)(e) or (2)(e), the chief of police, deputy chief of police or police officer, as the case may be, may elect to satisfy the penalty by working without pay or by applying the penalty to his or her vacation, overtime or sick leave credits or entitlements.

(5) **Additional powers.**— In addition to or instead of a penalty described in subsection (1) or (2), the board or chief of police, as the case may be, may,

(*a*) reprimand the chief of police, deputy chief of police or other police officer;

(*b*) direct that the chief of police, deputy chief of police or other police officer undergo specified counselling, treatment or training;

(*c*) direct that the chief of police, deputy chief of police or other police officer participate in a specified program or activity;

(*d*) take any combination of actions described in clauses (a), (b) and (c).

(6) **Notice needed for dismissal or demotion.**— The chief of police or board, as the case may be, shall not impose the penalties of dismissal or demotion unless the notice of hearing or a subsequent notice served on the chief of police, deputy chief of police or other police officer indicated that they might be imposed if the complaint were proved on clear and convincing evidence.

(7) **Notice of any action taken.**— The chief of police or board, as the case may be, shall promptly give written notice of the action taken under subsection (1), (2) or (5) with reasons, to the chief of police, deputy chief of police or other police officer who is the subject of the complaint and, in the case of an action taken by a municipal chief of police, to the board.

(8) **Same.**— If the action was taken as a result of a complaint made by a member of the public, the chief of police or board, as the case may be, shall also give written notice of the action taken, with reasons, to the complainant.

(9) **Police officer's employment record.**— The chief of police or board, as the case may be, may cause an entry concerning the matter, the action taken and the reply of the chief of police, deputy chief of police or other police officer against whom the action is taken, to be made in his or her employment record, but no

reference to the allegations of the complaint or the hearing shall be made in the employment record, and the matter shall not be taken into account for any purpose relating to his or her employment unless,

> (a) the complaint is proved on clear and convincing evidence; or

> (b) the chief of police, deputy chief of police or other police officer resigns before the matter is finally disposed of.

69. (1) *Statutory Powers Procedure Act* **applies to hearings by chief of board.**— A hearing held under subsection 64(7) or 65(9) shall be conducted in accordance with the *Statutory Powers Procedure Act*.

(2) **Application of this section to hearings under this Part.**— Subsections (3), (4), (5), (6), (7), (12), (13), (14), (15), (16) and (17) apply to any hearing held under this Part.

(3) **Parties.**— The parties to the hearing are the prosecutor, the police officer who is the subject of the hearing and, if the complaint was made by a member of the public, the complainant.

(4) **Notice to parties and right to counsel.**— The parties to the hearing shall be given reasonable notice of the hearing and each party may be represented by counsel or an agent.

(5) **Examination of evidence.**— Before the hearing, the police officer shall be given an opportunity to examine any physical or documentary evidence that will be produced or any report whose contents will be given in evidence.

(6) **Same.**— If the hearing is being conducted as a result of a public complaint, the complainant shall likewise be given an opportunity to examine evidence and reports before the hearing.

(7) **Police officer not required to give evidence.**— The police officer who is the subject of the hearing shall not be required to give evidence at the hearing.

(8) **Non-compellability.**— No person shall be required to testify in a civil proceeding with regard to information obtained in the course of his or her duties, except at a hearing held under this Part.

(9) **Inadmissibility of documents.**— No document prepared as the result of a complaint is admissible in a civil proceeding, except at a hearing held under this Part.

(10) **Inadmissibility of statements.**— No statement made during an attempt at informal resolution of a complaint is admissible in a civil proceeding, including a proceeding under subsection 64(15) or 65(17) or a hearing held under this Part, except with the consent of the person who made the statement.

(11) **Recording of evidence.**— The oral evidence given at the hearing shall be recorded and copies of transcripts shall be provided on the same terms as in the Ontario Court (General Division).

(12) **Release of exhibits.**— Within a reasonable time after the matter has been finally determined, documents and things put in evidence at the hearing shall, on request, be released to the person who produced them.

(13) **No communication without notice to parties.**— The person conducting the hearing shall not communicate directly or indirectly in relation to the subject-matter of the hearing with any person or person's counsel or agent, unless the parties receive notice and have an opportunity to participate.

(14) **Exception.**— However, the person conducting the hearing may seek legal advice from an advisor independent of the parties, and in that case the nature of

the advice shall be communicated to them so that they may make submissions as to the law.

(15) **Hearing may proceed on part if Crown Attorney consulted.**— If a Crown Attorney has been consulted, the person conducting the hearing may proceed to deal with the part of the complaint that, in his or her opinion, constitutes misconduct, as defined in section 74, or unsatisfactory work performance, unless the Crown Attorney directs otherwise.

(16) **Hearing to continue.**— If the police officer who is the subject of the hearing is charged with an offence under a law of Canada or of a province or territory in connection with the conduct that was the subject of the complaint, the hearing shall continue unless the Crown Attorney advises the chief of police or board, as the case may be, that it should be stayed until the conclusion of the proceedings dealing with the offence.

(17) **Photography at hearing.**— Subsections 136(1), (2) and (3) of the *Courts of Justice Act* (photography at court hearing) apply with necessary modifications to the hearing and a person who contravenes subsection 136(1), (2) or (3) of the *Courts of Justice Act*, as it is made to apply by this subsection, is guilty of an offence and on conviction is liable to a fine of not more than $2,000.

(18) **Six-month limitation period, exception.**— If six months have elapsed since the facts on which a complaint is based first came to the attention of the chief of police or board, as the case may be, no notice of hearing shall be served unless the board (in the case of a municipal police officer) or the Commissioner (in the case of a member of the Ontario Provincial Police) is of the opinion that it was reasonable, under the circumstances, to delay serving the notice of hearing.

70. (1) **Appeal to Commission.**— A police officer or complainant may, within 30 days of receiving notice of the decision made after a hearing held under subsection 64(7) or 65(9), appeal the decision to the Commission by serving on the Commission a written notice stating the grounds on which the appeal is based.

(2) **Commission to hold hearing on notice from police officer.**— The Commission shall hold a hearing upon receiving a notice under subsection (1) from a police officer.

(3) **Commission to hold hearing on notice from complainant, limitation.**— The Commission shall hold a hearing upon receiving a notice under subsection (1) from a complainant if the appeal is from the finding that misconduct or unsatisfactory work performance was not proved on clear and convincing evidence.

(4) **Commission may hold hearing.**— The Commission may hold a hearing, if it considers it appropriate, upon receiving a notice under subsection (1) from a complainant with respect to an appeal other than an appeal described in subsection (3).

(5) **Appeal on the record.**— A hearing held under this section shall be an appeal on the record, but the Commission may receive new or additional evidence as it considers just.

(6) **Powers of Commission.**— The Commission may confirm, vary or revoke the decision being appealed or may substitute its own decision for that of the chief of police or board, as the case may be.

71. (1) **Appeal to Divisional Court.**— A party to a hearing under section 70 may appeal the Commission's decision to the Divisional Court within 30 days of receiving notice of the Commission's decision.

(2) **Grounds for appeal.**— An appeal may be made on a question that is not a question of fact alone, from a penalty imposed or from any other action taken, or all of them.

(3) **Solicitor General may be heard.**— The Solicitor General is entitled to be heard, by counsel or otherwise, on the argument of the appeal. ...

72. (1) **Request for review of decision by Commission.**— If a complainant disagrees with the decision of a chief of police to deal with his or her complaint as a complaint about the policies of or services provided by the police force or as a complaint about the conduct of a police officer, the complainant may, within 30 days of receiving notice under subsection 59(2), ask the Commission to review the decision.

(2) **Same.**— If a complainant has been notified under subsection 59(6), 62(5) or 65(3) that his or her complaint will not be dealt with because it is frivolous or vexatious or made in bad faith, the complainant may, within 30 days of such notification, ask the Commission to review the decision.

(3) **Same.**— If a complainant has been notified under subsection 59(6), 62(5) or 65(4) that his or her complaint will not be dealt with because it was made more than six months after the facts on which it is based occurred the complainant may, within 30 days of such notification, ask the Commission to review the decision.

(4) **Same.**— If a complainant has been notified under subsection 59(6), 62(5) or 65(5) that his or her complaint will not be dealt with because he or she was not directly affected by the policy, service or conduct that is the subject of the complaint, the complainant may, within 30 days of such notification ask the Commission to review the decision.

(5) **Same.**— If a complainant has been notified under subsection 64(6) or (12) or 65(8) or (14) that his or her complaint is unsubstantiated or that the conduct he or she complained of has been determined to be not of a serious nature, the complainant may, within 30 days of such notification, ask the Commission to review the decision.

(6) **Request in writing.**— The request for a review must be in writing.

(7) **Commission to review.**— Upon receiving a request for a review under this section, the Commission shall review the decision, taking into account any material provided by the complainant or the chief of police, detachment commander or board, and shall endeavour to complete its review within 30 days of receiving the request, but the Commission shall not hold a hearing into the matter.

(8) **Commission's powers.**— Upon completion of the review, the Commission may confirm the decision or may direct the chief of police, detachment commander or board to process the complaint as it specifies or may assign the review or investigation of the complaint or the conduct of a hearing in respect of the complaint to a police force other than the police force in respect of which the complaint is made.

(9) **Cost of complaints process.**— If the Commission assigns the review or investigation of a complaint or the conduct of a hearing in respect of a complaint to a police force under subsection (8), the police force in respect of which the complaint is made shall pay the costs of the review, investigation or hearing incurred by the police force to which the matter is assigned.

(10) **Notice.**— The Commission shall notify the complainant and the chief of police, detachment commander or board, as the case may be, and the police officer who is the subject of the complaint of its decision and the action taken by it under subsection (8).

(11) **Complaint to be processed as specified.**— If notified by the Commission that the complaint is to be processed as specified, the chief of police, detachment commander or board shall immediately so process the complaint.

(12) **Final decision.**— The Commission's decision under subsection (8) is final and binding and there is no appeal therefrom.

73. (1) **Commission may direct complaint process.**— The Commission may, on its own motion and at any stage in the complaints process, direct a chief of police or board to process a complaint as it specifies or assign the review or investigation of a complaint or the conduct of a hearing in respect of a complaint to a police force other than the police force in respect of which the complaint is made.

(2) **Cost of complaints process.**— If the Commission assigns the review or investigation of a complaint or the conduct of a hearing in respect of a complaint to a police force under subsection (1), the police force in respect of which the complaint is made shall pay the costs of the review, investigation or hearing incurred by the police force to which the matter is assigned.

74. (1) **Misconduct.**— A police officer is guilty of misconduct if he or she,

    (*a*) commits an offence described in a prescribed code of conduct;

    (*b*) contravenes section 46 (political activity);

    (*c*) engages in an activity that contravenes subsection 49(1) (secondary activities) without the permission of his or her chief of police or, in the case of a chief of police, without the permission of the board, being aware that the activity may contravene that subsection;

    (*d*) contravenes subsection 55(5) (resignation during emergency);

    (*e*) contravenes section 75 (inducing misconduct, withholding services);

    (*f*) contravenes section 117 (trade union membership);

    (*g*) deals with personal property, other than money or a firearm, in a manner that is not consistent with section 132;

    (*h*) deals with money in a manner that is not consistent with section 133;

    (*i*) deals with a firearm in a manner that is not consistent with section 134;

    (*j*) contravenes a regulation made under paragraph 15 (equipment), 16 (use of force), 17 (standards of dress, police uniforms), 20 (police pursuits) or 21 (records) of subsection 135(1).

(2) **Off-duty conduct.**— A police officer shall not be found guilty of misconduct if there is no connection between the conduct and either the occupational requirements for a police officer or the reputation of the police force.

75. (1) **Inducing misconduct.**— No person, including a member of a police force, shall,

    (*a*) induce or attempt to induce a member of a police force to withhold his or her services; or

    (*b*) induce or attempt to induce a police officer to commit misconduct.

(2) **Withholding services.**— No member of a police force shall withhold his or her services.

(3) **Offence.**— A person who contravenes subsection (1) or (2) is guilty of an offence and on conviction is liable to a fine of not more than $2,000 or to imprisonment for a term of not more than one year, or to both.

(4) **Consent of Solicitor General.**— No prosecution shall be instituted under this section without the consent of the Solicitor General.

76. (1) **Delegation of chief's powers and duties.**— A chief of police may authorize a police officer or a former police officer of the rank of inspector or higher to conduct a hearing under subsection 64(7) or to act under subsection 64(11) or (15).

(2) **Same.**— A chief of police may authorize any member of any police force to exercise a power or perform a duty of the chief of police under this Part, other than those described in subsection (1).

(3) **Officer from another force.**— If a chief of police authorizes a police officer from another police force, of the rank of inspector or higher, to conduct a hearing under subsection 64(7), that police officer may do so only with the approval of his or her chief of police.

77. (1) **Notice.**— Where a notice is required to be given to or served on a person, board or the Commission under this Part, it may be served personally, by regular letter mail, by electronic transmission, by telephone transmission of a facsimile, or by some other method that allows proof of receipt.

(2) **Deemed receipt.**— Service by regular letter mail shall be deemed to be received by the person, board or Commission on the fifth day after it is mailed unless the person, board or Commission establishes that the person, board or Commission did not, acting in good faith, through absence, accident, illness or other cause beyond the person's, board's or Commission's control, receive the notice on that day.

(3) **Same.**— Service by electronic transmission or by telephone transmission of a facsimile shall be deemed to be received by the person, board or Commission on the day after it is sent or, if that day is a Saturday or holiday, on the next day that is not a Saturday or holiday, unless the person, board or Commission establishes that the person, board or Commission did not, acting in good faith, through absence, accident, illness or other cause beyond the person's, board's or Commission's control, receive the notice on that day. ...

78. *Ombudsman Act* **not to apply.**— The *Ombudsman Act* does not apply to anything done under this Part.

79. (1) **Transition, disciplinary proceedings.**— Disciplinary proceedings commenced before the coming into force of this section under Part V of the Act, as it then read, may continue to be dealt with in accordance with Part V, as it read immediately before the coming into force of this section, until January 1, 1998.

(2) **Transition, complaints.**— Public complaints made before the coming into force of this section under Part VI of the Act, as it then read, may continue to be dealt with in accordance with Part VI, as it read immediately before its repeal, until January 1, 1998.

(3) **Parties may elect to proceed under new Part V.**— If the parties to a disciplinary proceeding or public complaint described in subsection (1) or (2) agree, they may, before January 1, 1998, deal with the outstanding disciplinary proceeding or public complaint under Part V.

(4) **Proceed under new Part V from January 1, 1998.**— As of January 1, 1998, all outstanding disciplinary matters that commenced before the coming into force of this section and all proceedings with respect to public complaints that were made before the coming into force of this section shall be taken up and continued under Part V so far as consistently may be.

(5) **Saving.**— Despite subsection (4), a hearing that commenced but is not concluded before January 1, 1998 under Part V or VI of the Act, as it read immediately before its repeal by section 35 of the Police Services Amendment Act, 1997, may proceed to its conclusion after January 1, 1998 and Part V or VI of the Act, as the case may be, as it read immediately before its repeal, continues to apply to the hearing and to the powers of the chief of police, board, Commission or board of inquiry at the conclusion of the hearing.

(6) **Same.**— Despite subsection (4), an appeal made before January 1, 1998 to Divisional Court under section 98 of the Act, as it read immediately before its repeal, may proceed to its conclusion after January 1, 1998 as if section 98 of the Act had not been repealed.

80. (1) **Notice to potential complainant.**— If the complaint is made by a person who was not directly affected by the incident and did not observe it, the Commissioner shall, as soon as possible after receiving the complaint, attempt to find the person who was directly affected by the incident or who observed it and send him or her a notice.

(2) **Idem.**— The notice shall indicate that a complaint has been made, that the person is entitled to be the complainant in the matter and that the complaint will not be dealt with further unless he or she is the complainant.

(3) **Idem.**— The notice shall also include information about the procedures followed in dealing with a complaint and the rights of a complainant.

(4) **No further action.**— The complaint shall not be further dealt with under this Part if,

> (*a*) no person who was directly affected by the incident or who observed it can be found; or
>
> (*b*) the person to whom the Commissioner sends the notice does not, within thirty days of the date on which it is sent, file with the Commissioner a request to be the complainant in the matter.

(5) **Disciplinary proceeding.**— However, if a disciplinary proceeding is commenced against the police officer in respect of the complaint, the chief of police shall notify the Commissioner of the proceeding and of its result, and the Commissioner shall then notify the person who made the complaint.

(6) **Reopening of matter.**— If the person to whom the Commissioner sends the notice files a request to be the complainant in the matter after the thirty-day period referred to in subsection (4), the Commissioner may cause the matter to be reopened despite the late filing if he or she considers it advisable to do so.

81. (1) **Classification of complaint.**— When the bureau receives a complaint, the person in charge shall consider whether it relates to possible misconduct under section 56, to other matters or to both.

(2) **Idem.**— If the person in charge is of the opinion that all or part of the complaint relates only to other matters than possible misconduct, he or she may, with the Commissioner's consent, classify the complaint or part of the complaint as an inquiry.

(3) **Notice and investigation.**— When all or part of a complaint has been classified as an inquiry, the person in charge shall forthwith notify the complainant and the police officer of the fact and may cause the inquiry to be investigated.

(4) **Response to complainant.**— Not more than sixty days after the bureau receives the original complaint, the person in charge shall send the complainant a written response to the inquiry and shall also send the Commissioner a copy of the response, together with a summary of the results of any investigation.

(5) **Effect.**— A complaint or part of a complaint that is classified as an inquiry and not reclassified as a complaint and that is the subject of a response under this section need not be dealt with further under this Part.

82. (1) **Reclassification.**— During the course of the investigation of an inquiry, if the person in charge concludes that all or part of it relates to possible misconduct, he or she may reclassify the inquiry or part of the inquiry as a complaint.

(2) **Idem.**— After receiving a summary of the results of the investigation of an inquiry, the Commissioner may direct the person in charge to reclassify all or part of it as a complaint.

(3) **Notice.**— The person in charge shall forthwith notify the complainant and the police officer of the reclassification, and shall also notify the Commissioner in the case of a reclassification under subsection (1).

(4) **Effect.**— An inquiry or part of an inquiry that is reclassified as a complaint shall be dealt with as such under this Part.

INFORMAL RESOLUTION, WITHDRAWAL

83. (1) **Informal resolution by person in charge of bureau.**— If the complainant and the police officer consent, the complaint may be resolved informally by the person in charge of the bureau, before the chief of police gives notice of a decision under section 90, or by the Commissioner after that time.

(2) **Board's consent.**— If a board of inquiry has begun to hear evidence or argument in respect of the complaint, its consent is also required for an informal resolution.

(3) **Record.**— When a complaint is resolved informally, the resolution shall be recorded on a form provided by the Commissioner and signed by the complainant and police officer.

(4) **Copies.**— Copies of the record shall be provided to the complainant and the police officer, and to the Commissioner if the complaint was resolved by the person in charge of the bureau.

(5) **Commissioner's decision that complaint to continue.**— If the Commissioner is of the opinion that the informal resolution is the result of a misunderstanding or a threat or other improper pressure, he or she may decide that the complaint shall continue to be dealt with under this Part despite the informal resolution.

(6) **Notice.**— The Commissioner shall give notice of the decision, with reasons, to the complainant, the police officer, the chief of police and the person in charge of the bureau.

84. (1) **Withdrawal of complaint.**— The complainant may withdraw the complaint by giving a notice of withdrawal to the person in charge of the bureau, before the chief of police gives notice of a decision under section 90, or to the Commissioner after that time.

(2) **Idem, complaint made by Commissioner.**— If the complaint was made under section 78, the Commissioner may withdraw it by giving a notice of withdrawal to the chief of police and a copy to the police officer; subsection (3) applies to the withdrawal but subsections (4) to (7) do not.

(3) **Board's consent.**— If a board of inquiry has begun to hear evidence or argument in respect of the complaint, it shall not be withdrawn without the board's consent.

(4) **Copies.**— A copy of the notice of withdrawal shall be provided to the police officer, and to the Commissioner if the person in charge of the bureau received the notice.

(5) **Form.**— The notice of withdrawal shall be written on a form provided by the Commissioner.

(6) **Commissioner's decision that complaint to continue.**— If the Commissioner is of the opinion that the withdrawal is the result of a misunderstanding or a threat or other improper pressure, he or she may decide that the complaint shall continue to be dealt with under this Part despite the withdrawal.

(7) **Notice.**— The Commissioner shall give notice of the decision, with reasons, to the complainant, the police officer, the chief of police and the person in charge of the bureau.

POWERS OF CHIEF OF POLICE

85. (1) **Decision re no further action.**— At any time before making a decision under section 90, the chief of police may decide that the complaint or part of it shall not be further dealt with under this Part, if he or she is of the opinion that the complaint or part is frivolous or vexatious or was made in bad faith.

(2) **Notice.**— The chief of police shall give the Commissioner, the complainant and the police officer notice of the decision.

86. (1) **Power to commence or continue disciplinary proceeding.**— The chief of police may commence or continue a disciplinary proceeding against a police officer under Part V even if,

   (*a*) the complaint is withdrawn or is resolved informally; or

   (*b*) the complaint is not to be further dealt with under this Part because of subsection 77(7) (complaint filed more than six months after incident) or section 80 (complaint made by person not directly affected), or because of a decision by the chief of police under section 85.

(2) **Notice to Commissioner and complainant.**— The chief of police shall give the Commissioner and the complainant notice of a decision to commence or continue a disciplinary proceeding in the circumstances described in subsection (1), and shall also give them notice of the results of the proceeding.

INVESTIGATION OF COMPLAINT

87. (1) **Investigation.**— The person in charge of the bureau shall cause an investigation to be conducted into the complaint in accordance with the prescribed procedures.

(2) **Interim reports.**— During the course of the investigation, the person in charge shall send the Commissioner, the complainant and the police officer interim reports on the investigation at monthly intervals.

(3) **Idem.**— The first interim report shall be sent not more than thirty days after the bureau receives the complaint.

(4) **Exception.**— If there are no new matters to report, the person in charge may send the Commissioner, the complainant and the police officer a notice to that effect instead of an interim report.

(5) **Idem.**— The person in charge may withhold an interim report from the complainant or the police officer if, in his or her opinion, it is desirable to do so in order to avoid prejudicing the investigation, but in that case shall forthwith notify the Commissioner of the decision and the reasons for it.

(6) **Final report.**— When the investigation has been completed, the person in charge shall cause a final report to be prepared and shall send copies of it to the Commissioner, the chief of police, the complainant and the police officer.

(7) **Contents.**— The final report shall contain,

(*a*) a summary of the complaint, including a description of the police officer's alleged misconduct;

(*b*) a summary of the investigation, including summaries of the information obtained from the complainant, the police officer and any witnesses; and

(*c*) a description and analysis of any physical evidence obtained.

(8) **Further investigation.**— After receiving a final report, the Commissioner may require the chief of police to have the complaint investigated further.

(9) **Idem.**— A summary of the results of any further investigation shall be sent to the persons who received the final report.

(10) **Forms.**— The interim reports and final report shall be written on forms provided by the Commissioner.

88. (1) **Investigation by Commissioner.**— The Commissioner may conduct the investigation into the complaint, instead of the bureau,

(*a*) for any reason, after receiving the first interim report or after the thirty-day period referred to in subsection 87(3) has expired;

(*b*) if the complainant has commenced a court proceeding against the police officer, the police force or the chief of police, the police services board or the municipality (in the case of a municipal police force) or the Crown in right of Ontario (in the case of the Ontario Provincial Police) in connection with the incident to which the complaint relates;

(*c*) if the Commissioner has reasonable grounds to believe that undue delay or other unusual circumstances have affected the bureau's investigation or the preparation of its final report; or

(*d*) if the chief of police requests that the Commissioner conduct the investigation.

(2) **Duty of chief of police.**— The chief of police, if he or she becomes aware that the complainant has commenced a court proceeding of the kind described in clause (1)(b), shall forthwith notify the Commissioner of the fact.

(3) **Complaints concerning more than one police force.**— If the complaint concerns more than one police force, the Commissioner shall conduct the investigation.

(4) **Notice.**— When the Commissioner decides to conduct the investigation, he or she shall forthwith notify the chief of police, giving reasons in the case of a decision under clause (1)(a) or (c).

(5) **Effect on bureau.**— When the Commissioner notifies the chief of police of a decision to conduct the investigation, the person in charge of the bureau shall forthwith end any investigation begun by the bureau and send to the Commissioner the evidence that has been gathered and the documents relating to the complaint.

(6) **Manner of conducting investigation.**— Section 87 applies to the Commissioner's investigation, with necessary modifications, except that the Commissioner shall send the first interim report not more than thirty days after giving notice of the decision to conduct the investigation.

89. (1) **Investigation of complaint made by Commissioner.**— If the complaint was made under section 78, the Commissioner shall conduct the investigation in accordance with the prescribed procedures, and section 87 does not apply.

(2) **Interim reports.**— The Commissioner shall send the police officer and the chief of police interim reports on the investigation at monthly intervals.

(3) **Idem.**— The first interim report shall be sent not more than thirty days after the Commissioner makes the complaint.

(4) **Exception.**— If there are no new matters to report, the Commissioner may send the police officer and the chief of police a notice to that effect instead of an interim report.

(5) **Idem.**— The Commissioner may withhold an interim report from the police officer if, in his or her opinion, it is desirable to do so to avoid prejudicing the investigation, but in that case shall forthwith notify the chief of police of the decision and the reasons for it.

(6) **Final report.**— When the investigation has been completed, the Commissioner shall cause a final report to be prepared and shall send copies of it to the chief of police and the police officer.

(7) **Contents.**— The final report shall contain,

   (*a*) a summary of the complaint, including a description of the police officer's alleged misconduct;

   (*b*) a summary of the investigation, including summaries of the information obtained from the police officer and any witnesses; and

   (*c*) a description and analysis of any physical evidence obtained.

DECISION BY CHIEF OF POLICE

90. (1) **Review of final report.**— The chief of police shall review the final report of the investigation of a complaint and may order further investigation if he or she considers it advisable.

(2) **Results of further investigation.**— A summary of the results of any further investigation shall be sent to the persons who received the final report, and to the Commissioner if he or she conducted the original investigation.

(3) **Decision.**— After reviewing the final report and the results of any further investigation, the chief of police shall,

   (*a*) decide that no further action is necessary;

   (*b*) admonish the police officer regarding the matter in accordance with subsection 59(1);

   (*c*) hold a disciplinary hearing under section 60;

   (*d*) order that all or part of the complaint be the subject of a hearing by a board of inquiry; or (*e*) cause an information to be laid against the police officer and refer the matter to the Crown Attorney for prosecution.

(4) **Idem.**— If the chief of police decides to hold a disciplinary hearing under section 60 or orders a hearing by a board of inquiry, he or she may at the same time cause an information to be laid against the police officer.

(5) **Notice.**— The chief of police shall give written notice of the decision to the Commissioner, the complainant and the police officer, with reasons in the case of a decision that no further action is necessary or a decision to admonish the police officer.

(6) **Idem.**— If the chief of police orders a hearing by a board of inquiry, he or she shall also notify the chair appointed under subsection 103(9).

(7) **Six-month time limit.**— The chief of police shall give notice of the decision within six months of receiving the final report, unless the Commissioner grants an extension.

(8) **Deemed decision.**— If the chief of police does not give notice of the decision within the six-month period and is not granted an extension, he or she shall be deemed to have decided that no further action is necessary.

REVIEW BY COMMISSIONER

91. (1) **Review by Commissioner.**— The Commissioner shall review the decision of the chief of police,

(*a*) at the complainant's or police officer's request, in the case of a decision under section 90 to admonish the police officer;

(*b*) at the complainant's request, in the case of a decision under section 90 that no further action is necessary;

(*c*) at the complainant's request, in the case of a decision under section 85 that the complaint or part of it not be further dealt with under this Part.

(2) **Idem.**— The Commissioner may, if in his or her opinion it is in the public interest to do so, review the decision of the chief of police,

(*a*) in the case of a decision under section 90 to admonish the police officer;

(*b*) in the case of a decision under section 90 that no further action is necessary;

(*c*) in the case of a decision under section 85 that the complaint or part of it not be further dealt with under this Part.

(3) **Idem.**— The Commissioner shall, at the complainant's request, review the decision made in a disciplinary hearing under section 60 arising out of a complaint.

(4) **Thirty-day limit.**— The complainant or police officer may request a review by the Commissioner only within thirty days of receiving notice of the decision, unless the Commissioner grants an extension.

(5) **Complaint made by Commissioner.**— In the case of a complaint made under section 78, the Commissioner may review,

(*a*) a decision by the chief of police to admonish the police officer;

(*b*) a decision by the chief of police that no further action is necessary;

(*c*) the decision made in a disciplinary hearing under section 60 arising out of the complaint.

(6) **Commissioner's decision.**— After conducting the review, the Commissioner may decide to take no further action, or may order a hearing by a board of inquiry if he or she believes it to be necessary in the public interest.

(7) **Notice.**— The Commissioner shall forthwith give written notice of his or her decision, with reasons in the case of a decision to take no further action, to the chief of police, the complainant and the police officer.

(8) **Idem.**— If the Commissioner orders a hearing by a board of inquiry, he or she shall also notify the chair appointed under subsection 103(9).

HEARING BY BOARD OF INQUIRY

92. (1) **Police officer's appeal to board.**— If a penalty is imposed on a police officer after a disciplinary hearing under section 60 that was conducted as a result of the complaint, he or she may appeal to a board of inquiry by serving a notice of appeal on the Commissioner, the chair of the panel and the chief of police within fifteen days of receiving notice of the decision.

(2) **Notice to complainant.**— The Commissioner shall forthwith notify the complainant of the appeal.

(3) **Extension of time for appeal.**— A member of the panel who was appointed on a recommendation made under subsection 103(2) may grant an extension of the time provided for serving a notice of appeal, before or after the expiry of the time, and may give directions in connection with the extension.

(4) **Appeal to be combined with other hearing.**— The hearing of the police officer's appeal and any hearing ordered by the Commissioner under section 91 shall be combined.

93. (1) **Constitution of board.**— A board of inquiry shall be constituted,

  (*a*) when the chief of police orders under section 90 that a matter be heard by a board of inquiry;

  (*b*) when the Commissioner orders a hearing under section 91; and

  (*c*) when a police officer appeals under section 92.

(2) **Assignment of members to board.**— The chair of the panel shall assign the following members of the panel to the board of inquiry, choosing members from the area where the complaint arose if possible:

1. As presiding officer, a member who was appointed on a recommendation made under subsection 103(2).

2. A member who was appointed on a recommendation made under subsection 103(3).

3. A member who was appointed on a recommendation made under subsection 103(4).

(3) **Complaint against chief of police.**— In the case of a complaint against a chief of police, the board of inquiry shall include, instead of a member of the panel who was appointed on a recommendation made under subsection 103(3), a person, other than a police officer or a member of the Law Society of Upper Canada, appointed to the board of inquiry by the chair of the panel on the recommendation of the Ontario Association of Chiefs of Police.

94. (1) **New hearing, exception.**— The hearing before the board of inquiry shall be a new hearing, unless it follows a disciplinary hearing under section 60; in that case it shall be on the record, but the board may receive new or additional evidence as it considers just.

(2) **Record of disciplinary hearing.**— If a board is constituted following a disciplinary hearing, the chief of police shall cause a record of the hearing to be prepared, at the Commissioner's expense if the Commissioner ordered the hearing before the board.

(3) **Idem.**— The record shall include a transcript and shall be accompanied by the documents, physical evidence and exhibits considered at the disciplinary hearing.

95. (1) **Parties.**— The parties to a hearing are,

(*a*) the complainant;

(*b*) the police officer;

(*c*) the Commissioner; and

(*d*) the chief of police, in the case of an appeal by the police officer.

(2) **Idem.**— The board of inquiry may add parties at any stage of the hearing on the conditions it considers proper.

(3) **Carriage.**— In the case of a hearing ordered by the chief of police or by the Commissioner, the Commissioner has carriage of the matter and, in the case of an appeal by the police officer, the police officer has carriage.

(4) **Statement of alleged misconduct.**— In the case of a hearing ordered by the chief of police or by the Commissioner, the chief of police or the Commissioner, as the case may be, shall provide the parties with a concise statement of the allegations of misconduct to be heard.

96. (1) **Notice of hearing.**— The board of inquiry shall appoint a time for the hearing and notify the parties.

(2) **Examination of evidence.**— Before the hearing, the police officer and the complainant shall be given an opportunity to examine any physical or documentary evidence that will be produced or any report whose contents will be given in evidence at the hearing.

(3) **Recording of evidence.**— The oral evidence given at the hearing shall be recorded and copies of transcripts shall be provided on the same terms as in the Ontario Court (General Division).

(4) **Application.**— Section 136 of the *Courts of Justice Act* (photography at court hearing) applies with necessary modifications to the hearing.

(5) **Police officer not required to give evidence.**— Despite section 12 of the *Statutory Powers Procedure Act*, the police officer shall not be required to give evidence at the hearing.

(6) **Limited admissibility of certain statements.**— No statement made by the police officer or complainant in the course of an attempt to resolve the complaint informally shall be admitted in evidence at the hearing, except with the consent of the person who made the statement.

(7) **Board not to communicate in relation to subject-matter of hearing.**— The board of inquiry shall not communicate directly or indirectly in relation to the subject-matter of the hearing with any person or party or party's counsel or representative, unless all parties receive notice and have an opportunity to participate.

(8) **Exception.**— However, the board may seek legal advice from an adviser independent of the parties, and in that case the nature of the advice shall be communicated to the parties so that they may make submissions as to the law.

(9) **Adjournment for view.**— If it appears to be in the interests of justice, the board may direct that the board, the parties and their counsel or representatives shall have a view of any place or thing, and may adjourn the hearing for that purpose.

(10) **Release of exhibits.**— Within a reasonable time after the matter has been finally determined, documents and things put in evidence at the hearing shall, on request, be released to the person who produced them.

(11) **Stay.**— If the police officer is charged with an offence under a law of Canada or of a province or territory in connection with the misconduct or possible misconduct to which the complaint relates, the hearing shall continue unless the Crown Attorney advises the presiding officer that it should be stayed until the conclusion of the court proceedings.

(12) **Only members at hearing to participate in decision.**— No member of the board shall participate in a decision unless he or she was present throughout the hearing and heard the parties' evidence and argument; except with the parties' consent, no decision shall be given unless all the members so present participate in it.

(13) **Decision.**— The decision of a majority of the members of the board is the board's decision.

97. (1) **Penalties.**— If misconduct is proved at the hearing on clear and convincing evidence, the chief of police may make submissions as to penalty and the board of inquiry may,

   (*a*) dismiss the police officer from the police force;

   (*b*) direct that the police officer be dismissed in seven days unless he or she resigns before that time;

   (*c*) demote the police officer, specifying the manner and period of the demotion;

   (*d*) suspend the police officer without pay for a period not exceeding thirty days or 240 hours, as the case may be;

   (*e*) direct that the police officer forfeit not more than five days' or forty hours' pay, as the case may be; or

   (*f*) direct that the police officer forfeit not more than twenty days or 160 hours off, as the case may be.

(2) **Calculation.**— Penalties imposed under clauses (1)(d), (e) and (f) shall be calculated in terms of days if the police officer normally works eight hours a day or less and in terms of hours if he or she normally works more than eight hours a day.

(3) **Idem.**— Instead of or in addition to a penalty described in subsection (1), the board may reprimand the police officer.

(4) **Notice of decision.**— The board shall promptly give written notice of the decision, with reasons, to the parties and the Attorney General.

98. (1) **Appeal to Divisional Court.**— A party to a hearing before a board of inquiry may appeal to the Divisional Court within thirty days of receiving notice of the board's decision.

(2) **Grounds for appeal.**— An appeal may be made on a question that is not a question of fact alone, or from a penalty, or both.

(3) **Attorney General.**— The Attorney General is entitled to be heard, by counsel or otherwise, on the argument of the appeal.

POLICE COMPLAINTS COMMISSIONER

99. (1) **Appointment of Commissioner.**— The Lieutenant Governor in Council shall appoint a Police Complaints Commissioner, to hold office for a term not exceeding five years.

(2) **Reappointment.**— The Commissioner may be reappointed for a further term or terms not exceeding five years in each case.

(3) **Employees.**— Such employees as are considered necessary for the purposes of this Part may be appointed under the *Public Service Act*.

(4) **Remuneration.**— The Commissioner shall be paid such remuneration and allowance for expenses as may be fixed by the Lieutenant Governor in Council.

(5) **Records.**— The Commissioner shall maintain copies of all records, reports and other materials received under this Part.

(6) **Monitoring handling of complaints.**— The Commissioner shall monitor the handling of complaints by bureaus and chiefs of police.

(7) **Local offices.**— The Commissioner may establish local offices.

(8) **Idem.**— Anything that is given to or served upon the Commissioner under this Part may be given or served at one of the local offices.

(9) **Annual report.**— The Commissioner shall report annually to the Attorney General.

(10) **Audit.**— The Commissioner's accounts shall be audited annually by the Provincial Auditor.

100. (1) **Powers on investigation or review.**— For the purposes of an investigation under section 88 or 89 or a review under section 91, the Commissioner may, if he or she has reasonable grounds to believe that it is necessary to do so in furtherance of the investigation or review, enter a police station after informing the chief of police and examine there documents and things related to the complaint.

(2) **Powers on inquiry.**— For the purposes of an investigation or review, the Commissioner has the powers of a commission under Part II of the *Public Inquiries Act*, which Part applies to the investigation or review as if it were an inquiry under that Act.

(3) **Appointment of person to make investigation or review.**— The Commissioner may, in writing, appoint a person to make any investigation or review the Commissioner is authorized to make and the person has all the powers and duties of the Commissioner relating to the investigation and the review.

(4) **Identification.**— The person shall be provided with a certificate of appointment containing his or her photograph, and while exercising any powers or performing any duties in respect of the investigation or review shall produce the certificate of appointment upon request.

(5) **Report.**— The person shall report the results of the investigation or review to the Commissioner.

(6) **Obstruction.**— No person shall obstruct the Commissioner or a person appointed under subsection (3) or withhold from the Commissioner or person or conceal or destroy any documents or things related to the investigation or review.

(7) **Search warrant.**— If a justice of the peace is satisfied, on an application made without notice by the Commissioner or a person appointed under subsection (3), that there are reasonable grounds to believe that there are in any place documents or things relating to an investigation or review, the justice of the peace may make an order authorizing the applicant, together with such persons as he or she calls on for assistance, to enter the place, by force if necessary, search for the documents or things and examine them.

(8) **Entry and search at night restricted.**— The entry and search shall not be made between the hours of 9 p.m. and 6 a.m. unless the order so authorizes.

(9) **Removal of books, etc.**— The Commissioner may, upon giving a receipt, remove any documents or things examined under subsection (1) or (7) relating to the investigation or review, shall cause them to be copied with reasonable dispatch and shall then return them promptly to the person from whom they were removed.

(10) **Admissibility of copies.**— A copy made as provided in subsection (9) and certified to be a true copy by the Commissioner is admissible in evidence in any proceeding and is proof, in the absence of evidence to the contrary, of the original document and its contents.

(11) **Appointment of expert.**— The Commissioner may appoint an expert to examine documents or things examined under subsection (1) or (7).

101. (1) **Recommendations concerning police practices or procedures.**— The Commissioner may make recommendations with respect to the practices or procedures of a police force by sending the recommendations, with any supporting documents, to,

      (*a*) the Attorney General;

      (*b*) the Solicitor General;

      (*c*) the chief of police;

      (*d*) the association, if any; and

      (*e*) the police services board, in the case of a municipal police force.

(2) **Comments.**— Within ninety days of receiving the recommendations, the chief of police, association and police services board shall send their comments to the Attorney General, the Solicitor General and the Commissioner.

102. Judicial review of Commissioner's decisions.— The Commissioner's decisions under subsection 83(5) (complaint to continue to be dealt with despite informal resolution), subsection 84(6) (complaint to continue to be dealt with despite withdrawal) and clause 88(1)(c) (decision to conduct investigation because of undue delay) shall be deemed to be made in the exercise of a statutory power of decision.

BOARDS OF INQUIRY

103. (1) **Panel for boards of inquiry.**— The Lieutenant Governor in Council shall appoint a panel of persons to act as members of boards of inquiry to conduct hearings in connection with complaints.

(2) **Recommendations for appointment.**— One-third of the members of the panel shall be members of the Law Society of Upper Canada who are recommended for appointment by the Attorney General.

(3) **Idem.**— One-third of the members of the panel shall be persons, other than police officers and members of the Law Society of Upper Canada, who are recommended for appointment by the Police Association of Ontario.

(4) **Idem.**— One-third of the members of the panel shall be persons, other than police officers and members of the Law Society of Upper Canada, who are recommended for appointment by the Association of Municipalities of Ontario.

(5) **Failure to make recommendations.**— The Attorney General may make the recommendations under subsection (3) or (4) if the Police Association of Ontario or the Association of Municipalities of Ontario, as the case may be, do not submit written recommendations to the Attorney General within the time that he or she specifies.

(6) **Term.**— Appointments to the panel shall be for a term not exceeding three years and a member may be reappointed for a further term or terms.

(7) **Continuance in office for uncompleted assignments.**— A member of the panel whose term expires without reappointment continues in office for the purpose of completing the work of a board to which he or she was assigned before the expiration of the term.

(8) **Remuneration.**— The members of the panel shall be paid such remuneration and expenses as may be fixed by the Lieutenant Governor in Council.

(9) **Chair.**— The Lieutenant Governor in Council shall appoint a person to be the chair of the panel.

(10) **Annual summary of decisions.**— The chair shall cause to be prepared and published an annual summary of the decisions of boards, with reasons.

GENERAL MATTERS

104. Police officer's employment record.— No reference to a complaint, a hearing held under this Part or a disciplinary hearing conducted under section 60 as a result of the complaint shall be made in the police officer's employment record, and the matter shall not be taken into account for any purpose related to his or her employment, unless,

(*a*) the police officer is convicted of an offence in connection with the incident;

(*b*) misconduct is proved on clear and convincing evidence at a hearing held under this Part or at a disciplinary hearing;

(*c*) the chief of police admonishes the police officer in connection with the incident, in accordance with subsection 59(1);

(*d*) the police officer admits misconduct in the course of attempts to resolve the complaint informally; or

(*e*) the police officer resigns before the complaint is finally disposed of.

105. (1) **Resignation after hearing ordered.**— This section applies to a police officer who resigns from the police force after a hearing is ordered under section 90 or 91.

(2) **Idem.**— If the police officer resigns before a board of inquiry is constituted under section 93, the following rules apply:

1. No board of inquiry shall be constituted unless the police officer, within twelve months of the resignation, applies for employment with a police force or is employed by a police force.

2. In that case, the board acquires jurisdiction over the police officer despite the earlier resignation.

(3) **Idem.**— If the police officer resigns after a board of inquiry is constituted, the following rules apply:

1. The board of inquiry loses jurisdiction over the police officer.

2. If the police officer, within twelve months of the resignation, applies for employment with a police force or is employed by a police force, the board's jurisdiction is revived.

106. (1) **Notice.**— A notice or other document required to be given or sent under this Part is sufficiently given if delivered personally or sent by prepaid registered mail addressed to the person.

(2) **Notice by mail.**— Notice that is given by mail shall be deemed to be given on the fifth day after the day of mailing, unless the person to whom the notice is to be given establishes that he or she, acting in good faith, through absence, accident, illness or other cause beyond his or her control failed to receive the notice until a later date.

107. (1) **Delegation by chief of police.**— The chief of police may authorize any police officer of the rank of inspector or higher (from another police force if there is none in the chief's own police force) to exercise any power or perform any duty of the chief of police referred to in this Part.

(2) **Delegation by Commissioner.**— The Commissioner may authorize any member of his or her staff to exercise any power or perform any duty of the Commissioner referred to in this Part.

108. (1) **Application of section.**— This section applies to every person engaged in the administration of this Part, including a member of a police force.

(2) **Confidentiality, exceptions.**— A person shall preserve secrecy in respect of all information obtained in the course of his or her duties and not contained in a record as defined in the *Freedom of Information and Protection of Privacy Act*, and shall not communicate such information to any other person except,

(*a*) in accordance with subsection (3);

(*b*) as may be required for law enforcement purposes; or

(*c*) with the consent of the person, if any, to whom the information relates.

(3) **Permitted disclosure.**— A person may communicate information obtained in the course of his or her duties,

(*a*) as may be required in connection with the administration of this Act and the regulations; or

(*b*) to his or her counsel.

(4) **Non-compellability.**— No person shall be required to testify in a civil proceeding with regard to information obtained in the course of his or her duties, except at a hearing held under this Part or at a disciplinary hearing held under Part V.

(5) **Inadmissibility of documents.**— No document prepared under this Part as the result of a complaint and no statement referred to in subsection 96(6) (statements made during attempt at informal resolution) is admissible in a civil proceeding, except at a hearing held under this Part or at a disciplinary hearing held under Part V.

109. *Ombudsman Act* **not to apply.**— The *Ombudsman Act* does not apply to anything done under this Part.

110. Agreement for contributions.— The Attorney General may, with the approval of the Lieutenant Governor in Council, enter into an agreement with a municipality providing for its payment to the Treasurer of Ontario, on such conditions as may be agreed upon, of contributions in respect of the amounts required for the purposes of this Part.

111. Offence.— A person who contravenes subsection 96(4) (photography at hearing), 100(6) (obstructing Commissioner) or 108(2) (confidentiality) is guilty of an offence and on conviction is liable to a fine of not more than $2,000.

112. (1) **Definition.**— In this section , "former Act" means the *Metropolitan Toronto Police Force Complaints Act, 1984* being chapter 63.

(2) **Transition, complaints under former Act.**— Despite the repeal of the former Act, complaints made under the former Act before the 31st day of December, 1990 shall be dealt with in accordance with the former Act, except that hearings before boards of inquiry that are constituted after the 31st day of December, 1990 shall be conducted in accordance with this Part.

(3) **Transition, boards of inquiry.**— Members of boards of inquiry constituted under the former Act before the 31st day of December, 1990 are continued in office for the purpose of completing the work of the boards to which they were assigned. ...

PART VII
SPECIAL INVESTIGATIONS

113. (1) **Special investigations unit.**— There shall be a special investigations unit of the Ministry of the Solicitor General.

(2) **Composition.**— The unit shall consist of a director appointed by the Lieutenant Governor in Council on the recommendation of the Solicitor General and investigators appointed under the *Public Service Act.*

(3) **Idem.**— A person who is a police officer or former police officer shall not be appointed as director, and persons who are police officers shall not be appointed as investigators.

(4) **Peace officers.**— The director and investigators are peace officers.

(5) **Investigations.**— The director may, on his or her own initiative, and shall, at the request of the Solicitor General or Attorney General, cause investigations to be conducted into the circumstances of serious injuries and deaths that may have resulted from criminal offences committed by police officers.

(6) **Restriction.**— An investigator shall not participate in an investigation that relates to members of a police force of which he or she was a member.

(7) **Charges.**— If there are reasonable grounds to do so in his or her opinion, the director shall cause informations to be laid against police officers in connection with the matters investigated and shall refer them to the Crown Attorney for prosecution.

(8) **Report.**— The director shall report the results of investigations to the Attorney General.

(9) **Co-operation of police forces.**— Members of police forces shall co-operate fully with the members of the unit in the conduct of investigations.

PART VIII
LABOUR RELATIONS

114. Definitions.— In this Part,
"Arbitration Commission" means the Ontario Police Arbitration Commission continued by subsection 131(1);
"senior officer" means a member of a police force who has the rank of inspector or higher or is employed in a supervisory or confidential capacity.

115. (1) **Exclusion of O.P.P.**— This Part, except section 117, does not apply to the Ontario Provincial Police.

(2) **Exclusion of chief of police and deputy.**— The working conditions and remuneration of the chief of police and deputy chief of police of a police force shall be determined under clause 31(1)(d) (responsibilities of board) and not under this Part.

116. (1) **Hearing re person's status.**— If there is a dispute as to whether a person is a member of a police force or a senior officer, any affected person may apply to the Commission to hold a hearing and decide the matter.

(2) **Decision final.**— The Commission's decision is final.

117. Membership in trade union prohibited, exception.— A member of a police force shall not become or remain a member of a trade union or of an organization that is affiliated directly or indirectly with a trade union, unless the membership is required for secondary activities that do not contravene section 49 and the chief of police consents.

118. (1) **Categories.**— If a majority of the members of a police force, or an association that is entitled to give notices of desire to bargain, assigns the members of the police force to different categories for the purposes of this Part, bargaining, conciliation and arbitration shall be carried on as if each category were a separate police force.

(2) **Senior officers.**— If at least 50 per cent of the senior officers of a police force belong to an association composed only of senior officers, bargaining, conciliation and arbitration shall be carried on as if the senior officers were a separate police force.

(3) **Restriction.**— Bargaining, conciliation and arbitration may be carried on with more than two categories within a police force (apart from senior officers) only if the Commission has approved the creation of the categories.

119. (1) **Notice of desire to bargain.**— If no agreement exists or at any time after ninety days before an agreement would expire but for subsection 129(1) or (2), a majority of the members of a police force may give the board notice in writing of their desire to bargain with a view to making an agreement, renewing the existing agreement, with or without modifications, or making a new agreement.

(2) **Bargaining.**— Within fifteen days after the notice of desire to bargain is given or within the longer period that the parties agree upon, the board shall meet with a bargaining committee of the members of the police force.

(3) **Idem.**— The parties shall bargain in good faith and make every reasonable effort to come to an agreement dealing with the remuneration, pensions, sick leave credit gratuities and grievance procedures of the members of the police force and, subject to section 126, their working conditions.

(4) **Filing of agreement.**— The board shall promptly file a copy of any agreement with the Arbitration Commission.

(5) **Association.**— If at least 50 per cent of the members of the police force belong to an association, it shall give the notice of desire to bargain.

(6) **Municipal plans, notice to Minister.**— If the notice of desire to bargain involves pensions under a pension plan established or to be established under the *Municipal Act*, it shall also be given to the Minister of Municipal Affairs, who may determine the maximum pension benefits that may be included in any agreement or award with respect to the pension plan.

120. (1) **Bargaining committee.**— The members of the bargaining committee shall be members of the police force.

(2) **Counsel and advisors.**— One legal counsel and one other advisor for each of the bargaining committee and the board may participate in the bargaining sessions.

(3) **Police organization.**— If the notice of desire to bargain is given by an association that is affiliated with a police organization, or if at least 50 per cent of the members of the police force belong to a police organization, a member of the organization may attend the parties' bargaining sessions in an advisory capacity.

(4) **Chief of police.**— The chief of police or, if the parties consent, another person designated by the chief of police may also attend the parties' bargaining sessions in an advisory capacity.

121. (1) **Appointment of conciliation officer.**— The Solicitor General shall appoint a conciliation officer, at a party's request, if a notice of desire to bargain has been given.

(2) **Duty of conciliation officer.**— The conciliation officer shall confer with the parties and endeavour to effect an agreement and shall, within fourteen days after being appointed, make a written report of the results to the Solicitor General.

(3) **Extension of time.**— The fourteen-day period may be extended if the parties agree or if the Solicitor General extends it on the advice of the conciliation officer that an agreement may be made within a reasonable time if the period is extended.

(4) **Report.**— When the conciliation officer reports to the Solicitor General that an agreement has been reached or that an agreement cannot be reached, the Solicitor General shall promptly inform the parties of the report.

(5) **No arbitration until after conciliation.**— Neither party shall give a notice requiring matters in dispute to be referred to arbitration under section 122 until a conciliation officer has been appointed, endeavoured to effect an agreement and reported to the Solicitor General and the Solicitor General has informed the parties of the conciliation officer's report.

122. (1) **Arbitration.**— If matters remain in dispute after bargaining under section 119 and conciliation under section 121, a party may give the chair of the Arbitration Commission and the other party a written notice referring the matters to arbitration.

(2) **Composition of arbitration board.**— The following rules apply to the composition of the arbitration board:

1. The parties shall determine whether it shall consist of one person or of three persons. If they are unable to agree on this matter, or if they agree that the arbitration board shall consist of three persons but one of the parties then fails to appoint a person in accordance with the agreement, the arbitration board shall consist of one person.

2. If the arbitration board is to consist of one person, the parties shall appoint him or her jointly. If they are unable to agree on a joint appointment, the person shall be appointed by the chair of the Arbitration Commission.

3. If the arbitration board is to consist of three persons, the parties shall each appoint one person and shall jointly appoint a chair. If they are unable to agree on a joint appointment, the chair shall be appointed by the chair of the Arbitration Commission.

4. If the arbitration board consists of one person who was appointed by the chair of the Arbitration Commission or if the arbitration board consists of three persons and the chair was appointed by the chair of the Arbitration Commission, the chair of the Arbitration Commission shall select the method of arbitration and shall advise the arbitration board of the selection. The method selected shall be mediation-arbitration unless the chair of the Arbitration Commission is of the view that another method is more appropriate. The method selected shall not be final offer selection without mediation and it shall not be mediation-final offer selection unless the chair of the Arbitration Commission in his or her sole discretion selects that method because he or she is of the view that it is the most appropriate method having regard to the nature of the dispute. If the method selected is mediation-final offer selection, the chair of the arbitration board shall be the mediator or, if the arbitration board consists of one person, that person shall be the mediator.

(3) **When hearings commence.**— The arbitration board shall hold the first hearing within 30 days after the chair is appointed or, if the arbitration board consists of one person, within 30 days after that person is appointed.

(3.1) **Exception.**— If the method of arbitration selected by the chair of the Arbitration Commission is mediation-arbitration or mediation-final offer selection, the time limit set out in subsection (3) does not apply in respect of the first hearing but applies instead, with necessary modifications, in respect of the commencement of mediation.

(3.2) **Time for submission of information.**— If the method of arbitration selected by the chair of the Arbitration Commission is mediation-arbitration or mediation-final offer selection, the chair of the arbitration board or, if the arbitration board consists of one person, that person may, after consulting with the parties, set a date after which a party may not submit information to the board unless, (*a*) the information was not available prior to the date;

    (*b*) the chair or, if the arbitration board consists of one person, that person permits the submission of the information; and

    (*c*) the other party is given an opportunity to make submissions concerning the information.

(3.3) **Hearing.**— If the method of arbitration selected by the chair of the Arbitration Commission is conventional arbitration, the arbitration board shall hold a hearing, but the chair of the arbitration board or, if the arbitration board consists of one person, that person may impose limits on the submissions of the parties and the presentation of their cases.

(3.4) **Consolidation of disputes.**— Disputes may be arbitrated together only if all the parties to the disputes agree.

(3.5) **Time for decision.**— The arbitration board shall give a decision within 90 days after the chair is appointed or, if the arbitration board consists of one person, within 90 days after that person is appointed.

(3.6) **Extension.**— The parties may agree to extend the time described in subsection (3.5), either before or after the time has passed.

(3.7) **Remuneration and expenses.**— The remuneration and expenses of the members of an arbitration board shall be paid as follows:

    1. A party shall pay the remuneration and expenses of a member appointed by or on behalf of the party.

    2. Each party shall pay one-half of the chair's remuneration and expenses or, if the arbitration board consists of one person, one-half of that person's remuneration and expenses.

(4) **Representations by council.**— The municipal council may make representations before the arbitration board if it is authorized to do so by a resolution.

(5) **Criteria.**— In making a decision or award, the arbitration board shall take into consideration all factors it considers relevant, including the following criteria:

    1. The employer's ability to pay in light of its fiscal situation.

    2. The extent to which services may have to be reduced, in light of the decision or award, if current funding and taxation levels are not increased.

    3. The economic situation in Ontario and in the municipality.

    4. A comparison, as between the employees and other comparable employees in the public and private sectors, of the terms and conditions of employment and the nature of the work performed.

    5. The employer's ability to attract and retain qualified employees.

    6. The interest and welfare of the community served by the police force.

    7. Any local factors affecting that community.

(5.1) **Transition.**— Subsection (5) does not apply if, on or before the day the *Savings and Restructuring Act, 1996* receives Royal Assent,

    (*a*) an oral or electronic hearing has begun; or

(*b*) the arbitration board has received all the submissions, if no oral or electronic hearing is held.

(5.2) **Restriction.**— Nothing in subsection (5) affects the powers of the arbitration board.

(6) **Filing of award.**— The arbitration board shall promptly file a copy of its decision or award with the Arbitration Commission. ...

122.1 (1) **Existing proceedings discontinued.**— Proceedings before an arbitrator or arbitration board under this Act in which a hearing commenced before the date on which subsection 5(6) of the *Public Sector Dispute Resolution Act, 1997* comes into force are terminated and any decision in such proceedings is void.

(2) **Exception, completed proceedings.**— This section does not apply with respect to proceedings if,

(*a*) a final decision is issued on or before June 3, 1997; or

(*b*) a final decision is issued after June 3, 1997 and the decision is served before the date on which subsection 5(6) of the *Public Sector Dispute Resolution Act, 1997* comes into force.

(3) **Exception, by agreement.**— This section does not apply if the parties agree in writing after June 3, 1997 to continue the proceedings.

123. (1) **Dispute, appointment of conciliation officer.**— The Solicitor General shall appoint a conciliation officer, at a party's request, if a difference arises between the parties concerning an agreement or an arbitrator's decision or award made under this Part, or if it is alleged that an agreement or award has been violated.

(2) **Duty of conciliation officer.**— The conciliation officer shall confer with the parties and endeavour to resolve the dispute and shall, within fourteen days after being appointed, make a written report of the results to the Solicitor General.

(3) **Extension of time.**— The fourteen-day period may be extended if the parties agree or if the Solicitor General extends it on the advice of the conciliation officer that the dispute may be resolved within a reasonable time if the period is extended.

(4) **Report.**— When the conciliation officer reports to the Solicitor General that the dispute has been resolved or that it cannot be resolved by conciliation, the Solicitor General shall promptly inform the parties of the report.

(5) **No arbitration during conciliation.**— Neither party shall give a notice referring the dispute to arbitration until the Solicitor General has informed the parties of the conciliation officer's report.

124. (1) **Arbitration after conciliation fails.**— If the conciliation officer reports that the dispute cannot be resolved by conciliation, either party may give the Solicitor General and the other party a written notice referring the dispute to arbitration.

(2) **Idem.**— The procedure provided by subsection (1) is available in addition to any grievance or arbitration procedure provided by the agreement, decision or award.

(3) **Composition of arbitration board.**— The following rules apply to the composition of the arbitration board:

1. The parties shall determine whether it shall consist of one person or of three persons. If they are unable to agree on this matter, or if they

agree that the arbitration board shall consist of three persons but one of the parties then fails to appoint a person in accordance with the agreement, the arbitration board shall consist of one person.

2. If the arbitration board is to consist of one person, the parties shall appoint him or her jointly. If they are unable to agree on a joint appointment, the person shall be appointed by the Solicitor General.

3. If the arbitration board is to consist of three persons, the parties shall each appoint one person and shall jointly appoint a chair. If they are unable to agree on a joint appointment, the chair shall be appointed by the Solicitor General.

(4) **Time for arbitration.**— The arbitration board shall commence the arbitration within thirty days after being appointed, in the case of a one-person board, or within thirty days after the appointment of the chair, in the case of a three-person board, and shall deliver a decision within a reasonable time.

(5) **Filing of decision.**— The arbitration board shall promptly file a copy of its decision with the Arbitration Commission.

(6) **Costs and expenses.**— The following rules apply with respect to the costs and expenses of the arbitration:

1. The Arbitration Commission shall pay the fees of any person the Solicitor General appoints to the arbitration board.

2. Each party shall pay its own costs incurred in the arbitration, including the fees of any person it appoints to the arbitration board.

ONTARIO REGULATION 546/99

made under the
POLICE SERVICES ACT

SUSPECT APPREHENSION PURSUITS

1. For the purposes of this Regulation, a suspect apprehension pursuit occurs,

(a) when a police officer attempts to direct the driver of a motor vehicle to stop;

(b) the driver refuses to obey the police officer; and

(c) the police officer pursues in a motor vehicle for the purpose of stopping the fleeing motor vehicle or identifying the fleeing motor vehicle or an individual in the fleeing motor vehicle.

2. A suspect apprehension pursuit is discontinued when police officers are no longer pursuing a fleeing motor vehicle for the purpose of stopping the fleeing motor vehicle or identifying the fleeing motor vehicle or an individual in the fleeing motor vehicle.

3. (1) A police officer may pursue, or continue to pursue, a fleeing motor vehicle that fails to stop,

(a) if the police officer has reason to believe that a criminal offence has been committed or is about to be committed; or

(b) for the purposes of motor vehicle identification or the identification of an individual in the vehicle.

(2) A police officer shall, before initiating a suspect apprehension pursuit, determine that there are no alternatives available as set out in the written procedures of the police force established under subsection 7(1).

(3) A police officer shall, before initiating a suspect apprehension pursuit, determine whether in order to protect public safety the immediate need to apprehend an individual in the fleeing motor vehicle or the need to identify the fleeing motor vehicle or an individual in the fleeing motor vehicle outweights the risk to public safety that may result from the pursuit.

(4) During a suspect apprehension pursuit, a police officer shall continually reassess the determination made under subsection (3) and shall discontinue the pursuit when the risk to public safety that may result from the pursuit outweighs the risk to public safety that may result if an individual in the fleeing motor vehicle is not immediately apprehended or if the fleeing motor vehicle or an individual in the fleeing motor vehicle is not identified.

(5) No suspect apprehension pursuit shall be initiated for a non-criminal offence if the identity of an indivdual in the fleeing motor vehicle is known.

(6) All suspect apprehension pursuits for a non-criminal offence shall be discontinued once the fleeing motor vehicle or an individual in the fleeing motor vehicle is identified.

4. (1) A police officer shall notify a dispatcher when the officer initiates a suspect apprehension purusit.

(2) The dispatcher shall notify a communications supervisor or road supervisor, if a supervisor is available, that a suspect apprehension pursuit has been initiated.

5. A communications or road supervisor shall order police officers to discontinue a suspect apprehension pursuit if, in his or her opinion, the risk to public safety that may result from the pursuit outweighs the risk to public safety that may result if an individual in the fleeing motor vehicle is not immediately apprehended or if the fleeing motor vehicle or an individual in the fleeing motor vehicle is not identified.

6. Every police services board shall establish policies that are consistent with this Regulation about suspect apprehension pursuits.

7. (1) Every police force shall establish written procedures that set out the tactics that may be used in its jurisdiction,

(a) as an alternative to suspect apprehension pursuit; and

(b) for following or stopping a fleeing motor vehicle.

(2) Every police force shall establish written procedures that are consistent with this Regulation about suspect apprehension pursuits in its jurisdiction.

8. A police officer shall not discharge his or her firearm for the sole purpose of attempting to stop a fleeing motor vehicle.

9. A police officer in an unmarked police vehicle shall not engage in a suspect apprehension pursuit unless a marked police vehicle is not readily available and the police officer believes that it is necessary to immediately apprehend an individual in the fleeing motor vehicle or to identify the fleeing motor vehicle or an individual in the fleeing motor vehicle.

10. (1) During a suspect apprehension pursuit, a police officer shall consider the tactics for stopping a vehicle as set out in the written procedures referred to in subsection 7(1).

(2) A police officer may only intentionally cause a police motor vehicle to come into physical contact with a fleeing motor vehicle for the purposes of stopping it where the officer believes on reasonable grounds that to do so is necessary to immediately protect against loss of life or serious bodily harm.

(3) In considering the action referred to in subsection (2), a police officer shall assess the impact of the action on the safety of other members of the public and police officers.

(4) Despite subsection (2), a police officer may cause a police motor vehicle to come into physical contact with a fleeing motor vehicle for the purposes of pinning it if the fleeing motor vehicle has lost control or collided with an object and come to a stop and the driver of the motor vehicle continues to try to use it to flee.

(5) Nothing in subsectin (2) precludes police officers involved in a pursuit, with assistance from other police officers in motor vehicles, from attempting to safely position the police vehicles in such a manner as to prevent the movement either forward, backward or sideways of a fleeing motor vehicle.

(6) Every police force shall ensure that its police officers receive training about the intentional contact between vehicles that is described in subsection (2). The training must address the matters described in subsections (2) and (3).

11. (1) Every police force shall establish written procedures on the management and control of suspect apprehension pursuits.

(2) The procedures must describe the responsibilities of police officers, dispatchers, communications supervisors and road supervisors.

(3) The procedures must describe the equipment that is available for implementing alternative tactics.

12. (1) If more than one jurisdiction is involved in a suspect apprehension pursuit, the supervisor in the jurisdiction in which the pursuit begins has decision-making responsibility for the pursuit.

(2) The supervisor may hand over decision-making responsibility to a supervisor in another jurisdiction involved in the pursuit.

13. A police officer does not breach the code of conduct when he or she decides not to initiate or chooses to discontinue a suspect apprehension pursuit because he or she has reason to believe that the risk to public safety that may result from the pursuit outweighs the risk to public safety that may result if an individual in the fleeing motor vehicle is not immediately apprehended or if the fleeing motor vehicle or an individual in the fleeing motor vehicle is not identified.

14. Every police force shall ensure that its police officers, dispatchers, communications supervisors and road supervisors receive training accredited by the Solicitor General about suspect apprehension pursuits.

15. A police force shall ensure that the particulars of each suspect apprehension pursuit are recorded on a form and in a manner approved by the Solicitor General.

16. This Regulation comes into force on January 1, 2000.

EXERCISES

■ TRUE OR FALSE

____ 1. Municipalities that are served by the OPP must establish a community policing advisory committee to comply with the provisions of the *Police Services Act*.

____ 2. The OPP must provide assistance to any Ontario police service that requests assistance in an emergency.

____ 3. The OPP's responsibilities include bylaw enforcement in the communities with which they have contracted.

____ 4. All bodies of water that surround municipalities are the responsibility of the OPP for enforcement purposes.

____ 5. The Special Investigation Unit falls under the supervision of the OPP.

____ 6. The solicitor general of the province may give approval to a municipality to increase the number of members on its police services board.

____ 7. A municipality with a population of 100 000 people shall have a police services board that consists of at least three members who are appointed by city council.

____ 8. Municipalities that have populations in excess of 500 000 people will always have at least nine members on their police services boards.

____ 9. Police officers or former police officers are not eligible to be members of a police services board.

____ 10. Police services boards have the authority to direct the chief of police with respect to the day-to-day operation of the police service.

____ 11. A municipal police officer from Toronto has the authority to act as a police officer anywhere in the province.

____ 12. No person shall be appointed as a police officer in the province of Ontario unless he or she is a citizen or permanent resident of Canada.

____ 13. A person must complete at least two years of community college to be eligible for employment with an Ontario police service.

____ 14. A person convicted of a criminal offence would not be considered for employment with an Ontario police service.

____ 15. A special constable who is employed on a full-time basis may perform all of the usual duties of a police officer, provided that he or she has taken an oath of office as a special constable.

____ **16.** At any time before or during an investigation into a complaint of police misconduct, if the complaint appears to be of a minor nature, the chief of police may resolve the matter informally.

____ **17.** A police officer who receives a complaint from a member of the public about police services has the discretion to report the complaint to the chief, where he or she believes that the complaint is frivolous.

____ **18.** A police officer against whom a complaint of misconduct has been proved on clear and convincing evidence may have entries related to the complaint, action taken, and the reply of the chief included in his or her employment record unless the officer resigns prior to disposition of the matter.

____ **19.** Police officers who work in high-risk jurisdictions are encouraged to carry a second, smaller firearm that can easily be concealed.

■ MULTIPLE CHOICE

Circle the correct response(s).

1. The five core police services are crime prevention, law enforcement, assistance to victims of crime, emergency response, and:

    a. levying of fines

    b. maintenance of public order

    c. maintenance of public infrastructure

2. A municipality that has a population of 23 000 will have a police services board consisting of:

    a. 5 members

    b. 3 members

    c. 7 members

3. A municipal police officer's probationary period begins on the day that he or she is appointed and ends on the later of:

    a. the first anniversary of the day of appointment

    b. 6 months after appointment

    c. the first anniversary of the day the officer completes an initial period of training at the Ontario Police College

    d. any of the above

    e. a or c

4. A police officer must complete his or her initial training within:

    a. 1 year of appointment

    b. 6 months of appointment

    c. 3 months of appointment

    d. at whatever time his or her police service deems necessary

5. A municipal police officer who leaves to join the OPP must complete an additional probationary period of at least:

    a. 1 month

    b. 3 months

    c. no additional probationary period is required

    d. a period equivalent to that of a newly hired police officer

6. To hire police cadets, a police service requires the permission of:

   a. the police services board

   b. the solicitor general for the province

   c. the commissioner of the OPP

   d. no special permission is required

7. Auxiliary members of a police service have the same authority as a police officer if:

   a. they are accompanied by a police officer

   b. they are supervised by a police officer

   c. they are authorized to perform duties by the chief of police

   d. all of the above

   e. a and c

8. With the approval of the _____, a _____ may appoint a special constable to act for the period, area, and purpose that the _____ considers expedient.

   a. solicitor general, chief of police, police services board

   b. solicitor general, board, board

   c. attorney general, chief of police, police services board

9. A First Nations police officer has the powers of a police officer for the purpose of carrying out his or her specified duties:

   a. throughout the province of Ontario

   b. in the area to which the agreement for First Nations policing relates

   c. on any reserve in Canada, because First Nations policing is the responsibility of the federal government

10. A complaint may be made by a member of the public if the complainant was directly affected by:

    a. police service policy

    b. the quality of service that was received

    c. the conduct of a police officer

    d. an arrest that was believed to be unlawful

    e. a, b, or c

11. A chief of police has the right not to deal with any complaint made by a member of the public, if the complaint is made:

    a. 6 months after the facts on which it is based occurred

    b. 3 months after the facts on which it is based occurred

    c. 30 days after the facts on which it is based occurred

    d. 1 year after the facts on which it is based occurred

12. Complaints about OPP services must be referred to:

    a. the detachment commander

    b. the commissioner of the OPP

    c. the solicitor general

13. A chief of police who receives a complaint of police misconduct that he or she believes to be frivolous shall:

    a. dismiss the complaint and notify the complainant

    b. cause the complaint to be investigated and a written report to be completed

    c. meet with the complainant and notify him or her that the complaint is frivolous

14. In complaints of police misconduct, if the chief believes that an officer's conduct may constitute misconduct, the chief shall designate a prosecutor and hold a hearing. The prosecutor may be:

    a. a police officer from any rank equal to or higher than that of the police officer who is the subject of the hearing

    b. a Crown attorney

    c. a legal counsel or agent

    d. any of the above

    e. a or c

15. After an investigation and review of a written report, the chief of police has the option of resolving a complaint of police misconduct informally if the complaint was not of a serious nature and:

    a. the police services board agrees to this type of disposition

    b. the police officer and the complainant consent to the proposed resolution

    c. a and b

16. If an informal resolution is attempted but not achieved, the chief of police may:

    a. summarily dismiss the complaint

    b. impose a penalty that he or she deems appropriate for the alleged misconduct

    c. hold a hearing if the police officer does not consent to the penalty imposed

17. Members of the Ontario Civilian Commission on Police Services are appointed by:

    a. the solicitor general

    b. the attorney general

    c. the lieutenant governor in council

    d. the commissioner of the OPP

18. The powers and duties of the Ontario Civilian Commission on Police Services include conducting investigations with respect to police matters involving:

    a. the police needs of a municipality

    b. the conduct or the performance of duties of a police officer

    c. the administration of a municipal police service

    d. all of the above

19. The powers and duties of the Ontario Civilian Commission on Police Services include:

    a. hearing and disposing of major charges of police misconduct against a member of a municipal police service

    b. conducting inquiries into matters relating to crime and law enforcement

    c. ensuring that police services are complying with prescribed standards

    d. all of the above

    e. b and c

20. A member of a police service shall not engage in any activity that:

    a. interferes with his or her performance of duties as a police officer

    b. places him or her in a conflict of interest

    c. allows him or her to gain advantage because of his or her position as a police officer

    d. all of the above

    e. a and b

21. A police officer who engages in misconduct while off duty:

    a. can be convicted of misconduct under the *Police Services Act*

    b. shall not be found guilty of misconduct if there is no connection between the conduct and the reputation of the police service

    c. can be dealt with through informal resolution if the officer agrees to this method

    d. any of the above

22. The offence of inducing misconduct under the *Police Services Act* can be applied to:

    a. police officers

    b. civilian members of the police services

    c. members of the general public

    d. all of the above

    e. a and b

23. To commence a proceeding under the section dealing with inducing misconduct or inducing an officer to withhold services, the consent of the _____ is required.

    a. chief of police

    b. solicitor general of the province

    c. Crown attorney

    d. chair of the local police services board

24. The Special Investigations Unit (SIU) was assembled to:

    a. investigate complaints of major misconduct by police officers

    b. conduct investigations into circumstances of serious injuries or death that may have resulted from criminal offences committed by police officers

    c. conduct investigations of police officers as requested by the solicitor general

25. Members of a police service who are the subject of an SIU investigation:

    a. must cooperate fully with the unit in the conduct of investigations

    b. should follow the advice of their lawyer as to the level of cooperation to be given the SIU

26. A member of the OPP must give _____ notice in writing prior to resignation.

    a. 30 days'

    b. 2 weeks'

    c. 3 months'

27. A member of a police service may draw and discharge his or her firearm to:

    a. issue a warning to a dangerous offender

    b. stop a fleeing suspect

    c. protect against loss of life or serious bodily harm

    d. all of the above

28. A member of a police service may draw and discharge his or her firearm to:

    a. call for assistance in a critical situation

    b. destroy an animal that is potentially dangerous or is so badly injured that humanity dictates that its suffering be ended

    c. use during training sessions

    d. all of the above

    e. b and c

29. A police officer must complete a use-of-force report to the chief of police or the commissioner of the OPP whenever a member of the police service:

   a. draws a handgun in the presence of a member of the public

   b. discharges a firearm

   c. uses a weapon other than a firearm on another person

   d. all of the above

   e. b or c

30. With respect to political activity, a municipal police officer who is not on duty or in uniform may:

   a. act as scrutineer for a candidate in an election

   b. solicit or receive campaign funds

   c. engage in any political activity

   d. all of the above

   e. a and b

31. A municipal police officer may be a candidate in a municipal election, provided that:

   a. he or she has received permission from the chief of police

   b. he or she has received permission from the police services board

   c. he or she resides in another jurisdiction and the election campaign does not interfere with his or her duties as a police officer

■ SHORT ANSWER

1. List the activities that constitute misconduct under the *Police Services Act*:

    a.

    b.

    c.

    d.

    e.

    f.

    g.

    h.

    i.

    j.

    k.

    l.

    m.

    n.

2. The duties of police officers include the preserving of the peace and apprehending criminals. List the seven other duties of police officers:

    a.

    b.

    c.

    d.

    e.

    f.

    g.

3. Along with maintaining traffic patrol on the King's Highway and providing police services to parts of Ontario that do not have municipal police services, the OPP are responsible for:

    a.

    b.

    c.

4. List, in descending order, from chief of police to constable, the ranks that are available in a police service:

    a. chief of police

    b.

    c.

    d.

    e.

    f.

    g.

    h.

    i. constable

CHAPTER 12

What Is the Appropriate Role of the Police?

CHAPTER OBJECTIVES

After completing this chapter, you should be able to:

♦ Identify three sources of guidance for the appropriate exercise of police powers with respect to provincial offences.

♦ Identify three examples of the inappropriate exercise of police powers, and explain the possible consequences of these mistakes.

♦ Describe the source(s) and the scope of authority for making an arrest in connection with a provincial offence.

♦ Describe any special rules relating to the arrest of a young person suspected of committing a provincial offence.

♦ Describe the source(s) and the scope of authority for conducting a search in relation to a provincial offence.

INTRODUCTION TO POLICE POWERS

This chapter discusses appropriate police powers and responsibilities and touches on two of the most important justice reports of the century.

The Martin Report

The *Report of the Attorney General's Advisory Committee on Charge Screening, Disclosure, and Resolution Discussions* ("the Martin report") is applicable to criminal matters, as opposed to provincial offences matters, but its underlying principles have application to all prosecutions. This advisory committee was chaired by the Honourable G. Arthur Martin, after whom the report is named. The Martin report discusses the responsibilities of the various players in the justice system and sets out the role the police should play in criminal matters, which are in some ways analogous to provincial offences.

Some of the Martin committee's recommendations are set out below:

Both Crown counsel and the police are concerned with the due enforcement of the criminal law, and both Crown Counsel and the police are duty bound to discharge their duties objectively, with integrity, and with fairness. (p. 134)

It is important to prevent one's personal feelings and desire to "win" from interfering with the obligation to act fairly and dispassionately.

The commission provides further guidance on the need to act in a responsible, appropriate manner:

Like counsel, the police are also under the highest of duties to discharge their function in the criminal justice system responsibly... The need for the criminal investigators to act responsibly flows from three basic facts. The first basic fact, already stated above, is that there is a tremendously important societal need to apprehend and convict perpetrators of criminal acts, that is, the *actual* perpetrators of criminal acts. Thus, the first responsibility of the criminal investigator is to pursue his or her investigative duties skilfully and diligently, yet with the scrupulous dispassion that permits the evidence to tell its own story. The codes of conduct to which the police are subject speak directly to this need to be *diligent, impartial, honourable and incorruptible* [emphasis added].

The second and third basic facts that, in the Committee's view, most directly inform an understanding of the criminal investigator's responsibility, are that the investigator may exercise many broad powers, and that in many circumstances the investigator may exercise these powers at his or her discretion. (p. 35)

The committee explains that the sources of the general duty on the police to discharge their functions responsibly are statutory codes of conduct and decisions of the courts:

Codes of conduct are applied through disciplinary proceedings internal to the police community, while the decisions of the courts, often in the context of sections 7 to 10 of the Charter [*Canadian Charter of Rights and Freedoms*], are an external source of guidance, indirectly constraining particular exercises of power when the consequences are inconsistent with someone's legal rights. Case law that prescribes the realm of responsible conduct on the part of the police is legion. It is essentially the jurisprudence of sections 7 through 10 of the Charter. The extent of the case law on this aspect of police responsibility bespeaks, in the Committee's view, the great importance of an unfailing respect by the police for the legal rights of all persons, as those rights are contained in the Charter. This respect for legal rights, then, along with scrupulous and scrupulously impartial investigation of crimes, are the two pillars of a criminal investigator's responsibilities. (p. 36)

The Commission on Proceedings Involving Guy Paul Morin

Another significant report that all police officers should be aware of is the report of the Commission on Proceedings Involving Guy Paul Morin (Kaufman commission), which was chaired by the Honourable Fred Kaufman. It evaluated the reasons for the miscarriage of justice in the Guy Paul Morin case.

One of the findings of the Kaufman commission was the tendency on the part of police and prosecutors who work on a case—particularly if the case is long and difficult and they have invested a lot of time and energy in it—to develop tunnel vision. Tunnel vision is simply the tendency, after formulating a belief, to continue to adhere to that belief, even in the face of conflicting evidence or the emergence of possible alternatives. This is a dangerous tendency and one that all police officers and prosecutors must continuously guard against.

The most important thing for you as a police officer to bear in mind during your investigations of provincial offences and all other cases is your duty to be fair and to act with integrity in all of your dealings with the defendant and all members of the public. This duty to be fair and act with integrity also extends to the prosecution of your cases. You must be fair and scrupulous in all of your dealings with all of the players in the court system—the prosecution, the defence, and, of course, the judiciary.

The material that follows discusses your obligations in specific, defined areas, but this fundamental behaviour is really at the heart of all the case law and rules for police behaviour that have developed throughout the years. The best police officers are those who use the discretion that they possess wisely and who always strive to do what is right. If you keep these principles in mind and strive to behave decently and honourably, you will necessarily follow the formal rules in place and, in fact, be the kind of police officer that our society and our justice system most need and desire.

POWERS OF ARREST

Powers of arrest, as opposed to powers to "ticket" an offender for a provincial offence are limited under the *Provincial Offences Act* (POA). As emphasized throughout this book, there is a significant difference between crimes and provincial offences. Because provincial offences are less serious than crimes, police officers are not afforded the same powers of arrest for provincial offences as for criminal charges. Part VIII of the POA limits police powers of arrest to well-defined circumstances.

First, there must be lawful authority for the arrest, which means that the charging statute must allow for the defendant to be arrested. That is because there is no general power of arrest under the POA.

Second, even if the charging statute authorizes arrest, this right can be exercised only when the arrest occurs at the same time the offence is committed—for example, when, immediately after committing an offence, the defendant is attempting to escape from a police officer. Section 145 of the Act stipulates that only where a person has reasonable and probable grounds to believe an individual has committed an offence and is escaping from and freshly pursued by a police officer who has lawful authority to arrest that person, is there a power to arrest that individual without a warrant. This power is given to both police officers and average citizens; but where the citizen who makes the arrest is not a police officer, that citizen must deliver the person under arrest to a police officer.

Where a warrant is outstanding, however, police powers under the POA are much broader. Pursuant to s. 144, a police officer may arrest an individual against whom a warrant is directed regardless of where he or she is found in Ontario. In addition, where a police officer does not have the warrant, but believes on reasonable and probable grounds that there is a warrant in force in Ontario for an individual, the officer may arrest that individual.

A police officer has the power to use as much force as is necessary to do what the officer is required or authorized to do by law. The requirements of the *Police Services Act* should, however, be kept in mind when assessing the level of force necessary and the appropriate limitations on the use of force.

BAIL

Unless a police officer believes that the public interest would not be served, the officer, acting under either the authority of a warrant or other power of arrest, shall normally release a person from custody after serving him or her with a summons or offence notice.

Sometimes, however, detention is perceived by the officer to be necessary "in the public interest" having regard to all the circumstances, including the need to establish the individual's identity; the need to secure or preserve evidence of the offence; the need to prevent the continuation or repetition of some offence; or where the defendant is ordinarily resident outside Ontario and will not respond to a summons or offence notice (s. 149 POA). In such cases, the police officer shall deliver the defendant to the officer in charge who shall consider whether the conditions set out in s. 149 still apply. If the conditions no longer exist, the officer in charge will release the defendant upon (1) serving him or her with a summons or offence notice, or (2) upon having the defendant enter into a recognizance without sureties. If the person lives outside Ontario, a cash bail may also be set.

BAIL HEARINGS

Where a defendant is not released under s. 149 of the POA, the officer in charge must, pursuant to s. 150 of the POA, take the defendant before a justice within 24 hours of his or her arrest in order that he or she may have a bail hearing. Section 10 of the Charter also gives the defendant this right:

> Everyone has the right on arrest or detention
>
>> (a) to be informed promptly of the reasons therefor;
>>
>> (b) to retain and instruct counsel without delay and to be informed of that right; and
>>
>> (c) to have the validity of the detention determined by way of *habeas corpus* and to be released if the detention is not lawful.

Habeas corpus means the right, within 24 hours, to a bail hearing, which will then determine whether the individual will be detained or released from custody and if released, under what terms and conditions.

At the bail hearing, the justice will release the defendant unless the prosecutor shows cause as to why he should be detained. Section 150 of the POA sets out the possible forms of release available, which differ depending on the maximum penalty available for the offence in question.

The rules of evidence are far more relaxed at a bail hearing than at a trial. At the bail hearing, the justice may consider any information he or she considers credible or trustworthy, except that the defendant shall not be examined or cross-examined in respect of the offence with which he or she is charged. Pursuant to s. 151(2), both the prosecutor and the defendant have the right to review any bail order or detention order made.

SEARCH AND SEIZURE

Another possible Charter motion that may be brought by the defence relates to an improper search or seizure. Section 8 of the Charter states: "Everyone has the right to be secure against unreasonable search or seizure."

The law of search and seizure is extremely complicated and beyond the scope of this book. However, you should bear in mind that generally, for a search to be considered reasonable under s. 8 of the Charter, it must be authorized by law, the law itself must be reasonable, and the search must be conducted in a reasonable manner.

As emphasized throughout this book, there is a significant difference between provincial offences and crimes. Accordingly, the powers to search in relation to provincial offences violations are far narrower than those in relation to criminal matters (see s. 158 of the POA). The *Provincial Offences Act* does not contain a general power to search for and seize items without a warrant. You must, therefore, look to the specific charging legislation to determine whether there is some power within it to search without a warrant.

To obtain a search warrant, you must attend before a justice of the peace and swear an information. If the justice believes that the search is appropriate, he or she will issue a search warrant.

If, at trial, the defendant shows that a search was conducted without a warrant, the prosecution must show, on a balance of probabilities, that the search was reasonable. If a court decides that the search was unreasonable, the evidence obtained by the search is likely to be excluded, so it is important to proceed carefully in this area. If you are in doubt about the validity of a search that you are considering, ask the advice of senior police officers and/or senior members of the provincial prosecutor's office or the local Crown attorney's office.

DISCLOSURE

In any criminal prosecution, the individual who is charged has a right to know the case against him or her. This principle gives rise to an obligation on the part of the prosecution to *disclose* or provide *disclosure* of the entire case against the defendant, *if requested*.

What is disclosure? Disclosure consists of all relevant information that the prosecution intends to use at trial, including all documents, police notes, witness statements, and all other evidence against the defendant that is in the hands of the prosecution (including the police), whether favourable or unfavourable to the defence.

In the case of *R v. Stinchcombe*, the Supreme Court of Canada ruled that every piece of information in a criminal prosecution, whether damaging or helpful to the prosecution, should be provided to the defence, unless there are clear public policy reasons for not doing so—for example, in the case of an informant whose safety may be at risk. Although the court in *Stinchcombe* was dealing with a criminal matter, not a provincial offences matter, the same disclosure principle commonly applies to provincial offences. Provincial prosecutors routinely provide basic disclosure upon request. Police officers should, therefore, provide any information pertaining to the case to the Crown or provincial prosecutor, who will provide it to the defence.

In a simple provincial prosecution, it is possible that full disclosure will consist only of the police notes of the investigation and the charging documents, because that is all of the material relevant to the investigation. In a more complicated offence, in addition to police notes, full disclosure could include any witness statements, documents, papers, and physical evidence. No matter how trivial or serious the case, full disclosure means providing any relevant material pertaining to the case in your possession to the Crown or provincial prosecutor. The prosecutor or Crown will then turn the material over to the defence.

Disclosure should be provided unless there are clear public policy reasons for not doing so (for example, an informant's safety is at risk). If you are unsure about disclosure, you should obtain advice from the office of the Crown or provincial prosecutor.

Generally, it is better to err on the side of disclosing too much (as long as there are no public policy reasons against disclosure) than to hold information back. Although it may seem to you that a given piece of information is of dubious relevance, you have no way of knowing what defences the defendant may put forward, and the information in your possession may actually be very relevant to the defendant or his or her agent or counsel.

The Martin report stresses the important role that the police have to play in ensuring that investigatory materials provided to the prosecution are complete and appropriate. Numerous criminal cases have been stayed (that is, the prosecution was stopped) simply because the prosecution failed to disclose a single piece of information. Cases have also been stayed where the police or a third party has kept some information from the prosecution, even where the prosecutor disclosed everything of which he or she was aware. The prosecution can only disclose information of which it is aware, so it is up to you as a police officer to disclose everything in your possession to the Crown so that the Crown, in turn, can disclose everything in its possession to the defence. Therefore, full communication and cooperation between the police and the Crown or provincial prosecutor is essential.

QUASHING THE INFORMATION OR CERTIFICATE OF OFFENCE: THE SUFFICIENCY OF THE CHARGES

In addition to any possible Charter defences that may be raised, the defence may also try to have the charging document quashed. This is not, technically speaking, a defence, but if the charging document is quashed, the whole process must be started again, which will cause complications.

If an information or certificate of offence is too vague, the defence may object to it at trial. If the justice of the peace (known colloquially as the JP) or the judge hearing the case agrees that the offence is too vague or failed to include a relevant piece of information, the JP or the judge may quash the information or certificate. It is important, therefore, that you as a police officer complete the information or certificate of offence carefully, accurately, and completely.

Whether a defective information may be amended to cure the defect is within the sole discretion of the JP or the judge hearing the matter. He or she may decline to amend the charging document and quash it instead.

You should ensure that the charging document contains the date, time, and place of the offence and clearly identifies the alleged wrong so that the defendant can adequately prepare to make full answer and defence. The document must also comply with all of the requirements as set out in the *Provincial Offences Act* and in the charging legislation.

Depending on the nature of the charge and the circumstances underlying the charge, you will have to make a reasoned decision as to the appropriate method of charging the defendant. Chapter 1 sets out in detail the appropriate methods of charging and how to determine which charging document to use, in the context of the different types of offences—part I, part II, and part III. Remember always to refer to the *Provincial Offences Act* as well as the law that covers the particular area in question—for example, the *Trespass to Property Act*—to determine the requirements.

SITUATIONS REQUIRING PARTICULAR CARE

Delay in Laying of Charges

It is improper to delay the laying of charges solely to hurt the defendant's chances of making full answer and defence. Charges should be investigated promptly and thoroughly and within the time limitations specified within the *Provincial Offences Act* and the charging legislation.

Res Judicata

The principle of *res judicata*, or double jeopardy, is the well-known legal principle that an individual cannot be charged more than once for the same offence. This principle is not only rooted in common law but also enshrined in s. 11(h) of the Charter. Section 11(h) of the Charter states:

> Any person charged with an offence has the right ... (h) if finally acquitted of the offence, not to be tried for it again and, if finally found guilty and punished for the offence, not to be tried or punished for it again.

Even though this doctrine is well known and accords with common sense, there have been situations where police officers have directly or indirectly charged an individual with the same offence more than once. In the case of *R v. Keyowski*, for example, the Supreme Court of Canada held that successive prosecutions for the same offence are oppressive.

Charging someone twice for the same offence but using a slightly different date or wording of the offence in each charging document is not acceptable. Doing this will result in either a withdrawal of the charges if the prosecutor is fair and astute or, much worse, a finding by the court that there was an abuse of process, leading to a stay of the charges at the very least and possibly to an award of costs in favour of the defendant.

Delay in Advising the Individual Under Arrest of the Charge Against Him or Her

Section 11(a) of the Charter states:

Any person charged with an offence has the right ... (a) to be informed without delay of the specific offence.

You must immediately advise the individual of the offence with which he or she is being charged.

REFERENCES

Canadian Charter of Rights and Freedoms, part I of the *Constitution Act, 1982*, RSC 1985, app. II, no. 44.

Keyowski, R v., [1988] 1 SCR 657.

Ontario Ministry of the Attorney General. (1993). *The Report of the Attorney General's Advisory Committee on Charge Screening, Disclosure, and Resolution Discussions, chaired by the Honourable G. Arthur Martin*. Toronto: Queen's Printer for Ontario.

Ontario Ministry of the Attorney General. (1998). *The Commission on Proceedings Involving Guy Paul Morin, chaired by the Honourable Fred Kaufman*. Toronto: Queen's Printer for Ontario.

Stinchcombe, R v., (1991), 68 CCC (3d) 1 (SCC).

APPENDIX
Provincial Offences Forms

■ Forms 1 and 2   Certificate of Parking Infraction and Parking Infraction Notice

Form 1
Formule 1

Provincial Offences Act
Loi sur les infractions provinciales

CERTIFICATE OF PARKING INFRACTION
PROCÈS–VERBAL D'INFRACTION DE STATIONNEMENT

Form 1 – Provincial Offences Act
Formule 1 – Loi sur les infractions provinciales

CERTIFICATE OF PARKING INFRACTION
PROCÈS-VERBAL D'INFRACTION DE STATIONNEMENT

ONTARIO COURT   COUR DE L'ONTARIO
(PROVINCIAL DIVISION)   (DIVISION PROVINCIALE)
PROVINCE OF ONTARIO   PROVINCE DE L'ONTARIO

I _____ believe from my personal
Je soussigné(e)   (Print Name/Nom en lettres moulées)   crois, en me fondant sur ma

knowledge and certify that
connaissance directe de faits, et atteste que

On the ___ day of _____ 19 ___ Time _____   M
Le   jour de   À (heure)

the owner (or operator) of the vehicle upon which was displayed the number plate:
le propriétaire (ou l'utilisateur) du véhicule portant la plaque d'immatriculation suivante :

Plate No. N° de plaque d'immatriculation	Province	Expiry Date Date d'expiration M/M Y/A

did commit the parking infraction of : _____
a commis l'infraction de stationnement suivante :

at/à : _____

Municipality/Municipalité

Contrary to _____
Contrairement à

Section _____
Article

I further certify that I: **J'atteste en outre que j'ai :**

A. served a parking infraction notice on the owner of the vehicle identified herein by affixing it to the vehicle in a conspicuous place at the time of this alleged infraction or,

☐ A. signifié un avis d'infraction de stationnement au propriétaire du véhicule ci-identifié en apposant cet avis sur ce véhicule à un endroit bien en vue au moment de l'infraction reprochée ou;

B. served a parking infraction notice on the owner (or operator) of the vehicle identified herein by delivering it personally to the person having care and control (or operator) of the vehicle at the time of the alleged infraction.

☐ B. signifié un avis d'infraction de stationnement au propriétaire (ou à l'utilisateur) du véhicule ci-identifié en remettant cet avis en mains propres à la personne qui a la garde et le contrôle (ou à l'utilisateur) du véhicule au moment de l'infraction reprochée.

Signature of Issuing Provincial Offences Officer
Signature de l'agent des infractions provinciales

SET FINE/AMENDE FIXÉE
$ _____ $ _____

Officer No.
N° de l'agent

Unit
Unité

Complete only if operator is charged
Ne remplir que si l'utilisateur est inculpé

Name of Operator
Nom de   (Last   (First   (Middle)
L'utilisateur   Nom)   Prénom)   Initiale)

Address
Adresse

(Municipality /   (Province)   (Postal Code /
Municipalité)   Code Postal)

Driver's Licence No. / N° du permis de conduire

Sex Sexe	Birth Date/Date de naissance Day/Jour Mo./Mois Yr./Année	Province

O. Reg. 494/94, s. 3

Form 2
Formule 2

Provincial Offences Act
Loi sur les infractions provinciales

PARKING INFRACTION NOTICE
AVIS D'INFRACTION DE STATIONNEMENT

Form 2 – Provincial Offences Act
Formule 2 – Loi sur les infractions provinciales

PARKING INFRACTION NOTICE
AVIS D'INFRACTION DE STATIONNEMENT

ONTARIO COURT   COUR DE L'ONTARIO
(PROVINCIAL DIVISION)   (DIVISION PROVINCIALE)
PROVINCE OF ONTARIO   PROVINCE DE L'ONTARIO

believes from personal
crois, en me fondent sur ma

knowledge and certifies that
connaissance directe de faits, et atteste que

On the   day of   19   Time   M
Le   jour de   À (heure)

the owner (or operator) of the vehicle upon which was displayed the number plate:
le propriétaire (ou l'utilisateur) du véhicule portant la plaque d'immatriculation suivante :

Plate No. N° de plaque d'immatriculation	Province	Expiry Date Date d'expiration M/M Y/A

did commit the parking infraction of :
a commis l'infraction de stationnement suivante :

at/à :

Municipality/Municipalité

Contrary to
Contrairement à

Section
Article

Notice

Within 15 days of the date noted above, choose one of the options on the back of this Notice. If you do not pay the set fine shown below or if you do not deliver a Notice of Intention to Appear in court, or if you do not appear for trial, you will be deemed not to dispute this charge and a conviction may be entered against you. Upon conviction you will be required to pay the set fine plus court costs. An administrative fee is payable if the fine goes into default and the information may be provided to a credit bureau.

Avis

Dans les 15 jours de la date indiquée ci-dessus, veuillez choisir l'une des options figurant au verso de la présente formule. Si vous n'acquittez pas le montant de l'amende fixée qui est indiqué ci-dessous ou si vous ne remettez pas un avis d'intention de comparaître ou si vous ne comparaissez pas, vous serez réputé(e) ne pas contester cette accusation et une déclaration de culpabilité pourrait être inscrite contre vous. Sur déclaration de culpabilité, vous serez tenu(e) de payer l'amende fixée ainsi que les frais judiciaires. Des frais administratifs sont payables en cas de défaut de paiement de l'amende et les renseignements pourraient être communiqués à un service d'informations financières.

Signature of Issuing Provincial Offences Officer *Signature de l'agent des infractions provinciales*	SET FINE/*AMENDE FIXÉE*
	$ $
Officer No. *N° de l'agent*	Unit *Unité*

IMPORTANT - Please read carefully - Within 15 days of the date of the Parking Infraction Notice choose one of the following options. Complete the selected option (sign where necessary) and deliver it (and payment where applicable) to the address shown below. All enquiries concerning this infraction should be made to:

IMPORTANT - Veuillez lire attentivement - Dans les quinze jours qui suivent la date à laquelle vous recevez le présent avis, choisissez l'une des options suivantes. Remplissez l'option choisie (signez là où c'est nécessaire) et remettez l'avis (avec votre paiement, le cas échéant) à l'adresse indiquée ci-dessous. Pour tous renseignements concernant l'infraction, veuillez vous adresser à :

(Address and telephone number of police force or other agency that issued the Parking Infraction Notice.)
(adresse et numéro de téléphone du corps de police ou d'une autre agence qui a délivré l'avis d'infraction de stationnement)

Defendant's Options – Choose One Only
Options du défendeur – N'en choisir qu'une

❶ **Option 1 – Voluntary Payment:** I do not wish to dispute the charge and I enclose the amount of the set fine indicated on the front of this notice.

Paiement volontaire: Je ne désire pas contester l'accusation et joins à la présente le montant de l'amende fixée qui est indiqué au recto de cet avis.

Signature _____

Write the number of the Parking Infraction Notice on the front of your cheque or money order and make it payable to:
Inscrivez le numéro de l'avis d'infraction de stationnement au recto de votre chèque ou mandat, libellé à l'ordre de :

and mail or deliver your payment along with this notice to the address shown below. Dishonoured cheques will be subject to an administrative charge. An administrative fee is payable if the fine goes into default and the information may be provided to a credit bureau. Please allow sufficient time for your payment to be delivered.
et postez votre paiement ou remettez-le, accompagné de cet avis, à l'adresse indiquée ci-dessous. Les chèques refusés sont assujettis à des frais administratifs. Des frais administratifs s'appliquent également si l'amende reste impayée et les renseignements pourraient être communiqués à un service d'informations financières. Veuillez prévoir assez de temps pour que votre paiement soit délivré.

❷ **Option 2 – Trial Option – Notice of Intention to Appear in Court:**
1. I intend to appear in court to enter a plea at the time and date set for trial.
2. I intend to challenge the evidence of the officer who completed the Parking Infraction Notice. ☐ No   ☐ Yes
If you indicated "NO" above, the officer may not attend and the prosecutor may rely on certified statements as evidence against you.

Demande de procès – Avis d'intention de comparaître :
1. *J'ai l'intention de comparaître devant le tribunal pour inscrire un plaidoyer aux date et heure fixées pour le procès.*
2. *J'ai l'intention de contester la preuve de l'agent qui a rempli l'avis d'infraction de stationnement.* ☐ Non   ☐ Oui
Si vous avez coché la case «Non» ci-dessus, il se peut que l'agent ne soit pas présent et que le poursuivant s'appuie sur les déclarations certifiées pour prouver votre culpabilité.

I request my trial be held in the : / *Je demande que mon procès ait lieu :*

☐ English language/*en anglais*   ☐ French language/*en français*

Signature _____

Name / *Nom* _____ (Please Print / *Lettres moulées*)

Address / *Adresse* _____   Postal Code/*Code postal*

Deliver this signed notice (and payment where applicable) to the:
Remettez cet avis signé (avec votre paiement le cas échéant) à :

NOTICE – Ontario Motorists	*AVIS – Automobilistes de l'Ontario*
Failure to pay the fine imposed upon conviction will result in your Ontario Vehicle Permit not being renewed and no new permit being issued to you until the fine and all court costs and fees have been paid.	*Si l'amende imposée sur déclaration de culpabilité est impayée, votre certificat d'immatriculation de l'Ontario ne sera pas renouvelé et aucun nouveau certificat d'immatriculation ne vous sera délivré jusqu'à ce que l'amende, les frais judiciaires et autres frais aient été acquittés en totalité.*

O. Reg. 494/94, s. 3.

■ **Form 4   Notice of Impending Conviction**

Form 4
Formule 4

Provincial Offences Act
Loi sur les infractions provinciales

NOTICE OF IMPENDING CONVICTION
AVIS DE DÉCLARATION DE CULPABILITÉ IMMINENTE

ONTARIO COURT (PROVINCIAL DIVISION)
COUR DE L'ONTARIO (DIVISION PROVINCIALE)

NOTICE OF IMPENDING CONVICTION
AVIS DE DÉCLARATION DE CULPABILITÉ IMMINENTE
Form/*Formule* 4
O. Reg./*Règl.* O. 949

FROM / *DE*

ADDRESS / *ADRESSE*

(PLEASE INDICATE CHANGE OF NAME OR ADDRESS
HERE IF APPLICABLE
*VEUILLEZ INSCRIRE TOUT CHANGEMENT DE NOM OU
D'ADRESSE, LE CAS ÉCHÉANT)*

(NAME AND ADDRESS OF DEFENDANT / *NOM ET ADRESSE DU DÉFENDEUR)*

TO / *À*

Location _____   Set Fine Amount _____   Date of Infraction _____
Lieu   *Montant d'amende fixée*   *Date de l'infraction*

Parking Infraction No. _____   Licence Plate No. _____   Due Date _____
N° d'infraction de stationnement   *N° de plaque d'immatriculation*   *Date d'échéance*

The vehicle bearing the license plate mentioned above was unlawfully parked or stopped.

The amount of the fine indicated on the Parking Infraction Notice has not been paid. Unless payment or a Notice of Intention to Appear in court for the purpose of entering a plea and having a trial of the matter is received by the above due date a conviction will be recorded against you without further notice. On conviction you will be required to pay the set fine plus court costs. An administrative fee is payable if the fine goes into default and the information may be provided to a credit bureau.

If you do not wish to dispute the charge, you may pay the set fine amount above.

Write the Parking Infraction number on the front of your cheque or money order and make it payable to:

Le véhicule portant la plaque d'immatriculation susmentionnée était stationné ou arrêté illégalement.

Le montant de l'amende inscrit sur l'avis d'infraction de stationnement n'a pas été payé. À moins que le paiement ou un avis d'intention de comparaître au tribunal pour inscrire un plaidoyer et faire instruire la question ne soit reçu avant la date d'échéance, une déclaration de culpabilité sera enregistrée contre vous, sans autre avis. Sur déclaration de culpabilité, vous devrez payer l'amende fixée, plus des frais de justice. Vous devrez payer des droits administratifs, en cas de non-paiement de l'amende, et l'information peut être transmise à un service d'informations financières.

Si vous ne désirez pas contester l'accusation, vous pouvez payer le montant d'amende fixée, indiqué ci-dessus.

Écrivez le numéro de l'infraction de stationnement au recto de votre chèque ou de votre mandat libellé à l'ordre de :

DO NOT SEND CASH IN THE MAIL

Deliver this form and your payment to the address indicated below. If you would like to request a trial regarding this matter, complete the Notice of Intention to Appear below and deliver this form to the address below:

N'ENVOYEZ PAS D'ARGENT COMPTANT PAR LA POSTE

Si vous désirez qu'il y ait un procès sur cette question, remplissez l'avis d'intention de comparaître, ci-dessous. Faites parvenir la présente formule et votre paiement ou votre avis d'intention de comparaître à l'adresse suivante :

Please allow sufficient time for your payment or Notice to be delivered. If you have any further questions regarding this Notice, please call:

Veuillez prévoir un délai suffisant pour la livraison de votre paiement ou de votre avis. Pour toute question sur le présent avis, veuillez appeler:

◼ **Form 1   Certificate of Offence**

Form 1
Formule 1

Provincial Offences Act
Loi sur les infractions provinciales

CERTIFICATE OF OFFENCE
PROCÈS-VERBAL D'INFRACTION

ICON LOCATION CODE	OFFENCE NUMBER N° D'INFRACTION

FORM 1   PROVINCIAL OFFENCES ACT   ONTARIO COURT (PROVINCIAL DIVISION)
FORMULE 1   LOI SUR LES INFRACTIONS PROVINCIALES   COUR DE L'ONTARIO (DIVISION PROVINCIALE)

CERTIFICATE OF OFFENCE/*PROCÈS-VERBAL D'INFRACTION*

I _____   BELIEVE AND CERTIFY THAT
JE SOUSSIGNÉ(E)   (PRINT NAME/*NOM EN LETTRES MOULÉES*)   *CROIS ET ATTESTE QUE*

ON THE   DAY OF   19   TIME   **M**
LE   *JOUR DE*   *À (HEURE)*

NAME
NOM   FAMILY/*NOM DE FAMILLE*   GIVEN/*PRÉNOM*   INITIALS/*INITIALES*

ADDRESS
ADRESSE   NUMBER AND STREET/*N° ET RUE*

MUNICIPALITY/*MUNICIPALITÉ*   P.O./C.P.   PROVINCE   POSTAL CODE/*CODE POSTAL*

AT/*À*

DID COMMIT THE OFFENCE OF: MUNICIPALITY / *MUNICIPALITÉ*
A COMMIS L'INFRACTION SUIVANTE :

CONTRARY TO:
CONTRAIREMENT A :

SECT./*ART.*

DRIVER'S LICENCE NO./*NUMÉRO DE PERMIS DE CONDUIRE*		CVOR/*ICVU*
SEX *SEXE* BIRTHDATE/*DATE DE NAISSANCE* D/J M/M Y/A MOTOR VEHICLE INVOLVED *VÉHICULE IMPLIQUÉ* ☐ YES *OUI* ☐ NO *NON*	PLATE NUMBER N° DE PLAQUE D'IMMATRICULATION	PROVINCE

AND I FURTHER CERTIFY THAT I SERVED AN   *JE CERTIFIE EN OUTRE QUE J'AI SIGNIFIÉ UN*
OFFENCE NOTICE   *AVIS D'INFRACTION*
PERSONALLY UPON THE PERSON CHARGED ON THE OFFENCE DATE /*EN MAINS PROPRES À L'ACCUSÉ(E) LE JOUR DE L'INFRACTION.*

SIGNATURE OF ISSUING PROVINCIAL OFFENCES OFFICER *SIGNATURE DE L'AGENT DES INFRACTIONS PROVINCIALES*	OFFICER NO. AGENT N°	PLATOON PELOTON	UNIT UNITÉ

SIGNATURE OF PERSON CHARGED (OPTIONAL)/*SIGNATURE DE L'ACCUSÉ(E) (FACULTATIF)*

SET FINE OF/*L'AMENDE FIXÉE DE* $ $	**TOTAL PAYABLE**
(INCLUDING COSTS) IS INCLUDED IN THE TOTAL PAYABLE ALONG WITH THE APPLICABLE VICTIM FINE SURCHARGE *(INCLUANT LES FRAIS) ET LA SURAMENDE COMPENSATOIRE APPLICABLE SONT COMPRISES DANS LE MONTANT TOTAL À PAYER.*	**$** **$** **MONTANT TOTAL EXIGIBLE**

SUMMONS ISSUED FOR/*ASSIGNATION DÉLIVRÉE POUR* | CT.ROOM *SALLE D'AUDIENCE* | CODE |
     M

THE ___ DAY OF _____ 19 ___ AT _____
LE   *JOUR DE*   *À (HEURE)*
ONTARIO COURT (PROVINCIAL DIVISION) AT/*COUR DE L'ONTARIO (DIVISION PROVINCIALE) À*

CONVICTION ENTERED. SET FINE (INCLUDING COSTS) IMPOSED. *CONDAMNATION INSCRITE. AMENDE FIXÉE (Y COMPRIS LES FRAIS) IMPOSÉE*	DATE	D/J	M/M	Y/A

_____ JUSTICE/*JUGE*	C.V.O.R. NUMBER (COMMERCIAL VEHICLES ONLY) *N° DE L'ICVU (VÉHICULES UTILITAIRES SEULEMENT)*

■ Form 3   Offence Notice

Form 3
Formule 3

Provincial Offences Act
Loi sur les infractions provinciales

OFFENCE NOTICE
AVIS D'INFRACTION

ICON LOCATION CODE	OFFENCE NUMBER N° D'INFRACTION

FORM 3   REG. 950   PROVINCIAL OFFENCES ACT   ONTARIO COURT (PROVINCIAL DIVISION)
FORMULE 3   RÉGL. 950   LOI SUR LES INFRACTIONS PROVINCIALES   COUR DE L'ONTARIO (DIVISION PROVINCIALE)

OFFENCE NOTICE/*AVIS D'INFRACTION*

BELIEVES AND CERTIFIES THAT
CROIT ET ATTESTE QUE

ON THE / *LE*   DAY OF / *JOUR DE*   19   TIME / *À (HEURE)*   ☐ M

NAME / *NOM*   FAMILY/*NOM DE FAMILLE*   GIVEN/*PRÉNOM*   INITIALS/*INITIALES*

ADDRESS / *ADRESSE*   NUMBER AND STREET/*N° ET RUE*

MUNICIPALITY/*MUNICIPALITÉ*   PO/*C P*   PROVINCE   POSTAL CODE/*CODE POSTAL*

AT/*À*

MUNICIPALITY / *MUNICIPALITÉ*

DID COMMIT THE OFFENCE OF:
A COMMIS L'INFRACTION SUIVANTE :

CONTRARY TO:
CONTRAIREMENT À :

SECT./*ART.*

DRIVER'S LICENCE NO./*NUMÉRO DE PERMIS DE CONDUIRE*		CVOR/*ICVU*
SEX/*SEXE* · BIRTHDATE/*DATE DE NAISSANCE* D/J M/M Y/A · MOTOR VEHICLE INVOLVED/*VÉHICULE IMPLIQUE* ☐ YES/OUI ☐ NO/NON	PLATE NUMBER N° DE PLAQUE D'IMMATRICULATION	PROVINCE

I BELIEVE AND CERTIFY THAT THE ABOVE OFFENCE HAS BEEN COMMITTED
je crois et atteste que l'INFRACTION CI-DESSUS A ÉTÉ COMMISE

SIGNATURE OF ISSUING PROVINCIAL OFFENCES OFFICER / *SIGNATURE DE L'AGENT DES INFRACTIONS PROVINCIALES*	OFFICER NO. *AGENT N°*	PLATOON *PELOTON*	UNIT *UNITÉ*

SIGNATURE OF PERSON CHARGED (OPTIONAL)/*SIGNATURE DE L'ACCUSÉ(E) (FACULTATIF)*

SET FINE OF/*L'AMENDE FIXÉE DE $* $ **TOTAL PAYABLE**

(INCLUDING COSTS) IS INCLUDED IN THE TOTAL PAYABLE ALONG WITH THE APPLICABLE VICTIM FINE SURCHARGE *(INCLUANT LES FRAIS) ET LA SURAMENDE COMPENSATOIRE APPLICABLE SONT COMPRISES DANS LE MONTANT TOTAL À PAYER.*   **$ $**
MONTANT TOTAL EXIGIBLE

SUMMONS ISSUED FOR/*ASSIGNATION DÉLIVRÉE POUR*   CT ROOM *SALLE D'AUDIENCE* ☐ M   CODE

THE / *LE*   DAY OF / *JOUR DE*   19   AT / *À (HEURE)*

ONTARIO COURT (PROVINCIAL DIVISION) AT/*COUR DE L'ONTARIO (DIVISION PROVINCIALE) À*

DATE OF SERVICE IF OTHER THAN OFFENCE DATE
DATE DE LA SIGNIFICATION DE L'AVIS SI ELLE DIFFÈRE DE CELLE DE L'INFRACTION

D/J   M/M   Y/A

■ **Form 6   Summons**

Form 6
Formule 6

Provincial Offences Act
Loi sur les infractions provinciales

SUMMONS
ASSIGNATION

ICON
LOCATION
CODE

FORM 6   PROVINCIAL OFFENCES ACT   ONTARIO COURT (PROVINCIAL DIVISION)
FORMULE 6   LOI SUR LES INFRACTIONS PROVINCIALES   COUR DE L'ONTARIO (DIVISION PROVINCIALE)

SUMMONS/ASSIGNATION

BELIEVES AND CERTIFIES THAT
CROIT ET ATTESTE QUE

| ON THE *LE* | DAY OF *JOUR DE* | 19 | TIME *À (HEURE)* | M |

NAME *NOM*   FAMILY/*NOM DE FAMILLE*   GIVEN/*PRÉNOM*   INITIALS/*INITIALES*

ADDRESS *ADRESSE*   NUMBER AND STREET/*N° ET RUE*

MUNICIPALITY/*MUNICIPALITÉ*   P.O./*C.P.*   PROVINCE   POSTAL CODE/*CODE POSTAL*

AT/*À*

DID COMMIT THE OFFENCE OF:
A COMMIS L'INFRACTION SUIVANTE :

MUNICIPALITY / *MUNICIPALITÉ*

CONTRARY TO:
CONTRAIREMENT À :

SECT./*ART.*

DRIVER'S LICENCE NO./*NUMÉRO DE PERMIS DE CONDUIRE*					CVOR/*CVU*
SEX *SEXE*	BIRTHDATE/*DATE DE NAISSANCE* D/J M/M Y/A	MOTOR VEHICLE INVOLVED *VÉHICULE IMPLIQUÉ* ☐ YES *OUI* ☐ NO *NON*		PLATE NUMBER *N° DE PLAQUE D'IMMATRICULATION*	PROVINCE

OFFICER NO. *AGENT N°*	PLATOON *PELOTON*	UNIT *UNITÉ*

THIS IS THEREFORE TO COMMAND YOU IN HER MAJESTY'S NAME TO APPEAR BEFORE
THE ONTARIO COURT (PROVINCIAL DIVISION)
POUR CES MOTIFS, ORDRE VOUS EST DONNÉ, AU NOM DE SA MAJESTÉ, DE COMPARAÎTRE
DEVANT LA COUR DE L'ONTARIO (DIVISION PROVINCIALE)

| M | CT.ROOM *SALLE D'AUDIENCE* | CODE |

| ON THE *LE* | DAY OF *JOUR DE* | 19 | AT *À (HEURE)* |

ONTARIO COURT (PROVINCIAL DIVISION) AT/*COUR DE L'ONTARIO (DIVISION PROVINCIALE) À*

AND TO ATTEND THEREAFTER AS REQUIRED BY THE COURT IN ORDER TO BE DEALT WITH ACCORD-
ING TO LAW. THIS SUMMONS IS SERVED UNDER PART I OF THE PROVINCIAL OFFENCES ACT.
ET D'Y ÊTRE PRÉSENT(E) PAR LA SUITE LORSQUE LE TRIBUNAL L'EXIGERA, DE FAÇON À ÊTRE
TRAITÉ(E) SELON LA LOI. CETTE ASSIGNATION VOUS EST SIGNIFIÉE AUX TERMES DE LA
PARTIE I DE LA LOI SUR LES INFRACTIONS PROVINCIALES.

SIGNATURE OF PROVINCIAL OFFENCES OFFICER/*SIGNATURE DE L'AGENT DES INFRACTIONS PROVINCIALES*

Form 8
Formule 8

Provincial Offences Act
Loi sur les infractions provinciales

NOTICE OF TRIAL
AVIS DE PROCÈS

ONTARIO COURT (PROVINCIAL DIVISION)
COUR DE L'ONTARIO (DIVISION PROVINCIALE)

Notice of Trial/*Avis de procès*
Form/*Formule* 8
Reg./*Règl.* 950

To
À

You are charged with the following offence:/*Vous êtes accusé(e) de l'infraction suivante* :

On the/*Le* .... day of / *jour de* ...., 19 ... , at/à ...... am/pm/*(heure)*

at / *à* ....

you did commit the offence of speeding contrary to the Section 128 of the *Highway Traffic Act*.
vous avez commis l'infraction d'excès de vitesse, en contravention de l'article 128 du Code de la route.

Set fine of $ _____ (including costs) is included in the total payable along
with the applicable victim fine surcharge.
*L'amende fixée de _____ $ (incluant les frais) et la suramende compensatoire
applicable sont comprises dans le montant total exigible.*

Total Payable
***Montant total exigible* $**_____ $

TAKE NOTICE that on the ············· day

of ·······················, 19 ···· ,

at ······ am/pm, your trial will be held at:

AVIS VOUS EST DONNÉ que le ....

....,19 .... ,

à ...... heure, votre procès sera tenu à

Court Address/*Adresse du tribunal*

This will confirm that you have (chosen to/have chosen not to)
(delete inapplicable)
challenge the evidence of the Photo-Radar System Operator.
*Note: Section 205.9 of the Highway Traffic Act provides that you must
apply to the justice at trial if you wish to compel the attendance of
the Provincial Offences Officer who issued the certificate of offence.*

Your trial will be held on the date and time noted above at the Ontario
Court (Provincial Division) shown. You and your witnesses should
be ready for your trial at that time. If you do not appear, you will be
deemed not to dispute the charge and the court may convict you in
your absence without further notice.

Ceci confirme que vous avez choisi (de contester/de ne pas contester)
(biffez la mention inutile)
la preuve de l'opérateur du système de radar photographique.
*Remarque : L'article 205.9 du Code de la route prévoit que vous devez vous
adresser au juge du procès si vous désirez obtenir la comparution de l'agent
des infractions provinciales qui a délivré le certificat d'infraction.*

*Votre procès se tiendra à la date et à l'heure mentionnées ci-dessus à la Cour
de l'Ontario (Division provinciale) susmentionnée. Vos témoins et vous-même
devrez être prêts pour votre procès à cette date. Si vous ne comparaissez pas,
vous serez réputé(e) ne pas contester l'accusation, et le tribunal pourra vous
déclarer coupable en votre absence, sans autre avis.*

Issued at ....
Décerné à

this .... day of ...., 19 ....
le   *jour de*

O. Reg. 786/94, s. 1
Règl. de l'Ont. 786/94, art. 1

■ **Form 104   Summons to Defendant Under Section 22 of the Provincial Offences Act**

Courts of Justice Act

Ontario Court (Provincial Division) — Province of Ontario

You are charged with the following offence:

On the .... day of ...., 19....., at ....M

Name ....

Address ....

At ....

Did commit the offence of ....

Contrary to .... section ....

Therefore you are commanded in Her Majesty's name to appear before the Ontario Court (Provincial Division) at .... on the .... day of ...., 19..... at ....M at .... (courtroom) and to appear thereafter as required by the court in order to be dealt with according to law.

Issued this .... day of ...., 19.....

....

Provincial Offences Officer

■ Form 105 Information Under Section 23 of the Provincial Offences Act

Courts of Justice Act

Ontario Court (Provincial Division) — Province of Ontario

This is the information of .... of ....
(occupation)

I have reasonable and probable grounds to believe and do believe that
.... (name) on or about the .... day of ...., 19....., at
.... (location) .... did commit the offence of
.... contrary to .... section ....

....

(signature of informant)

Sworn before me at ...., this .... day of ...., 19.....

....

Provincial Judge or Justice of the Peace

■ **Form 137   Warrant for Arrest of Defendant Under Section 155 of the Provincial Offences Act**

Courts of Justice Act

Ontario Court (Provincial Division) — Province of Ontario

To all police officers in the Province of Ontario:

This warrant is for the arrest of ...., of ....
(location), ... (occupation), hereinafter called the
defendant.

Whereas .... (name of surety), a surety, has applied in writing
to be relieved of the surety's obligation under a recognizance dated the .....
day of ...., 19..... by the defendant.

Therefore, you are commanded in Her Majesty's name to arrest the defendant and
bring the defendant before a justice so that the defendant may be dealt with
under section 150 of the *Provincial Offences Act*.

This warrant is issued under section 155 of the *Provincial Offences Act*.

Issued at .... this .... day of ...., 19.....

....

Provincial Judge or Justice of the Peace

■ Form 140   Information To Obtain Search Warrant Under Section 158 of the Provincial Offences Act

Courts of Justice Act

Ontario Court (Provincial Division) — Province of Ontario

This is the information of .... (name) of ....
(address), ... (occupation)

I have reasonable ground to believe and do believe that in a certain building, receptacle, or place, namely, ... (building, receptacle or place), of .... (owner), at .... (address) there are the following thing(s): ....

(check appropriate box)

❑ upon or in respect of which an offence has been or is suspected to have been committed.

❑ that there are reasonable grounds to believe will afford evidence as to the commission of an offence.

And I further say that my grounds for so believing are:

....

Therefore I request that a search warrant by issued to search the said .... (building, receptacle, or place) for the said thing(s).

....

(signature of informant)

Sworn before me at ...., this .... day of ...., 19.....

....

Provincial Judge or Justice of the Peace

■ Form 141   Search Warrant Under Section 158 of the Provincial Offences Act

Courts of Justice Act

Ontario Court (Provincial Division) — Province of Ontario

To .... and to the police officers of Ontario.

Whereas, on the information upon oath of ...., I am satisfied that there are reasonable grounds to believe that ....
(describe things to be searched for) ....

(check appropriate box)

❏ upon or in respect of which the offence of .... contrary to .... section .... is suspected to have been committed, or

❏ that there is reasonable ground to believe will afford evidence as to the commission of the offence of .... contrary to................. section ....

may be found at .... (building, place, receptacle) of .... at .... (address) hereinafter called the premises.

This is therefore to authorize you to enter such ....
(name or location of building, receptacle or place)

.... between the hours of 6:00 a.m. and 9:00 p.m. standard time, or

.... (time warrant to be executed)

and to search there for the said things and to seize them and carry them before me or another justice so that they may be dealt with according to the law. This warrant expires on the .... day of ...., 19....., a day not later than the fifteenth day after its issue.

Issued at .... this .... day of ...., 19.....

....

Provincial Judge or Justice of the Peace